Hero Tales and Legends of the Rhine

Lewis Spence

Dover Publications, Inc.
New York

Published in Canada by General Publishing Company, Ltd., 30 Lesmill Road, Don Mills, Toronto, Ontario.
Published in the United Kingdom by Constable and Company, Ltd., 3 The Lanchesters, 162–164 Fulham Palace Road, London W6 9ER.

Bibliographical Note

This Dover edition, first published in 1995, is a slightly altered, unabridged republication of the work originally published by George C. Harrap & Company, London, in 1915. For the Dover edition, the original color plates have been reproduced in black and white, the sequence of the plates has been rearranged, and the map is reprinted on four pages instead of one foldout page.

Library of Congress Cataloging-in-Publication Data

Spence, Lewis, 1874–1955.
  [Hero tales & legends of the Rhine]
  Hero tales and legends of the Rhine / Lewis Spence.
      p.   cm.
  Originally published: Hero tales & legends of the Rhine. London ; New York : George C. Harrap, 1915.
  Includes index.
  ISBN 0-486-28870-6 (pbk.)
    1. Legends—Rhine River Valley.   2. Legends—Germany.   3. Legends—France.   I. Title.
  GR139.8.H47   1995
  398.2′0943′5502—dc20   95-19305
                                                                          CIP

Manufactured in the United States of America
Dover Publications, Inc., 31 East 2nd Street, Mineola, N.Y. 11501

INTRODUCTION

AN abundance of literature exists on the subject of the Rhine and its legends, but with few exceptions the works on it which are accessible to English-speaking peoples are antiquated in spirit and verbiage, and their authors have been content to accept the first version of such legends and traditions as came their way without submitting them to any critical examination. It is claimed for this book that much of its matter was collected on the spot, or that at least most of the tales here presented were perused in other works at the scene of the occurrences related. This volume is thus something more than a mere compilation, and when it is further stated that only the most characteristic and original versions and variants of the many tales here given have gained admittance to the collection, its value will become apparent.

It is, of course, no easy task to infuse a spirit of originality into matter which has already achieved such a measure of celebrity as have these wild and wondrous tales of Rhineland. But it is hoped that the treatment to which these stories have been subjected is not without a novelty of its own. One circumstance may be alluded to as characteristic of the manner of their treatment in this work. In most English books on Rhine legend the tales themselves are presented in a form so brief, succinct, and uninspiring as to rob them entirely of that mysterious glamour lacking which they become mere material by which to add to and illustrate the guide-book. The absence of the romantic spirit in most English and American compilations dealing with the Rhine legends is noteworthy, and in writing this book the author's intention has been to supply this striking defect by retaining as much of the atmosphere of mystery so dear to the German heart as will convey to the English-speaking reader a true conception of the spirit of German legend.

But it is not contended that because greater space and freedom of narrative scope than is usual has been taken by the author the volume would not prove itself an acceptable companion upon a voyage on Rhine waters undertaken in holiday times of peace. Indeed, every attempt has been made so to arrange the legends that they will illustrate a Rhine journey from sea to source—the manner in which the majority of visitors to Germany will make the voyage—and to this end the tales have been marshalled in such form that a reader sitting on the deck of a Rhine steamer may be able to peruse the legends relating to the various localities in their proper order as he passes them. There are included, however, several tales relating to places which cannot be viewed from the deck of a steamer, but which may be visited at the cost of a short inland excursion. These are such as from their celebrity could not be omitted from any work on the legends of Rhineland, but they are few in number.

The historical development, folklore, poetry, and art of the Rhine-country have been dealt with in a special introductory chapter. The history of the Rhine basin is a complicated and uneven one, chiefly consisting in the rapid and perplexing rise and fall of dynasties and the alternate confiscation of one or both banks of the devoted stream to the empires of France or Germany. But the evolution of a reasoned narrative has been attempted from this chaotic material, and, so far as the author is aware, it is the only one existing in English. The folklore and romance elements in Rhine legend have been carefully examined,

Introduction

and the best poetic material upon the storied river has been critically collected and reviewed.

To those who may one day visit the Rhine it is hoped that the volume may afford a suitable introduction to a fascinating field of travel, while to such as have already viewed its glories it may serve to renew old associations and awaken cherished memories of a river without peer or parallel in its wealth of story, its boundless mystery, and the hold which it has exercised upon all who have lingered by the hero-trodden paths that wind among its mysterious promontories and song-haunted strands.

L. S.

CONTENTS

ILLUSTRATIONS

CHAPTER I : TOPOGRAPHICAL AND HISTORICAL

THERE are many rivers whose celebrity is of much greater antiquity than that of the Rhine. The Nile and the Ganges are intimately associated with the early history of civilization and the mysterious beginnings of wisdom; the Tiber is eloquent of that vanished Empire which was the first to carry the torch of advancement into the dark places of barbarian Europe; the name of the Jordan is sacred to thousands as that first heard in infancy and linked with lives and memories divine. But, universal as is the fame of these rivers, none of them has awakened in the breasts of the dwellers on their banks such a fervent devotion, such intense enthusiasm, or such a powerful patriotic appeal as has the Rhine, at once the river, the frontier, and the palladium of the German folk.

The Magic of the Rhine

But the appeal is wider, for the Rhine is peculiarly the home of a legendary mysticism almost unique. Those whose lives are spent in their creation and interpretation know that song and legend have a particular affinity for water. Hogg, the friend of Shelley, was wont to tell how the bright eyes of his comrade would dilate at the sight of even a puddle by the roadside. Has water a hypnotic attraction for certain minds? Be that as it may, there has crystallized round the great waterways of the world a traditionary lore which preserves the thought and feeling of the past, and retains many a circumstance of wonder and marvel from olden epochs which the modern world could ill have spared.

Varied and valuable as are the traditional tales of other

streams, none possess that colour of intensity and mystery, that spell of ancient profundity which belong to the legends of the Rhine. In perusing these we feel our very souls plunged in darkness as that of the carven gloom of some Gothic cathedral or the Cimmerian depths of some ancient forest unpierced by sun-shafts. It is the Teutonic mystery which has us in its grip, a thing as readily recognizable as the Celtic glamour or the Egyptian gloom—a thing of the shadows of eld, stern, ancient, of a ponderous fantasy, instinct with the spirit of nature, of dwarfs, elves, kobolds, erlkings, the wraiths and shades of forest and flood, of mountain and mere, of castled height and swift whirlpool, the denizens of the deep valleys and mines, the bergs and heaths of this great province of romance, this rich satrapy of Faëry.

A Land of Legend

Nowhere is legend so thickly strewn as on the banks of the Rhine. Each step is eloquent of tradition, each town, village, and valley. No hill, no castle but has its story, true or legendary. The Teuton is easily the world's master in the art of conserving local lore. As one speeds down the broad breast of this wondrous river, gay with summer and flushed with the laughter of early vineyards, so close is the network of legend that the swiftly read or spoken tale of one locality is scarce over ere the traveller is confronted by another. It is a surfeit of romance, an inexhaustible hoard of the matter of marvel.

This noble stream with its wealth of tradition has made such a powerful impression upon the national imagination that it has become intimate in the soul of the people and commands a reverence and affection which is not given by any other modern nation to its greatest and

2

The Song of the Iron Chancellor

most characteristic river. The Englishman has only a mitigated pride in the Thames, as a great commercial asset or, its metropolitan borders once passed, a river of peculiarly restful character; the Frenchman evinces no very great enthusiasm toward the Seine; and if there are many Spanish songs about the " chainless Guadalquivir," the dons have been content to retain its Arabic name. But what German heart does not thrill at the name of the Rhine ? What German cheek does not flush at the sound of that mighty thunder-hymn which tells of his determination to preserve the river of his fathers at the cost of his best blood ? Nay, what man of patriotic temperament but feels a responsive chord awake within him at the thought of that majestic song, so stern, so strong, " clad in armour," vibrant with the clang of swords, instinct with the universal accord of a united people ? To those who have heard it sung by multitudinous voices to the accompaniment of golden harps and silver trumpets it is a thing which can never be forgotten, this world-song that is at once a hymn of union, a song of the deepest love of country, a defiance and an intimation of resistance to the death.

The Song of the ' Iron Chancellor '

How potent *Die Wacht am Rhein* is to stir the hearts of the children of the Fatherland is proven abundantly by an apposite story regarding the great Bismarck, the 'man of blood and iron.' The scene is the German Reichstag, and the time is that curious juncture in history when the Germans, having realized that union is strength, were beginning to weld together the petty kingdoms and duchies of which their mighty empire was once composed. Gradually this task was becoming accomplished,

3

and meanwhile Germany grew eager to assert her power in Europe, wherefore her rulers commenced to create a vast army. But Bismarck was not satisfied, and in his eyes Germany's safety was still unassured; so he appealed to the Reichstag to augment largely their armaments. The deputies looked at him askance, for a vast army meant ruinous taxation; even von Moltke and von Roon shook their heads, well aware though they were that a great European conflict might break out at any time; and, in short, Bismarck's proposal was met by a determined negative from the whole House. "*Ach, mein Gott!*" he cried, holding out his hands in a superb gesture of despair. "*Ach, mein Gott!* but these soldiers we *must* have." His hearers still demurred, reminding him that the people far and near were groaning under the weight of taxation, and assuring him that this could not possibly be increased, when he suddenly changed his despairing gesture for a martial attitude, and with sublime eloquence recited the lines:

> " Es braust ein Ruf wie Donnerhall,
> Wie Schwertgeklirr und Wogenprall;
> Zum Rhein, zum Rhein, zum deutschen Rhein,
> Wer will die Strömes Hüter sein?
> Lieb Vaterland, magst ruhig sein,
> Fest steht und treu die Wacht am Rhein."

The effect was magical; the entire House resounded with cheers, and the most unbounded enthusiasm prevailed. And ere the members dispersed they had told Bismarck he might have, not ten thousand, but a hundred thousand soldiers, such was the power of association awakened by this famous hymn, such the spell it is capable of exercising on German hearers.

Topography of the Rhine

Topography of the Rhine

Ere we set sail upon the dark sea of legend before us it is necessary that, like prudent mariners, we should know whence and whither we are faring. To this end it will be well that we should glance briefly at the topography of the great river we are about to explore, and that we should sketch rapidly the most salient occurrences in the strange and varied pageant of its history, in order that we may the better appreciate the wondrous tales of world-wide renown which have found birth on its banks.

Although the most German of rivers, the Rhine does not run its entire course through German territory, but takes its rise in Switzerland and finds the sea in Holland. For no less than 233 miles it flows through Swiss country, rising in the mountains of the canton of Grisons, and irrigates every canton of the Alpine republic save that of Geneva. Indeed, it waters over 14,000 square miles of Swiss territory in the flow of its two main branches, the Nearer Rhine and the Farther Rhine, which unite at Reichenau, near Coire. The Nearer Rhine issues at the height of over 7000 feet from the glaciers of the Rheinwaldhorn group, and flows for some thirty-five miles, first in a north-easterly direction through the Rheinwald Valley, then northward through the Schams Valley, by way of the Via Mala gorge, and Tomleschg Valley, and so to Reichenau, where it is joined by its sister stream, the Farther Rhine. The latter, rising in the little Alpine lake of Toma near the Pass of St. Gotthard, flows in a north-easterly direction to Reichenau. The Nearer Rhine is generally considered to be the more important branch, though the Farther Rhine is the longer by some seven miles. From Reichenau the Rhine flows north-eastward to Coire, and thence northward to the Lake of Constance, receiving on its way two tributaries, the Landquart and the Ill, both on the right bank. Indeed, from source to sea the Rhine receives a vast number of tributaries, amounting, with their branches, to over 12,000. Leaving the Lake of Constance at the town of that name, the river flows westward to Basel, having as the principal towns on its banks Constance, Schaffhausen, Waldshut, Laufenburg, Säckingen, Rheinfelden, and Basel.

Not far from the town of Schaffhausen the river precipitates itself from a height of 60 feet, in three leaps, forming the famous Falls of the Rhine. At Coblentz a strange thing happens, for at this place the river receives the waters of the Aar, swollen by the Reuss and the Limmat, and of greater volume than the stream in which it loses itself.

It is at Basel that the Rhine, taking a northward trend, enters Germany. By this time it has made a descent of nearly 7000 feet, and has traversed about a third of its course. Between Basel and Mainz it flows between the mountains of the Black Forest and the Vosges, the distance between which forms a shallow valley of some width. Here and there it is islanded, and its expanse averages about 1200 feet. The Taunus Mountains divert it at Mainz, where it widens, and it flows westward for about twenty miles, but at Bingen it once more takes its course northward, and enters a narrow valley where the enclosing hills look down sheer upon the water.

It is in this valley, probably one of the most romantic in the world, that we find the legendary lore of the river packed in such richness that every foot of its banks has its place in tradition. But that is not to say that this portion of the Rhine is wanting in natural beauty. Here are situated some of its sunniest vineyards, its most wildly romantic heights, and its most picturesque ruins. This part of its course may be said to end at the Siebengebirge, or 'Seven Mountains,' where the river again widens and the banks become more bare and uninteresting. Passing Bonn and Cologne, the bareness of the landscape is remarkable after the variety of that from which we have just emerged, and henceforward the river takes on what may be called a 'Dutch' appearance. After entering Holland it divides into two branches, the Waal flowing to the west and uniting with the Maas. The smaller branch to the right is still called the Rhine, and throws off another branch, the Yssel, which flows into the Zuider Zee. Once more the river bifurcates into insignificant streams, one of which is called the Kromme Rijn, and beyond Utrecht, and under the name of the Oude Rijn, or Old Rhine, it becomes so stagnant that it requires the aid of a canal to drain it into the sea. Anciently the Rhine at this part of its course was an abounding stream, but by the ninth century the sands at Katwijk had silted it up, and it was only in the beginning of last century that its way to the sea was made clear.

The Sunken City

More than six centuries ago Stavoren was one of the chief commercial towns of Holland. Its merchants traded with all parts of the world, and brought back their ships laden with rich cargoes, and the city became ever more prosperous.

The majority of the people of Stavoren were well-to-do, and as their wealth increased they became luxurious and dissipated, each striving to outdo the others in the magnificence of their homes and the extravagance of their hospitality.

Many of their houses, we are told, were like the palaces of princes, built of white marble, furnished with the greatest sumptuousness, and decorated with the costliest hangings and the rarest statuary.

But, says the legend, of all the Stavoren folk there was none wealthier than young Richberta. This maiden owned a fleet of the finest merchant-vessels of the city, and loved to ornament her palace with the rich merchandise which these brought from foreign ports.

With all her jewels and gold and silver treasures, however, Richberta was not happy. She gave gorgeous banquets to the other merchant-princes of the place, each more magnificent than the last, not because she received any pleasure from thus dispensing hospitality, but because she desired to create envy and astonishment in the breasts of her guests.

On one occasion while such a feast was in progress Richberta was informed that a stranger was waiting without who was desirous of speaking with her. When she was told that the man had come all the way from a distant land simply to admire her wonderful treasures, of which he had heard so much, the maiden was highly flattered and gave orders that he should be admitted without delay. An aged and decrepit man, clad in a picturesque Eastern costume, was led into the room, and Richberta bade him be seated at her side. He expected to receive from the young lady the symbol of welcome— bread and salt. But no such common fare was to be found on her table—all was rich and luxurious food.

The stranger seated himself in silence. At length he began to talk. He had travelled in many lands, and now
8

He rose abruptly and left the room

Hiram Ellis

(See page 9)

The Courtyard, Heidelberg Castle
Louis Weirter, R.B.A.

(See page 44)

The Sunken City

he told of his changing fortunes in these far-off countries, always drawing a moral from his adventures—that all things earthly were evanescent as the dews of morning. The company listened attentively to the discourse of the sage; all, that is, but their hostess, who was angry and disappointed that he had said no word of the wealth and magnificence displayed in her palace, the rich fare on her table, and all the signs of luxury with which he was surrounded. At length she could conceal her chagrin no longer, and asked the stranger directly whether he had ever seen such splendour in his wanderings as that he now beheld.

" Tell me," she said, " is there to be found in the courts of your Eastern kings such rare treasures as these of mine ? "

" Nay," replied the sage, " they have no pearls and rich embroideries to match thine. Nevertheless, there is one thing missing from your board, and that the best and most valuable of all earthly gifts."

In vain Richberta begged that he would tell her what that most precious of treasures might be. He answered all her inquiries in an evasive manner, and at last, when her question could no longer be evaded, he rose abruptly and left the room. And, seek as she might, Richberta could find no trace of her mysterious visitor.

Richberta strove to discover the meaning of the old man's words. She was rich—she possessed greater treasures than any in Stavoren, at a time when that city was among the wealthiest in Europe—and yet she lacked the most precious of earth's treasures. The memory of the words galled her pride and excited her curiosity to an extraordinary pitch. In vain she asked the wise men of her time—the priests and philosophers—to read her the riddle of the mysterious traveller. None could name a treasure that was not already hers.

In her anxiety to obtain the precious thing, whatever it might be, Richberta sent all her ships to sea, telling the captain of each not to return until he had found some treasure that she did not already possess. The vessels were victualled for seven years, so that the mariners might have ample time in which to pursue their quest. So their commander sent one division of the fleet to the east, another to the west, while he left his own vessel to the hazard of the winds, letting it drift wheresoever the fates decreed. His ship as well as the others was laden heavily with provisions, and during the first storm they encountered it was necessary to cast a considerable portion of the food overboard, so that the ship might right itself. As it was, the remaining provisions were so damaged by the sea-water that they rotted in a few days and became unfit for food. A pestilence would surely follow the use of such unwholesome stuff, and consequently the entire cargo of bread had to be cast into the sea.

The commander saw his crew ravaged by the dreaded scurvy, suffering from the lack of bread. Then only did he begin to perceive the real meaning of the sage's words. The most valuable of all earthly treasures was not the pearls from the depths of the sea, gold or silver from the heart of the mountains, nor the rich spices of the Indies. The most common of all earth's products, that which was to be found in every country, which flourished in every clime, on which the lives of millions depended —this was the greatest treasure, and its name was— *bread.*

Having reached this conclusion, the commander of Richberta's fleet set sail for a Baltic port, where he took on board a cargo of corn, and returned immediately to Stavoren.

Richberta was astonished and delighted to see that he had achieved his purpose so soon, and bade him tell her of what the treasure consisted which he had brought with him. The commander thereupon recounted his adventures—the storm, the throwing overboard of their store of bread, and the consequent sufferings of the crew —and told how he at length discovered what was the greatest treasure on earth, the priceless possession which the stranger had looked for in vain at her rich board. It was bread, he said simply, and the cargo he had brought home was corn.

Richberta was beside herself with passion. When she had recovered herself sufficiently to speak she asked him :

" At which side of the ship did you take in the cargo ? "

" At the right side," he replied.

" Then," she exclaimed angrily, " I order you to cast it into the sea from the left side."

It was a cruel decision. Stavoren, like every other city, had its quota of poor families, and these were in much distress at the time, many of them dying from sheer starvation. The cargo of corn would have provided bread for them throughout the whole winter, and the commander urged Richberta to reconsider her decision. As a last resort he sent the barefooted children of the city to her, thinking that their mute misery would move her to alleviate their distress and give them the shipload of corn. But all was in vain. Richberta remained adamantine, and in full view of the starving multitude she had the precious cargo cast into the sea.

But the curses of the despairing people had their effect. Far down in the bed of the sea the grains of corn germinated, and a harvest of bare stalks grew until it reached the surface of the water. The shifting quicksands at the bottom of the sea were bound together by the overspreading stalks into a mighty sand-bank which rose above the surface in front of the town of Stavoren.

No longer were the merchant-vessels able to enter the harbour, for it was blocked by the impassable bank. Nay, instead of finding refuge there, many a ship was dashed to pieces by the fury of the breakers, and Stavoren became a place of ill-fame to the mariner.

All the wealth and commerce of this proud city were at an end. Richberta herself, whose wanton act had raised the sand-bank, had her ships wrecked there one by one, and was reduced to begging for bread in the city whose wealthiest inhabitant she had once been. Then, perhaps, she could appreciate the words of the old traveller, that bread was the greatest of earthly treasures.

At last the ocean, dashing against the huge mound with ever-increasing fury, burst through the dyke which Richberta had raised, overwhelmed the town, and buried it for ever under the waves.

And now the mariner, sailing on the Zuider Zee, passes above the engulfed city and sees with wonderment the towers and spires of the 'Sunken Land.'

Historical Sketch

Like other world-rivers, the Rhine has attracted to its banks a succession of races of widely divergent origin. Celt, Teuton, Slav, and Roman have contested for the territories which it waters, and if the most enduring of these races has finally achieved dominion over the fairest

Prehistoric Miners

river-province in Europe, who shall say that it has emerged
from the struggle as a homogeneous people, having
absorbed none of the blood of those with whom it strove
for the lordship of this vine-clad valley? He would indeed be a courageous ethnologist who would suggest a
purely Germanic origin for the Rhine race. As the
historical period dawns upon Middle Europe we find the
Rhine basin in the possession of a people of Celtic blood.
As in Britain and France, this folk has left its indelible
mark upon the countryside in a wealth of place-names
embodying its characteristic titles for flood, village, and
hill. In such prefixes and terminations as *magh*, *brig*,
dun, and *ac* we espy the influence of Celtic occupants, and
Maguntiacum, or Mainz, and Borbetomagus, or Worms,
are examples of that 'Gallic' idiom which has indelibly
starred the map of Western Europe.

Prehistoric Miners

The remains of this people which are unearthed from
beneath the superincumbent strata of their Teutonic successors in the country show them to have been typical
of their race. Like their kindred in Britain, they had
successfully exploited the mineral treasures of the country,
and their skill as miners is eloquently upheld by the mute
witness of age-cold cinder-heaps by which are found the
once busy bronze hammer and the apparatus of the smelt-
ing-furnace, speaking of the slow but steady smith-toil
upon which the foundation of civilization arose. There
was scarcely a mineral beneath the loamy soil which
masked the metalliferous rock which they did not work.
From Schönebeck to Dürkheim lies an immense bed of
salt, and this the Celtic population of the district dug and
condensed by aid of fires fed by huge logs cut from the giant

13

trees of the vast and mysterious forests which have from time immemorial shadowed the whole existence of the German race. The salt, moulded or cut into blocks, was transported to Gaul as an article of commerce. But the Celts of the Rhine achieved distinction in other arts of life, for their pottery, weapons, and jewellery will bear comparison with those of prehistoric peoples in any part of Europe.

As has been remarked, at the dawn of history we find the Rhine Celts everywhere in full retreat before the rude and more virile Teutons. They lingered latterly about the Moselle and in the district of Eifel, offering a desperate resistance to the onrushing hordes of Germanic warriors. In all likelihood they were outnumbered, if not outmatched in skill and valour, and they melted away before the savage ferocity of their foes, probably seeking asylum with their kindred in Gaul.

Probably the Teutonic tribes had already commenced to apply pressure to the Celtic inhabitants of Rhineland in the fourth century before the Christian era. As was their wont, they displaced the original possessors of the soil as much by a process of infiltration as by direct conquest. The waves of emigration seem to have come from Rhaetia and Pannonia, broad-headed folk, who were in a somewhat lower condition of barbarism than the race whose territory they usurped, restless, assertive, and irritable. Says Beddoe: [1]

" The mass of tall, blond, vigorous barbarians multiplied, seethed, and fretted behind the barrier thus imposed. Tacitus and several other classic authors speak of the remarkable uniformity in their appearance; how they were all tall and handsome, with fierce blue eyes and

[1] *The Anthropological History of Europe*, p. 100.

The Graverow Type

yellow hair. Humboldt remarks the tendency we all have to see only the single type in a strange foreign people, and to shut our eyes to the differences among them. Thus some of us think sheep all alike, but the shepherd knows better; and many think all Chinamen are alike, whereas they differ, in reality, quite as much as we do, or rather more. But with respect to the ancient Germans, there certainly was among them one very prevalent form of head, and even the varieties of feature which occur among the Marcomans—for example, on Marcus Aurelius' column—all seem to oscillate round one central type.

The 'Graverow' Type

"This is the Graverow type of Ecker, the Hohberg type of His and Rutimeyer, the Swiss anatomists. In it the head is long, narrow (say from 70 to 76 in breadth-index), as high or higher than it is broad, with the upper part of the occiput very prominent, the forehead rather high than broad, often dome-shaped, often receding, with prominent brows, the nose long, narrow, and prominent, the cheek-bones narrow and not prominent, the chin well marked, the mouth apt to be prominent in women. In Germany persons with these characters have almost always light eyes and hair. . . . This Graverow type is almost exclusively what is found in the burying-places of the fifth, sixth, and seventh centuries, whether of the Alemanni, the Bavarians, the Franks, the Saxons, or the Burgundians. Schetelig dug out a graveyard in Southern Spain which is attributed to the Visigoths. Still the same harmonious elliptic form, the same indices, breadth 73, height 74."

Hero Tales & Legends of the Rhine

Early German Society

Tacitus in his *Germania* gives a vivid if condensed picture of Teutonic life in the latter part of the first century :

"The face of the country, though in some parts varied, presents a cheerless scene, covered with the gloom of forests, or deformed with wide-extended marshes; toward the boundaries of Gaul, moist and swampy ; on the side of Noricum and Pannonia, more exposed to the fury of the winds. Vegetation thrives with sufficient vigour. The soil produces grain, but is unkind to fruit-trees; well stocked with cattle, but of an under-size, and deprived by nature of the usual growth and ornament of the head. The pride of a German consists in the number of his flocks and herds ; they are his only riches, and in these he places his chief delight. Gold and silver are withheld from them: is it by the favour or the wrath of Heaven ? I do not, however, mean to assert that in Germany there are no veins of precious ore ; for who has been a miner in these regions ? Certain it is they do not enjoy the possession and use of those metals with our sensibility. There are, indeed, silver vessels to be seen among them, but they were presents to their chiefs or ambassadors; the Germans regard them in no better light than common earthenware. It is, however, observable that near the borders of the empire the inhabitants set a value upon gold and silver, finding them subservient to the purposes of commerce. The Roman coin is known in those parts, and some of our specie is not only current, but in request. In places more remote the simplicity of ancient manners still prevails : commutation of property is their only traffic. Where money passes in the way of barter our old coin is the most acceptable, particularly that which is indented at the edge,

Ancient German Weapons

or stamped with the impression of a chariot and two horses, called the Serrati and Bigati. Silver is preferred to gold, not from caprice or fancy, but because the inferior metal is of more expeditious use in the purchase of low-priced commodities.

Ancient German Weapons

" Iron does not abound in Germany, if we may judge from the weapons in general use. Swords and large lances are seldom seen. The soldier grasps his javelin, or, as it is called in their language, his *fram*—an instrument tipped with a short and narrow piece of iron, sharply pointed, and so commodious that, as occasion requires, he can manage it in close engagement or in distant combat. With this and a shield the cavalry are completely armed. The infantry have an addition of missive weapons. Each man carries a considerable number, and being naked, or, at least, not encumbered by his light mantle, he throws his weapon to a distance almost incredible. A German pays no attention to the ornament of his person ; his shield is the object of his care, and this he decorates with the liveliest colours. Breastplates are uncommon. In a whole army you will not see more than one or two helmets. Their horses have neither swiftness nor elegance, nor are they trained to the various evolutions of the Roman cavalry. To advance in a direct line, or wheel suddenly to the right, is the whole of their skill, and this they perform in so compact a body that not one is thrown out of his rank. According to the best estimate, the infantry comprise the national strength, and, for that reason, always fight intermixed with the cavalry. The flower of their youth, able by their vigour and activity to keep pace with the movements of the horse, are selected for this purpose, and placed in the front of the lines. The number of these is fixed and certain: each canton sends a hundred, from that circumstance called *Hundreders* by the army. The name was at first numerical only: it is now a title of honour. Their order of battle presents the form of a wedge. To give ground in the heat of action, provided you return to the charge, is military skill, not fear or cowardice. In the most fierce and obstinate engagement, even when the fortune of the day is doubtful, they make it a point to carry off their slain. To abandon their shield is a flagitious crime. The person guilty of it is interdicted from religious rites and excluded from the assembly of the state. Many who survived their honour on the day of battle have closed a life of ignominy by a halter."

Teutonic Customs

The kings of this rude but warlike folk were elected by the suffrages of the nobility, and their leaders in battle, as was inevitable with such a people, were chosen by reason of their personal prowess. The legal functions were exercised by the priesthood, and punishments were thus held to be sanctioned by the gods. Among this barbaric people the female sex was held as absolutely sacred, the functions of wife and mother being accounted among the highest possible to humanity, and we observe in ancient accounts of the race that typically Teutonic conception of the woman as seer or prophetess which so strongly colours early Germanic literature. Women, indeed, in later times, when Christianity had nominally conquered Paganism, remained as the sole conservators of the ancient Teutonic magico-religious lore, and in the curtained recesses of dark-timbered halls whiled away the white hours of winter by the painful spelling out of runic characters and the

18

practice of arts which they were destined to convey from the priests of Odin and Thor to the witches of medieval days.

Costume of the Early Teuton

The personal appearance of these barbarians was as rude and simple as were their manners. Says Tacitus:

"The clothing in use is a loose mantle, made fast with a clasp, or, when that cannot be had, with a thorn. Naked in other respects, they loiter away whole days by the fireside. The rich wear a garment, not, indeed, displayed and flowing, like the Parthians or the people of Sarmatia, but drawn so tight that the form of the limbs is palpably expressed. The skins of wild animals are also much in use. Near the frontier, on the borders of the Rhine, the inhabitants wear them, but with an air of neglect that shows them altogether indifferent about the choice, The people who live more remote, near the northern seas, and have not acquired by commerce a taste for new-fashioned apparel, are more curious in the selection. They choose particular beasts and, having stripped off the furs, clothe themselves with the spoil, decorated with parti-coloured spots, or fragments taken from the skins of fish that swim the ocean as yet unexplored by the Romans. In point of dress there is no distinction between the sexes, except that the garment of the women is frequently made of linen, adorned with purple stains, but without sleeves, leaving the arms and part of the bosom uncovered."

The Germanic Tribes

It is also from Tacitus that we glean what were the names and descriptions of those tribes who occupied the territory adjacent to the Rhine. The basin of the river between

Hero Tales & Legends of the Rhine

Strassburg and Mainz was inhabited by the Tribacci, Nemetes, and Vangiones, further south by the Matiacci near Wiesbaden, and the Ubii in the district of Cologne. Further north lay the Sugambri, and the delta of the river in the Low Countries was the seat of the brave Batavii, from whom came the bulk of the legions by means of which Agricola obtained a footing in far Caledonia. Before the Roman invasion of their territories these tribes were constantly engaged in internecine warfare, a condition of affairs not to be marvelled at when we learn that at their tribal councils the warrior regarded as an inspired speaker was he who was most powerfully affected by the potations in which all habitually indulged to an extent which seemed to the cultured Roman as bestial in the last degree. The constant bearing of arms, added to their frequent addiction to powerful liquors, also seemed to render the Germanic warriors quarrelsome to excess, and to provoke intertribal strife.

The Romans in the Rhine Country

Caesar is the first Roman writer to give us any historical data concerning the peoples who inhabited the basin of the Rhine. He conquered the tribes on the left bank, and was followed a generation or so later by Augustus, who established numerous fortified posts on the river. But the Romans never succeeded in obtaining a firm occupancy of the right bank. Their chief object in colonizing the Rhine territory was to form an effective barrier between themselves and the restless barbarian tribes of the Teutonic North, the constant menace of whose invasion lay as a canker at the heart of rich and fruitful Italy. With the terror of a barbarian inroad ever before their eyes, the cohorts of the Imperial City constructed a formidable

The Rebellion of the Barbarians

vallum, or earthen wall, from the vicinity of Linz to
Regensburg, on the Danube, a distance of three hundred
and fifty miles, for the purpose of raising a barrier against
the advance of the warlike men of the North. They further
planted a colony of veterans in the Black Forest neighbourhood in order that invasion might be resisted from
that side. But as the Empire began to exhibit signs of
decadence the barbarians were quick to recognize the
symptoms of weakness in those who barred their advance
to the wealthy South, the objective of their dreams, hurled
themselves against the boundary, now rendered feeble by
reason of the withdrawal of its most experienced defenders,
and, despite a stern resistance, flooded the rich valleys of
the Rhine, swamped the colonies on the left bank which
had imbibed Roman civilization, and made all wholly
Teutonic.

The Rebellion of the Barbarians

This was, however, a process of years, and by no means
a speedy conquest. The closing years of Augustus' reign
were clouded by a general rising of the Rhine peoples.
Quintilius Varus, an officer who had been entrusted with
the government of the provinces beyond the Rhine, proved
totally unequal to curbing the bolder spirits among the
Germans, who under their chief, Arminius, boldly challenged the forces of this short-sighted officer. Arminius
belonged to the Cherusci. He had served with the German horsemen in the Rhenish armies, and was conversant
with the Latin language. Observing that half, at least,
of the Roman forces were on leave, he incited the tribes
of Lower Saxony to revolt. The weak Varus, who had
under-estimated the influence of Arminius, attempted to
quell the rising, but without success, and the bank of the

river was the scene of a wholesale slaughter. Varus, completely losing his nerve, attempted to separate the cavalry from the infantry and endeavoured to escape with three squadrons of the former; but the Germans surrounded them, and after a hand-to-hand struggle of three days the Roman army was annihilated. The news of this disaster prompted the aged Emperor to dispatch his son Tiberius to suppress what appeared to be a general rising of the North. The Rhenish tribes, however, were too wary to meet the powerful force now sent against them in the open field, and during the remainder of the year Tiberius, left in peace, occupied himself in strengthening the Rhine fortifications.

He was soon after recalled to Rome to assume the purple on the death of Augustus. Germanicus, who had taken command of the legions on the Rhine, became conscious of discontent among the soldiers, who threatened to carry him into Rome and thrust him into the seat of empire. But he soothed the passions of his soldiers by gifts and promises. A road was opened from the Rhine into the German hinterland, and Germanicus led his army into the heart of a country of which he knew but little to avenge the disasters of the Varian legions. The forest folk eluded the invading host, which now sought to return to headquarters; but ere they had completed the journey they were assailed and suffered a severe reverse.

Numerous revolts occurred among the Gaulish legions in the service of the Roman Empire in Germany. But the stubborn and trained resistance of the Romans no less than the inexperience of the Gauls led to a cessation of hostilities. The secret of Roman power in Rhenish territory lay in the circumstance that the two great elements of German nationality, the nobility and the priesthood,

The Franks & Goths

were becoming Romanized. But a rude culture was beginning to blossom, and a desire arose among the barbarians for unity. They wished to band themselves into a nation.

The Franks and Goths

The most dangerous enemies of Rome during the reigns of Valerian and Gallienus were the Franks, the Alemanni, and the Goths, whose action finally decided the conquest of the Rhenish provinces of Rome. The name Frank, or Freedman, was given to a confederacy formed in A.D. 240 by the old inhabitants of the Lower Rhine and the Weser. It consisted of the Chauci, the Cherusci, and the Chatti, and of several other tribes of greater or less renown. The Romans foresaw the power of this formidable union and, by the presence of the Emperor himself and his son, endeavoured to stem the invasion, which threatened their suzerainty. The Franks, fond of liberty and imbued with a passion for conquest, crossed the Rhine, in spite of its strong fortifications, and carried their devastations to the foot of the Pyrenees. For twelve years Gallienus attempted to stem the torrent thus freed.

The Alemanni, who belonged to the Upper Rhine, between the Main and the Danube, were composed of many tribes, the most important of which was the celebrated Suevi. This people, who had now become a permanent nation, threatened the Empire with an invasion which was checked with difficulty after they had fought their way to the gates of Rome itself. In A.D. 271 Aurelian completely subdued the Rhenish peoples, numbers of whom were dragged in his triumph through the streets of Rome; but after his brief reign the old condition of things reasserted itself, until Probus, who assumed the purple in 276, restored peace and order by the construction of a massive wall between the Rhine and the Danube over two hundred miles in length. The barbarians were driven beyond the river, which had hitherto served as a boundary-line, even past the Elbe and the Neckar. Finally, however, the internecine strife in the Imperial City forced the Romans to return thence, and Rhineland was abandoned to the will of its semi-barbarian inhabitants.

The early Christian centuries are full of the sound of conflict. In the fourth century the principal tribes in Western Germany were the Franks and the Alemanni, the former of whom maintained a constant strife with the Saxons, who pressed heavily upon their rear. The Franks occupied the lower portion of the river, near to its mouth, whilst the Alemanni dwelt on the portion to the bounds of Helvetia and Switzerland. At this period great racial upheavals appear to have been taking place further east. By the beginning of the sixth century the Saxons seem to have penetrated almost to the north-western Rhine, where the Franks were now supreme.

The Merovingians

In the middle of the fifth century arose the powerful dynasty of the Merovingians, one of the most picturesque royal houses in the roll of history. In their records we see the clash of barbarism with advancement, the bizarre tints of a semi-civilization unequalled in rude magnificence. Giant shadows of forgotten kings stalk across the canvas, their royal purple intermingling with the shaggy fell of the bear and wolf. One, Chilperic, a subtle grammarian and the inventor of new alphabetic symbols, is yet the most implacable of his race, the murderer of his wife, the heartless slayer of hundreds, to whom human life is as that of cattle, skilled in the administration of poison, a picturesque cut-throat. Others are weaklings, *fainéants*; but one, the most dread woman in Frankish history, Fredegonda, the queen of Chilperic, towers above all in this masque of slaughter and treachery.

Tradition makes claim that Andernach was the cradle of the Merovingian dynasty. In proof of this are shown the extensive ruins of the palace of these ancient Frankish kings. Merovig, from whom the race derived its name, was said to be the son of Clodio, but legend relates far otherwise. In name and origin he was literally a child of the Rhine, his father being a water-monster who seized the wife of Clodio while bathing in that river. In time she gave birth to a child, more monster than man, the spine being covered with bristles, fingers and toes webbed, eyes covered with a film, and thighs and legs horny with large shining scales. Clodio, though aware of the real paternity of this creature, adopted it as his own son, as did King Minos in the case of the Minotaur, giving him the name Merovig from his piscatory origin. On Clodio's death the demi-monster succeeded to the throne, and from him sprang a long line of sovereigns, worthless and imbecile for the most part.

Childeric, the son and successor of Merovig, enraged his people to such a degree by his excesses that they drove him from throne and country. One friend alone remained to him, Winomadus, who, having no female relations to suffer by the king's attentions, did not find the friendship so irksome as others; indeed, had been a partner in his licentious pleasures. He undertook to watch over the interests of Childeric during his enforced absence in Thuringia at the court of Basium, king of that country. The Franks had elected Aegidius, a Roman general, to the sovereignty over them, but as he proved himself no better than Childeric, whom they had deposed, they once more essayed to choose another ruler. This was made known to Childeric through his friend Winomadus. He rapidly returned to the shores of the Rhine and, reinforcing his following as he proceeded on his march, appeared before Andernach at the head of a formidable force, composed of many of his former subjects, together with Thuringian auxiliaries. The people of Andernach, unable to resist this overwhelming argument, again accepted Childeric as their king.

Basina the Sorceress

While in Thuringia Childeric had seduced the affections of Basina, the queen of his protector. When he regained his throne he induced her to leave her husband, and made her his queen. Basina was a sorceress, one who could divine the future and also bestow the gift upon others. Through this she gained great influence over Childeric, who desired to see and know what fate had in store for himself and his race. Basina agreed to satisfy his curiosity, and one night, at the midnight hour, they climbed together to the summit of the hill behind Andernach. There she bade him stand and look out over the plain while she performed her magical operations. After some lengthy incantations she bade him look well and tell her what he saw.

In a trance-like voice the king replied:

"I see a great light upon the plain, although all around is blackest night."

He paused; then, at her bidding, proceeded again:

"I see an immense concourse of wild animals—the lion, the tiger, the spotted pard, the elephant, the unicorn—ah!

26

they are coming this way—they will devour us!" and he turned to flee in great terror.

Basina bade him stay in peremptory tones and again to look out over the plain. In a voice of alarm he cried out:

"I see bears and wolves, jackals and hyenas. Heaven help us, the others are all gone!"

Heedless of his terror, the queen bade him look again and, for the last time, tell her what he saw.

"I see now dogs and cats and little creatures of all kinds. But there is one small animal—smaller than a mouse—who commands them all. Ah! he is eating them up—swallowing them all—one after another."

As he looked the light, the plain, the animals all vanished, and darkness fell. Basina then read to him the meaning of his vision.

"The first vision you saw indicated the character of our immediate successors. They will be as bold as lions, terrible as tigers, strong as elephants, uncommon as unicorns, beautiful as the pard. These are the men of an age; for a century shall they rule over the land."

At this Childeric was delighted and ejaculated a fervent "Praise be to the gods!"

"The second," pursued Basina, "are the men of the following century—our more remote descendants—rude as the bear, fell as the wolf, fawning as the jackal, cruel as the hyena—the curse of their people and—themselves. The last one—the following century—they will be weak, timid, irresolute—the prey of every base and low thing, the victims of violence, deceit, and cunning; vanquished and destroyed at last by the smallest of their own subjects."

Such was Childeric's vision and his queen's interpretation.

As she had predicted, the Merovingian dynasty lasted three hundred years, when it was overturned by one Pepin of Heristal, the smallest man of his day—at least, so tradition tells.

At the death of Clovis his sons split up the kingdom, and from that epoch a deadly war was waged between the rival kingdoms of Neustria and Austrasia, the west and the east.

The wars of Neustria and Austrasia (*Ost Reich*, the Eastern Kingdom, which has, of course, no connexion with the modern Austria) are related by Gregory of Tours in his *Ecclesiastical History of the Franks*, one of the most brilliant pieces of historical and biographical writing to be discovered among the literature of Europe in the Dark Ages. Metz was the capital of this kingdom-province. Fredegonda, the queen of Chilperic of Neustria, had a deadly blood-feud with her sister-in-law of Austrasia, and in the event put her rival to death by having her torn asunder by wild horses (A.D. 613). Later Austrasia became incorporated with Franconia, which in 843 was included in the kingdom of Louis the German.

The Great Race of Charlemagne

The race of the Carolingians, whose greatest monarch was the famous Charlemagne, or Karl der Grosse, sprang from a family of usurpers known as the 'Mayors of the Palace,' who had snatched the crown from the *rois fainéants*, the last weakly shoots of the mighty line of Merovig. He was the elder son of Pepin the Short, and succeeded, on the death of his father in A.D. 768, to a kingdom which extended from the Low Countries to the borders of Spain. His whole life was

The Song of the Saxons

one prolonged war undertaken against the forces of paganism, the Moors of Spain who harassed his borders to the south, and the restless Saxon tribes dwelling between the Rhine, Weser, and Elbe. Innumerable are the legends and romances concerning this great, wise, and politic monarch and statesman, who, surrounding himself with warriors of prowess whom he called his paladins, unquestionably kept the light of Christianity and civilization burning in Western Europe. He was, however, quite as great a legislator as a warrior, and founded schools and hospitals in every part of his kingdom. He died at Aix-la-Chapelle in 814, and was buried there.[1]

The 'Song of the Saxons'

One of the most stirring of the romances which tell of the wars of Charlemagne in the Rhine country is the *Song of the Saxons*, fifth in number of the *Romans des Douze Pairs de France*, and composed by Jean Bodel, a poet of Artois, who flourished toward the middle of the thirteenth century. Charles, sitting at table in Laon one Whitsuntide with fourteen kings, receives news of an invasion of the Saxons, who have taken Cologne, killed many Frankish nobles, and laid waste the country. A racy epitome of the events which follow has been given by Ludlow in his *Popular Epics of the Middle Ages* (1865) as follows:
" Charles invades Saxony, and reaches the banks of ' Rune the Deep,' beyond which lies Guiteclin's palace of ' Tremoigne ' (supposed to be Dortmund, in Westphalia). The river is too deep to be crossed by the army, although

---

[1] For numerous critical articles upon Charlemagne and the epics or *chansons des gestes* connected with him see the author's *Dictionary of Medieval Romance.*

the two young knights, Baldwin and Berard, succeed in doing so in quest of adventure. The Saxons will not attack, trusting that the French will be destroyed by delay and the seasons. And, indeed, after two years and four months, the barons represent to the Emperor the sad plight of the host, and urge him to call upon the men of Herupe (North-west France) for performance of their warlike service. This is done accordingly, and the Herupe barons make all haste to their sovereign's aid, and come up just after the Saxons have made an unsuccessful attack. They send to ask where they are to lodge their troops. The Emperor points them laughingly to the other side of the Rune, where float the silken banners of the Saxons, but says that any of his men shall give up their camping-place to them. The Herupe men, however, determine to take him at his word and, whilst the Archbishop of Sens blesses the water, boldly fling themselves in and cross it, and end, after a tremendous struggle, in taking up the quarters assigned to them; but when he sees their prowess the Emperor recalls them to his own side of the river.

"A bridge is built, the army passes over it, the Saxons are discomfited in a great battle, and Guiteclin is killed in single combat by Charlemagne himself.

"By this time the slender vein of historic truth which runs through the poem may be considered as quite exhausted. Yet the real epic interest of the work centres in its wholly apocryphal conclusion, connected essentially with its purely romantic side.

"Sebile, the wife of Guiteclin, is a peerless beauty, wise withal and courteous; 'hair had she long and fair, more than the shining gold, a brow polished and clear, eyes blue and laughing, a very well-made nose, teeth small and white, a *savourous* mouth, more crimson than blood; and in body and limbs so winning was she that God never made the man, howsoever old and tottering, if he durst look at her, but was moved with desire.'"

Fair Helissend, the daughter of the murdered Milo of Cologne, is her captive at once and her favourite, and when the French host takes up its position before the Rune, names and points out young Baldwin to her.

With her husband's sanction, Sebile has her tent pitched on the bank, and establishes herself there with her ladies to act as decoys to the Franks; for "fair lady's look makes men undertake folly." She is taken, however, in her own toils; falls in love with Baldwin one summer's day on seeing him ride forth with hawk on wrist, and makes Helissend invite him over the river, under a very frank pledge that "she will be his, for loss or gain." Their first meeting apparently takes place in the presence of Sebile's ladies, and so little mystery is attached to their love that, on Baldwin's return to the Frank host after killing and despoiling of his armour a Saxon chief, he not only tells his adventure publicly to the Emperor, but the latter promises in a twelvemonth to have him crowned king of the country and to give him Sebile for wife, forbidding him, however, to cross the river any more—a command which Baldwin hears without meaning to obey. Nay, when Baldwin has once broken this injunction and escaped with great difficulty from the Saxons, the Emperor imposes on him the brutal penance of entering Sebile's tent to kiss her in the sight of the Saxons, and bringing back her ring—which Baldwin contrives to fulfil by putting on the armour of a Saxon knight whom he kills. As in *The Taking of Orange*, it never seems to occur to the poet that there can be any moral wrong in making love to a "Saracen's" wife, or in promising her hand in her husband's lifetime ; and, strange to say, so benignant are these much-wronged paynim that Guiteclin is not represented as offering or threatening the slightest ill-treatment to his faithless queen, however wroth he may be against her lover ; nor, indeed, as having even the sense to make her pitch her tent further from the bank. The drollest bit of sentimentality occurs, however, after the victory of the Franks and Guiteclin's death, when Sebile is taken prisoner. After having been bestowed in marriage on Baldwin by the Emperor, she asks one boon of both, which is that Guiteclin's body be sought for, lest the beasts should eat it—a request the exceeding nobleness of which strikes the Emperor and the Frank knights with astonishment. When the body is found and brought to Sebile, " the water of her eyes falls down her chin. 'Ha, Guiteclin,' said she, 'so gentle a man were you, liberal and free-spending, and of noble witness! If in heaven and on earth Mahomet has no power, even to pray Him who made Lazarus, I pray and request Him to have mercy on thee.'" The dead man is then placed in a great marble tomb ; Sebile is christened, marries her lover, and is crowned with him as Queen of Saxony, Helissend being in like manner given to Berard.

" It is now that the truly tragical part of the poem commences. Charles and his host depart, the Emperor warning his nephew to be courteous, loyal, and generous, to keep true faith to his wife, yet not to spend too much time in her arms, but to beware of the Saxons. The caution is needed, for already the two sons of Guiteclin, with one hundred thousand Russians and Bulgarians, and the giant Ferabras of Russia, a personage twelve feet high, with

The Song of the Saxons

light hair plaited together, reddish beard, and flattened face, are within a day and a half's journey of 'Tremoigne,' burning to avenge Guiteclin. One Thursday morning their invasion is announced to the young king, who has but fifteen thousand men to oppose to them. Sebile embraces her husband's knees, and entreats him to send at once for help to his uncle; the barons whom he has called to counsel favour her advice. 'Barons,' said Baldwin, 'I should fear the dishonour of it. It is too soon to seek and pray for succour. We have not yet unhorsed knights, cut arms from bodies, made bowels trail; we are fifteen thousand young men untried, who should buy our praise and our honour, and seize and acquire strange lands, and kill and shame and grieve our enemies, cleave the bright helmets, pierce the shields, break and tear the hauberks of mail, shed blood and make brains to fly. To me a pleasure it seems to put on hauberk, watch long nights, fast long days. Let us go strike upon them without more delay, that we may be able to govern this kingdom.' The barons listen with an ill-will to this speech; Baldwin himself, on viewing the paynim host, is staggered at their numbers, and lets Sebile persuade him to send a messenger to his uncle. However, with five thousand men he makes a vigorous attack on the vanguard of the Saxons, consisting of twenty thousand, and ends by putting them to flight. On the news of this repulse the two sons of Guiteclin come out, apparently with the bulk of the army. The French urge the young king to re-enter the city, but he refuses— Sebile would hold him for a sleepy coward. He kills Ferabras, unhorses one of Guiteclin's sons. But the disparity of numbers is too great; the French are obliged to retreat, and shut themselves up in the city.

" Meanwhile the messenger had reached Charlemagne at

Cologne with the news of the renewal of the war. Whilst all his barons are summoned, the Emperor starts in haste himself for Saxony with ten thousand men. Baldwin was seated in his tower, looking out upon a league of hostile tents, complaining to Sebile, who 'comforts him as a worthy lady,' bidding him trust in his uncle's succour. She is the first to descry the French host and to point it out to her husband. 'Ah, God!' said Charles's nephew, 'fair Father Creator, yet will I avenge me of the pagan people.' He goes down from his palace, and cries to his men, 'Arm ye, knights! Charles is returned.'

"The besieged prepare at once for a sally. Sebile places the helmet on her husband's head and kisses him, never to see him more alive. The enemy are disarmed; three thousand of them are killed by the time Baldwin cuts his way to his uncle, to whom, as his liege lord, he makes complaint against the Saxons. The Emperor's answer contains little but philosophic comfort: 'Fair nephew, so goes war; when your day comes, know that you will die; your father died, you will not escape. Yonder are your enemies, of whom you complain; I give you leave, go and strike them.' Uncle and nephew both perform wonders. But Berard is killed by Feramor, one of Guiteclin's sons, and the standard which he bore disappears under him. Baldwin engages Feramor; each severely wounds the other; the fight is so well contested that Baldwin offers to divide the land with him if he will make peace. The Saxon spurns the offer, and is killed.

" But 'Baldwin is wounded in the breast grievously; from thence to the spur his body is bloody.' Saxons, Lusatians, Hungarians perceive that his blows lessen and fall slow. '*Montjoie!*' he cries many a time, but the French hear him not. 'When Baldwin sees that he will have no succour,

The Song of the Saxons

as a boar he defends himself with his sword. . . . Who
should have seen the proud countenance of the king, how
he bears and defends himself against the paynim, great
pity should surely take his heart.' Struck with fifteen
wounds, his horse killed under him, he offers battle on
foot. They dare not approach, but they fling their swords
at him, and then go and hide beneath a rock. Baldwin,
feeling death approaching, 'from the fair eyes of his head
begins to weep' for sorrow and rage. He now addresses
an elaborate last prayer to God; but whilst he is on his
knees, looking toward the East, a Saxon comes to cut off
his head. Baldwin, furious, seizes his sword, which had
fallen from his hand on the green grass, and with a last
blow cleaves the Saxon to the shoulders, then dies.

" The news is carried to the Emperor, who laments his
ill fate. Rest he has never had; the paynim folk have
killed him the flower of his friends, Roland at Roncevaux
and now Baldwin. ' Ha, God! send me death, without
making long delay!' He draws his sword, and is about
to kill himself when Naymes of Bavaria restrains him
and bids him avenge his nephew's death. The old man,
however, exposes his life with such recklessness, the
struggle is so unequal, that Naymes himself has to
persuade him to leave the battle and enter the city until
the Herupe nobles come to his aid. ' Dead is Count
Roland and Count Oliver, and all the twelve peers, who
used to help in daunting that pride which makes us bend
so; no longer at your right hand is Baldwin the warrior;
the paynim have killed him and Berard the light; God
has their souls. . . . If you are killed . . . in your death
alone a hundred thousand will die.'

" They lead him away, unwilling, from the field. Baldwin's
corpse is carried by him on his shield. Sebile comes to

35

meet the Emperor and asks of her husband. Charles
bids her look at him. She faints to the ground. There
is true pathos (though somewhat wire-drawn) in her
lament, when she comes to herself:

"'Sir King Baldwin, for God's sake, speak! I am your
love, mistake me not. If I have offended you in aught,
it shall be made amends for wholly to your pleasure; but
speak to me. For you was my body baptized and lifted;
my heart leans on you, and all my affections, and if you
fail me, it will be ill done. Too soon it seems to me, if
already you repent. Baldwin, is it a trick? Are you
deceiving me? Speak to me, friend, if you can. . . .
I see your garments dyed and bloody, but I do not believe
that you are killed; there is no man so bold or so
outrageous who ever could kill you; he durst not do so.
But I think by such a will you wish to try me, how I
should behave if you were departed. Speak to me, for
God's sake who was born of virgin, and for that lady who
kept chastity, and for the holy cross whereon Jesus
suffered! Try me no more, friend, it is enough; I shall
die now if you tarry longer,' 'Naymes,' says the king,
'take this lady away; *if I see her grief any more, I shall
go mad.*'

"That night he ate no bread nor drank wine, but had the
city watched, and rode the rounds himself, with helmet
closed, his great buckler hanging to his neck, his sword
in his fist. All the night it rained and blew; the water
ran through the joints of his hauberk, and wetted his
ermine pelisse beneath. His beard swayed, whiter than
flax, his long moustache quivered; until dawn he lamented
his nephew, and the twelve peers, and all his next-of-kin
who were dead. From the gate at morn a Saxon, King
Dyalas, defies the old man, swearing that he will wear his

Fastrada: a Legend of Aix-la-Chapelle

crown in Paris. The Emperor has the gate opened, and
sallies forth to meet him. They engage in single combat;
the old Emperor kills the Saxon's horse, disarms him,
and only spares his life on condition of his embracing
Christianity and yielding himself prisoner.
"The rest of the poem has comparatively little interest.
Old Naymes in turn kills his man—a brother of Guiteclin
—in single combat. Dyalas, the Emperor's new vassal,
'armed in French fashion,' performs wonders in honour
of his new allegiance. Finally the Herupese come up, and
of course overthrow the Saxons. An abbey is founded on
the field of battle, which Sebile enters; Dyalas, baptized
as 'Guiteclin the convert,' receives charge of the kingdom,
and the Emperor returns, bearing with him the bodies of
Baldwin and Berard; after which 'well was France in
peace many a year and many a day; the Emperor found
not any who should make him wroth.'"

Fastrada: a Legend of Aix-la-Chapelle

Fastrada, we are told, was the fourth wife of the Emperor
Charlemagne and the best beloved. Historians have
judged that the lady was by no means worthy of the
extraordinary affection bestowed upon her by her husband,
some maintaining that she practised the arts of sorcery,
others crediting her with political intrigues, and still
others roundly asserting that she was not so virtuous as
she should have been.
History failing to account for Charlemagne's devotion to
his fourth wife, the task has devolved upon tradition.
Once upon a time (so runs the tale), when Charlemagne
dwelt at Zurich, he had a pillar erected before his house,
and on the top of the pillar a bell was placed, so that any
one desiring justice had but to ring it to be immediately

conducted before the Emperor, there to have his case considered.

One day, just as Charlemagne was about to dine, the bell was rung loudly. He at once dispatched his attendants to bring the importunate claimant into his presence. A moment later they re-entered with the assurance that no one waited outside. Even as they spoke the bell rang again, and again the attendants withdrew at the bidding of their royal master. Once more they returned with the information that none was to be seen. When the bell rang for the third time the Emperor himself rose from the table and went outside to satisfy himself as to the ringer's identity. This time the mystery was solved; for twining round the pillar was a great snake, which, before the astonished eyes of the Emperor and his suite, was lustily pulling the bell-rope.

"Bring the snake before me," said Charlemagne. "Whether to man or beast, I may not refuse justice."

Accordingly the snake was conducted with much ceremony into the Emperor's presence, where it was distinctly observed to make a low obeisance. The Kaiser addressed the animal courteously, as though it were a human being, and inquired what it wanted. Whereupon the snake made a sign which the company took to indicate that it desired the Emperor to follow it. Charlemagne did not hesitate, but followed the creature to the shores of the lake, attended by all his courtiers. Straight to its nest went the snake, and there, among the eggs, was an enormous toad, puffing out its bloated body and staring with glassy eyes at the company. The reason for the snake's appeal was at once apparent.

"Take away that toad," said the Emperor, as gravely as though he were pronouncing judgment in an important

Fastrada : a Legend of Aix-la-Chapelle

human case; "take away that toad and burn it. It has taken unlawful possession of the snake's nest."

The court listened to the Emperor's decree in respectful silence, and immediately carried out the sentence. The company thereupon re-entered the royal abode, and thought no more of the incident.

On the following day, however, at about the same hour, the serpent entered the chamber in which Charlemagne sat, and glided swiftly toward the table. The attendants were somewhat astonished at the unexpected appearance, but the Kaiser motioned to them to stand aside, for he was very curious to see what the reptile would do. Raising itself till its head was on a level with the table, it dropped into his plate a magnificent diamond of the first water, gleaming with the purest light. This done, the serpent bowed low, as on the previous occasion, and quitted the room as silently as it had entered.

The diamond, set in a gold ring of exquisite workmanship, Charlemagne presented to his wife, the beautiful Fastrada. But besides being a thing of beauty and of great value, the diamond was also a charm, for whoever received it from another received with it a wealth of personal affection. So was it with Charlemagne and Fastrada. On presenting the ring to his wife the Emperor straightway conceived for her a passion far more intense than he had hitherto experienced. From that time to the day of her death he was her devoted slave, blind and deaf to all her faults.

Nay, even when she died, he refused to quit the room in which she lay, or permit the interment of her body; refused to see the approach of corruption, which spares not youth or loveliness; seemed, in short, to have lost all count of the passage of time in his grief for the beloved Fastrada. At length he was approached by Turpin,

39

Archbishop of Rheims, who had learnt, by occult means, the reason for the Emperor's strange infatuation. Going up to the dead Empress, he withdrew from her mouth a large diamond. At the same moment Charlemagne regained his senses, made arrangements for the burial of his wife, and left for the Castle of Frankenstein.

The possessor of the ring was now the worthy archbishop, and to him the magically inspired affections of Charlemagne were transferred, much to the good man's annoyance. To rid himself of the unwelcome attentions and fulsome flatteries of his sovereign, he cast the ring into the lake which surrounded the castle. Once more the Emperor's affections changed their object, and this time it was the town of Aix-la-Chapelle with which he fell in love, and for which he retained a firm attachment all through his life, finally directing that he should be buried there. And so he was laid to rest in that wondrous old town in the church of St. Mary. In the year 1000 his tomb was opened by the Emperor Otto III, but the account that Otto found the body seated upon a throne with crown on head and sceptre in hand is generally regarded as legendary. The sarcophagus was once more opened by Frederick I in 1165, when the remains were transferred from the princely marble where they had hitherto rested and placed in a wooden coffin. Fifty years later, however, Frederick II had them placed in a splendid shrine. The original sarcophagus may still be seen at Aix, and the royal relics are exhibited every six years.

Louis, Charlemagne's son, lived to see the division of his Empire, brought about through his own weakness. His fair provinces were ravaged by the Danes and the Normans. Teuton and Frank were now for ever separated. Twice during Louis' reign his own sons dethroned him, but

The Last Carolingians

on his death in 840 the Empire became more firmly established.

Lothair I (840–855) succeeded to the imperial title, while Germany fell to the lot of his brother Louis. Charles the Bald ruled over France. Lothair's portion was limited to Lorraine, Burgundy, Switzerland, and Italy. Civil strife broke out, but Louis retained the whole of Germany with the provinces on the left bank of the Rhine. Louis II (856–875) ascended the throne as Roman Emperor, but died without any male issue, while Charles the Fat, who succeeded him, was removed from the throne by order of the Church on account of his insanity.

With Charles ended the Carolingian dynasty. From the death of the illustrious Charlemagne the race had gradually but surely declined. After the removal of Charles the Fat there came a lapse of seventy-four years.

Conrad I (911–919) founded the Gascon dynasty of Germany, and was succeeded by Henry the Fowler (919–936). His son, Otto I, called the Great (936–973), was crowned Roman Emperor in 962. In 936 his elevation to the Germanic kingdom was a popular one. A portion of Gaul to the west of the Rhine along the banks of the Meuse and the Moselle was ceded to the Germans. Otto's supremacy between the Rhine, the Rhone, and the Alps was acquired and held for his successors. With the sword he propagated Christianity, subdued Italy, and delivered the Pope from his enemies, who, to show his appreciation, invested him with the imperial title, which ever after belonged to the Germanic nation. The German Emperors, however, still continued to exercise the right of electing the Pope, thereby reducing the Roman Church to a level of servitude.

Toward the close of the Carolingian dynasty France

and Germany had become irrevocably detached; both nations suffered from internecine wars. The Slavonians penetrated into the Empire, even to the banks of the Rhine. Feudal princes began to make war upon each other, and, within their respective districts, were virtual sovereigns.

At the partition of the domains of Charlemagne in A.D. 843 the Rhine formed the boundary between Germany and the middle kingdom of Lotharingia, but by 870 the latter had been absorbed by the larger country. For a period verging upon eight hundred years it remained the frontier of the German Empire. In the early Middle Ages the heritage of the ancient Roman civilization rendered it the most cultured portion of Germany. By the time of Otto I (died 973) both banks of the Rhine had become German, and the Rhenish territory was divided between the duchies of Upper and Lower Lorraine, the one on the Moselle and the other on the Meuse. But, like other German states, on the weakening of the central power they split up into numerous petty independent principalities, each with its special history.

The Palatinate

Chief among these was the state known as the Palatinate, from the German word *Pfalz*, a name given generally to any district ruled by a count palatine. It was bounded by Prussia on the north, on the east by Baden, and on the south by Alsace-Lorraine. We first hear of a royal official known as the Count Palatine of the Rhine in the tenth century. Although the office was not originally an hereditary one, it seems to have been held by the descendants of the first count, until the continuity of the race of Hermann was broken by the election of Conrad,

A Tale of the Palatine House

stepbrother of the German king Frederick I, as Count Palatine. From that time till much later in German history the Palatinate of the Rhine appears to have been gifted during their lifetime to the nephews or sons-in-law of the reigning Emperor, and by virtue of his occupancy of the office the holder became an Elector, or voter in the election of an Emperor. The office was held by a large number of able and statesmanlike princes, as Frederick I, Frederick III, the champion of Protestantism, and Frederick V. In the seventeenth century the Palatinate was first devastated and then claimed by France, and later was disturbed by still more harassing religious strife. In 1777 it was united with Bavaria upon the reigning Elector falling heir to the Electorate of that state.

A Tale of the Palatine House

Throughout the Middle Ages the nobles of Rhineland were mostly notorious for their wild savagery and predatory habits, and thus the modern traveller on the famous river, admiring the many picturesque castles built on summits overlooking its banks, is prone to think of these places as having been the homes of men who were little better than freebooters. And in general this idea is just; yet Walter Pater's story, *Duke Karl of Rosenwald*—which tells how a medieval German baron discovered in himself a keen love of art, and sought to gather artists round him from France and Italy—may well have been culled from a veracious historical source. For at least a few of the German petty princes of the Middle Ages shared the aestheticism characterizing so many of their contemporaries among the noblemen of the Latin races, and it is interesting to find that among the old German courts where art was loved in this isolated fashion was

43

that of the Palatine house, which ultimately became related by marriage to the Royal Stuarts, a dynasty as eminently artistic as the Medicis themselves.

This Palatine house was regnant for many generations at Heidelberg Castle, and there, at a remote medieval date, reigned a prince named Louis III, who esteemed literature and painting. A fond parent he was besides, devoted to his two sons, the elder called Louis and the younger Frederick; and from the outset he attended carefully to the education of the pair, choosing as their tutor a noted scholar, one Kenmat, while he allowed this tutor's daughter Eugenia to be taught along with the princely pupils, and he also admitted to the group an Italian boy, Rafaello. These four children grew up together, and the Palatine prince was pleased to mark that Frederick, though full of martial ardour, showed intellectual tastes as well; yet the father did not live long to watch the growth of the boy's predilection therein, and there came a day when the crown of Louis III was acquired by his heir, Louis IV. Still quite young, the latter was already affianced to Margaret of Savoy; and this engagement had incensed various nobles of the Rhine, especially the Count of Luzenstein. He was eager that his own house should become affiliated with the Palatinate, and while he knew that there was little hope of frustrating Louis' prospective wedding, this did not nullify his ambitions. For was it not possible that the marriage might prove without issue? And, as that would ultimately set Frederick on the Palatine throne, Luzenstein determined that his daughter Leonora should wed the younger of the two princes. She herself was equally eager for the union, and though the affair was not definitely arranged in the meantime, it was widely

A Tale of the Palatine House

understood that at no very distant date Leonora's betrothal would be announced.

At length there came a day when the *noblesse* of the Rhine assembled at Heidelberg to celebrate the nuptials of Louis and Margaret. For a space the rejoicings went forward merrily, but, as Louis scanned the faces of his guests, he was surprised to find that Frederick was absent. Why was this? he mused; and going in search he soon found his brother in one of the smaller rooms of the castle, attended by Rafaello. Now the latter, who was developing a rare gift for sculpture, had lately made a statue to decorate this room; and on Louis entering Frederick was gazing with passionate fondness at this new work of art. Louis was straightway called upon to observe its loveliness, and even as Frederick was descanting thus, a number of the guests who had remarked their host's temporary absence trooped into the room, among them being Leonora of Luzenstein. She was in ill-temper, for Frederick had not so much as troubled to salute her on her arrival; and now, finding him deep in admiration of a statue, its subject a beautiful girl, her rancour deepened apace. But who was the girl? she wondered; and as divers other guests were also inquisitive on this head, it soon transpired that Rafaello's model had been Eugenia. Leonora knew that this girl had been Frederick's playmate in youth, so her wrath turned to fierce malice, for she suspected that in Eugenia she had a rival who might wreck all hopes of the Luzensteins becoming united to the Palatine house.

But Frederick regarded Eugenia only as a sister. He knew that she and the sculptor who had hewn her likeness loved one another, and he longed to see their union brought about, his genuine affection for the young Italian being the greater on account of Rafaello's blossoming talents as an artist. Leonora, however, knew nothing of the real situation; she fancied she had been insulted, and demanding of her father that he should cease all negotiations regarding Frederick's suggested engagement to her, she proceeded to take stronger measures. Readers of Sir Walter Scott's *Anne of Geierstein* will recall the *Vehmgericht*, that 'Secret Tribunal' whose deeds were notorious in medieval Germany, and it chanced that the Luzensteins were in touch with this body. Its minions were called upon to wreak vengeance on the younger Palatine prince. On several occasions his life was attempted, and once he would certainly have been killed had not Rafaello succoured him in the hour of need.

Meanwhile a son was born to Louis, and in celebration of the event a tourney was held at Heidelberg, competitors coming from far and near, all of them eager to win the golden sword which was promised to the man who should prove champion. One after another they rode into the lists, Frederick being among the number; and as each presented himself his name was called aloud by the herald. At length there came one of whom this functionary cried, "This is a nameless knight who bears a plain shield"; and at these words a murmur of disapproval rose from the crowd, while everyone looked up to where Louis sat, awaiting his verdict on the matter. But he signified that the mysterious aspirant should be allowed to show his prowess, and a minute later, all who were to take part being now assembled, Frederick and another competitor were stationed at opposite ends of the lists, and the signal given them to charge. Forward thundered their steeds, a fierce combat ensued; but Frederick proved victor, and so

A Tale of the Palatine House

another warrior came forward to meet him. He, too, was worsted, and soon it appeared as though the young Palatine prince would surely win the coveted golden sword; for foeman after foeman he vanquished, and eventually only two remained to confront him—the nameless knight and another who had entered the lists under a strange, though less suspicious, pseudonym. The latter expressed his desire to fight last of all, and so the nameless one galloped toward Frederick, and their lances clashed together. The Palatine prince bore his adversary to the ground, apparently conquering him with complete ease; and fearing he had wounded him mortally, Frederick dismounted with intent to succour him. But the speedy fall had been a feint, and as the victor bent down the mysterious knight suddenly drew a dagger, with intent to plunge it into the prince's heart. So stealthy a deed was unknown in the history of the tourney. The crowd gazed as though petrified, and Frederick's life would doubtless have been lost—for he was weak after his many joustings—had not he who had asked to fight last of all galloped forward instantly on marking the drawn weapon and driven his lance into the body of the would-be murderer !

It was Rafaello who had rescued the Palatine prince once again, and it was a member of the Luzenstein house who had sought to kill him thus. A crafty device in truth, and thenceforth the name of Luzenstein became abhorred throughout all Rhineland, while the brave Italian was honoured by knighthood, and arrangements were made for his speedy union with Eugenia. But, alas ! the fates were untoward ; for the ' Secret Tribunal,' having been baulked again and again, began to direct their schemes against the sculptor instead of his patron ; and one evening, as Rafaello was walking with his beloved one, a band of villains attacked and murdered the pair. They were buried together at a place known for many centuries after as 'The Lovers' Grave,' and here Frederick used to loiter often, musing fondly on the dear sister who had been snatched from him in this ruthless fashion, and dreaming of the lofty artistic career which he had planned in vain for his beloved Rafaello.

Bishops, Barons, and Bourgeois

To trace the fortunes, divisions, and junctions of the lesser Rhine principalities would be a work requiring a world of patience on the part of the reader as well as an amount of space which would speedily surpass the limits even of such an ample volume as the present. The constant changes of boundary of these tiny lordships, the hazy character of the powers possessed by their rulers, the multiplicity of free townships yielding obedience to none but their own civic rulers, the brief but none the less tyrannous rule of scores of robber barons who exercised a *régime* of blood and iron within a radius of five miles of their castellated eyries, render the tracing of the history of the Rhine during the Middle Ages a task of almost unequalled complexity, robbed of all the romance of history by reason of the necessity for constant attention to the details of dynastic and territorial changes and the petty squabblings and dreary scufflings of savage barons with their neighbours or with the scarcely less brutal ecclesiastical dignitaries, who, joining with gusto in the general *mêlée* of land-snatching, served to swell the tumult with their loud-voiced claims for land and lordship. Three of the Electors of Franconia, within the boundaries of which the Palatinate was included, were archbishops, and these were foremost in all dynastic and territorial bickerings.

The Rhine Hanse Towns

The growth of German municipalities since the days of their founder, Henry the Fowler, was not without effect upon the Empire. Distinctions of class were modified. The freeman became empowered to reserve to himself the right of going to war along with his lord. Imperial cities began to spring up; these were governed by a lieutenant of the Emperor, or by their own chief magistrate. They achieved confederation, thus guarding themselves against imperial and feudal encroachments. The 'League of the Rhine' and that of the Hanse Towns emerged as the fruit of this policy. The latter federation consisted of about four-score cities of Germany which under their charter enjoyed a commercial monopoly. This example succeeded so well that its promoter, Lübeck, had the satisfaction of seeing all cities between the Rhine and the Vistula thus connected. The clergy, jealous of this municipal power, besought the Emperor to repress the magistrates who had been called into being by the people, and who were closely allied to this commercial confederation. But the monarch advised the prelates to return to their churches lest their opulent friends became their enemies.

The Rhine Hanse Towns

The influence of the Hanseatic League of the Rhine district in the fourteenth century extended over the whole commercial radius of Germany, Prussia, Russia, the Netherlands, and Britain. It opened up new fields of commerce, manufacture, and industry. It paved the way for culture, it subdued the piracy which had existed in the Baltic, and it promoted a universal peace. On the other hand, it created jealousy; it boycotted the honest manufacturer and merchant who did not belong to the

League, and fostered luxury in the Rhenish cities, which did much to sap the sturdy character of the people. The celebrity which many of these municipalities attained through their magnificence can be gathered from the historic buildings of Worms, Spires, Frankfort, Cologne, Augsburg, and Nuremberg. The splendour of these edifices and the munificence of their wealthy inhabitants could only be equalled in the maritime regions of Italy. But in the fifteenth century the power of the League began to decline. The Russian towns, under the leadership of Novgorod the Great, commenced a crusade against the Hanse Towns' monopoly in that country. The general rising in England, which was one of the great warehouses, under Henry VI and Edward IV reflected upon them. The Netherlands followed England's example. In the seventeenth century their existence was confined to three German towns— Lübeck, Hamburg, and Bremen. These no longer had the power to exercise their influence over the nation, and soon the League dropped out of existence.

The Thirty Years' War

The protracted struggle known as the Thirty Years' War was most prejudicial to the interests of the Rhine valley, which was overrun by the troops of the several nationalities engaged. One phase of this most disastrous struggle— the War of the Palatinate—carried the rapine and slaughter to the banks of the Rhine, where, as has been said, they were long remembered. During the reign of Ferdinand III (1637–1659) a vigorous and protracted war broke out between France and Germany, the former assisted by her ally Sweden. Germany, seeing that unless peace were restored her ruin as a great power would be inevitable, entered into negotiations with France, and in 1648 the claims of France and Sweden were settled by the Peace of Westphalia. This treaty is particularly notable in the present instance because it gave to the former country the footing on the Rhine already mentioned as the beginning of French encroachments. Germany was forced to give up Alsace, on the left bank of the river. France, by the seizure of Strassburg, confirmed by the Treaty of Ryswick in 1695, extended her boundaries to the Rhine. At the beginning of the French Revolution Leopold II of Germany and other German monarchs agreed to support the cause of French royalty, a resolution which was disastrous to the Empire. In 1795 Prussia, for political reasons, withdrew from the struggle, ceding to France, in the terms of the Treaty of Basel, all her possessions on the left bank of the Rhine. In 1799 war again broke out; but in 1801 the Treaty of Lunéville gave to France the whole of the left bank of the river. Thus the historic stream became the boundary between France and Germany. In 1806 the humiliation of the latter country was complete, for in that year a number of German princes joined the Confederation of the Rhine, thus allying themselves with France and repudiating their allegiance to the Empire. In 1815, at the Congress of Vienna, the whole of the Lower Rhenish district was restored to Prussia, while Bavaria, a separate state, was put in possession of the greater part of the Palatinate on the left bank of the Rhine.

From that time onward the German national spirit flourished, but the future of the Empire was uncertain till its fate was decided by the Franco-Prussian War of 1870–71. In the great hall of the Palace of Versailles in 1871 William I, King of Prussia, proclaimed, in the hour of victory, the restoration of the confederated

51

German Empire. The French forfeited their Rhenish provinces, and once more the Rhine was restored to Germany.

That the Thirty Years' War did not fail to linger in the folk-memory is evidenced by the following gruesome legend of Oppenheim:

The Battle of Skeletons

The smoke and terror of the great struggle had surged over Oppenheim. A battle had been fought there, and the Swedes and Spaniards who had contested the field and had been slain lay buried in the old churchyard hard by the confines of the town. At least many had been granted the right of sepulture there, but in a number of cases the hasty manner in which their corpses had received burial was all too noticeable, and a stranger visiting the churchyard confines years after the combat could not fail to be struck by the many uncoffined human relics which met his gaze.

But an artist who had journeyed from far to see the summer's sun upon the Rhine water, and who came to Oppenheim in the golden dusk, was too intent on the search for beauty to remember the grisly reputation of the town. Moreover, on entering the place the first person by whom he had been greeted was a beautiful young maiden, daughter of the innkeeper, who modestly shrank back on hearing his confident tones and, curtsying prettily, replied to his questions in something like a whisper.

" Can you recommend me to a comfortable hostelry, my pretty maid, where the wine is good and the company jovial?"

" If the Herr can put up with a village inn, that of

Oppenheim Abbey

Louis Weirter, R.B.A.

(See page 52)

The Lorelei
Louis Weirter, R.B.A.

(See page 59)

my father is as good as any in the place," replied the maid.

"Good, my pretty," cried the bold painter, sending the ready blood to her face with a glance from his bright black eyes. "Lead the way, and I will follow. Or, better still, walk with me."

By the time they had reached the inn they felt like old friends. The girl had skilfully but simply discovered the reason for the young artist's sojourn in Oppenheim, and with glowing face and eyes that had grown brighter with excitement, she clasped her hands together and cried: "Oh, the Herr must paint my beloved Oppenheim. There is no such place by moonlight, believe me, and you will be amply repaid by a visit to the ruins of the old church to-night. See, a pale and splendid moon has already risen, and will light your work as the sun never could."

"As you ask me so prettily, Fräulein, I shall paint your beloved abbey," he replied. "But why not in sunlight, with your own sweet face in the foreground?"

"No, no," cried the girl hastily. "That would rob the scene of all its romance."

"As you will," said the artist. "But this, I take it, is your father's inn, and I am ready for supper. Afterward—well, we shall see!"

Supper over, the painter sat for some time over his pipe and his wine, and then, gathering together his sketching impedimenta, quitted the inn and took his way toward the ruins of Oppenheim's ancient abbey. It was a calm, windless night, and the silver moon sailed high in the heavens. Not a sound broke the silence as the young man entered the churchyard. Seating himself upon a flat tombstone, he proceeded to arrange his canvas and sketching materials; but as he was busied thus his foot struck something hard. Bending down to remove the obstacle, which he took for a large stone, he found, to his horror, that it was a human skull. With an ejaculation he cast the horrid relic away from him, and to divert his mind from the grisly incident commenced to work feverishly. Speedily his buoyant mind cast off the gloomy train of thought awakened by the dreadful find, and for nearly a couple of hours he sat sketching steadily, until he was suddenly startled to hear the clock in the tower above him strike the hour of midnight.

He was gathering his things preparatory to departure, when a strange rustling sound attracted his attention. Raising his eyes from his task, he beheld a sight which made his flesh creep. The exposed and half-buried bones of the dead warriors which littered the surface of the churchyard drew together and formed skeletons. These reared themselves from the graves and stood upright, and as they did so formed grisly and dreadful battalions—Swedes formed with Swedes and Spaniards with Spaniards. On a sudden hoarse words of command rang out on the midnight air, and the two companies attacked one another.

The luckless beholder of the dreadful scene felt the warm blood grow chill within his veins. Hotter and hotter became the fray, and many skeletons sank to the ground as though slain in battle. One of them, he whose skull the artist had kicked, sank down at the young man's feet. In a hollow voice he commanded the youth to tell to the world how they were forced to combat each other because they had been enemies in life, and that they could obtain no rest until they had been buried.

Directly the clock struck one the battle ceased, and the bones once more lay about in disorder. The artist (who, it need hardly be said, gave no more thought to his picture)

54

hastened back to the inn and in faltering accents related his experiences. When the Seven Years' War broke out, not long afterward, the people of Oppenheim declared that the apparition of the skeletons had foretold the event.

The Robbers of the Rhine

For many hundreds of years the valley of the Rhine itself, and the various valleys adjacent, were the haunt of numerous bodies of rapacious and desperate banditti. The rugged, mountainous nature of the country naturally made lawlessness the more easy there, and till so late as the beginning of the nineteenth century these gangs of robbers were a constant menace to the traveller in Rhineland. At the time of the French Revolution, indeed, and for some decades thereafter, the district was literally infested with thieves; for the unsettled state of Europe at this date perforce tended to bring desperadoes from far and near, and for a while the inhabitants of the different villages on the banks of the Rhine endured a veritable reign of terror.

But almost from the outset the brigands realized that they would soon be undone if they grew too numerous. They knew that, in that event, strong military measures would probably be taken against them; so they made every effort to practise that union which is proverbially strength, and to prevent the enlisting in their ranks of anyone likely to prove cowardly or perfidious. In some cases, too, they actually had a well and capably organized system whereby one of their number could escape quickly, if need be, from the scene of his crime; for, like the French prisoners described in Stevenson's *St. Ives*, they had a line of sanctuaries extending perhaps into Austria or Italy, the retreat in most instances being an inn whose keeper was sworn to hide and protect his robber guest at all costs. In short, there was honour among these thieves, and even certain spirit of freemasonry; while, more important still, the captain of a band was very often in league with the few police officials of the neighbourhood.

The great highwaymen of Stuart and Georgian England —for example, that gallant Beau Brocade of whom Mr. Austin Dobson writes—were mostly content with waylaying a chance passer-by; while their contemporaries in France usually worked on this principle also, as witness the deeds of the band who figure in Théophile Gautier's story *Le Capitaine Fracasse*. But the robbers of the Rhine were of different mettle from these, and often it was almost a predatory warfare rather than mere brigandage which they carried on. Frequently they had an agent in each of the villages on the river, this agent being usually a member of the scattered remnant of Israel; and the business of this person was to discover a house containing especial wealth, and then to inform the robbers accordingly. Having gleaned the requisite information in this wise, the gang would sally down from the mountains at dead of night; and it was customary, as they drew near to their prey, for the captain to call his henchmen to attention and see that each was ready for the imminent fray. Then, having gagged the village watchman and muffled his bell, they would proceed to surround the house they intended to rifle, and, should resistance be offered, to batter in the door with a log or other instrument. Sometimes it would transpire that the Jewish agent had misinformed them, telling them of booty where booty there was little, and woe betide him should this prove the state of affairs. Moreover, unlike the brigands in *Gil Blas*, these scoundrels of the Rhine would not be encumbered by prisoners, and they were wont to slay outright all who were minded to show fight.

Yet to their own brotherhood the robbers were invariably loyal, seldom failing to carry away with them such of their *confrères* as were wounded in the assault; for each was sworn to support his fellows under all circumstances, and awful was the fate of the marauder who violated this compact. It is told of a band commanded by one Picard, a cruel but brave leader, that one of its members chanced to be captured, and with a view to purchasing his freedom he gave information about the whereabouts of his chief. The next night, as the captive lay in his dungeon, a masked face suddenly appeared at the barred window, and in awestruck tones the prisoner asked the new-comer to declare his identity. "I am Picard, your captain," came the answer. "As in duty bound, I have risked my life to set you free," and having spoken thus, he proceeded to file through one of the bars, which being accomplished, the reprobate was drawn out of his cell by the aid of a rope. He breathed freely now, finding himself once more among some of his old comrades, but a moment later Picard addressed him again. "Traitor," he snarled, "do not think that your perfidy has failed to reach our ears; you must pay the full penalty." "Mercy," cried the unfortunate one; "at least let me die in action. Lead on against some foe, and let me fall at their hands." "Cowards," retorted Picard, "deserve no such gallant fate," and with these words he drove his sword deep into the heart of the traitor.

In general it was a point of honour among these bandits that none should reveal to a woman anything about the doings of his band, and one story relates how a young brigand, on the eve of setting out on his first predatory expedition, was rash enough to inform his sweetheart whither he and his mates were bound. Their commander was a Captain Jikjak, reputed something of a wit; and betimes, after the brigands had marched forward silently for a while, this worthy called upon them to halt. They imagined it was but the usual inspection of arms which was about to take place, but Jikjak, speaking in stentorian tones, told them that a traitor was in their midst, and pointing to the culprit, he bade him step forth. The young man pled his youth as an excuse for his fault, and he told the captain that, could he but get a chance to show his prowess once, they would soon see that he was as gallant a robber as any of them. But Jikjak laughed scornfully, saying he was anxious to find out which was stronger, the young man's legs or a pair of trees. The culprit quailed on hearing the verdict, and implored a less ghastly fate; but Jikjak was obdurate, and smiling blandly, he bade his followers bend a couple of stout branches to the ground and tie their tops to the ankles of the offender. . . .

Such, then, were the robbers of the Rhine, and such the code of honour which existed among them. A romantic institution they no doubt were, yet it was a form of picturesqueness whose disappearance can scarcely be regretted.

CHAPTER II : THE RHINE IN FOLKLORE AND LITERATURE

Affinities of the Rhine Legends

A CLOSE perusal of the body of tradition known as the legends of the Rhine displays one circumstance which is calculated to surprise the collector of these narratives not a little. It is generally represented —probably through ignorance of the real circumstances— that these tales abound in the matter of folklore. This is, however, by no means the case, and even a superficial examination of them will prove most of them to be allied to the matter of romance in a much more intimate way than they approach that of folklore. But this is not so as regards all of them, and it will be interesting to look into the character of those which present folklore affinities, whilst leaving the consideration of their romantic aspect for a later portion of this chapter.

By right of precedence, among the legends of the Rhine which possess folklore characteristics is the wonderful legend of the Lorelei, a word derived from the old High German *lur*, to lurk, and *lai*, a rock. The height from which the bewitching water-spirit sent her song floating over the waves of the Rhine is situated near St. Goar, and possesses a remarkable echo which may partly account for the legend.

The Lorelei

Many are the legends which cluster round the name of the Lorelei. In some of the earlier traditions she is represented as an undine, combing her hair on the Loreleiberg and singing bewitching strains wherewith to lure mariners to their death, and one such legend relates how an old soldier named Diether undertook to capture her.

Graf Ludwig, son of the Prince Palatine, had been caught in her toils, his frail barque wrecked, and he himself caught in the whirlpool and drowned. The prince, grievously stricken at the melancholy occurrence, longed to avenge his son's death on the evil enchantress who had wrought such havoc. Among his retainers there was but one who would undertake the venture—a captain of the guard named Diether—and the sole reward he craved was permission to cast the Lorelei into the depths she haunted should he succeed in capturing her.

Diether and his little band of warriors ascended the Lorelei's rock in such a way as to cut off all retreat on the landward side. Just as they reached the summit the moon sailed out from behind a cloud, and behold, the spirit of the whirlpool was seen sitting on the very verge of the precipice, binding her wet hair with a band of gleaming jewels.

"What wouldst thou with me?" she cried, starting to her feet.

"To cast thee into the Rhine, sorceress," said Diether roughly, "where thou hast drowned our prince."

"Nay," returned the maid, "I drowned him not. 'Twas his own folly which cost him his life."

As she stood on the brink of the precipice, her lips smiling, her eyes gleaming softly, her wet dark hair streaming over her shoulders, some strange, unearthly quality in her beauty, a potent spell fell upon the little company, so that even Diether himself could neither move nor speak.

"And wouldst thou cast me in the Rhine, Diether?" she pursued, smiling at the helpless warrior. "'Tis not I who go to the Rhine, but the Rhine that will come to me."

The Forsaken Bride

Then loosening the jewelled band from her hair, she flung it on the water and cried aloud: "Father, send me thy white steeds, that I may cross the river in safety."

Instantly, as at her bidding, a wild storm arose, and the river, overflowing its banks, foamed right up to the summit of the Lorelei Rock. Three white-crested waves, resembling three white horses, mounted the steep, and into the hollowed trough behind them the Lorelei stepped as into a chariot, to be whirled out into the stream. Meanwhile Diether and his companions were almost overwhelmed by the floods, yet they were unable to stir hand or foot. In mid-stream the undine sank beneath the waves: the spell was broken, the waters subsided, and the captain and his men were free to return home.

Nevermore, they vowed, would they seek to capture the Lorelei.

The Forsaken Bride

There is a later and more popular legend of the Lorelei than the foregoing.

According to this tale Lorelei was a maiden of surpassing beauty who dwelt in the town of Bacharach in medieval times. So potent were her attractions that every gallant on whom her eye rested fell hopelessly in love with her, while her ever-widening fame drew suitors in plenty from all parts of the country. The dismissed lovers wandered disconsolately in the neighbouring forests, vowing to take their lives rather than suffer the pangs of unrequited passion; while occasionally the threat was fulfilled, and a brave knight would cast himself into the Rhine and perish for love of the cold and cruel maid. Thus her fatal beauty played havoc among the flower of German chivalry. But she, dowered with virtue and goodness, as well as with

61

more transient charms, trembled when she saw the effect of her attractions on her many lovers, and secluded herself as closely as possible.

The truth was, she had given her heart into the keeping of a young knight who, after plighting his troth with her, had ridden away to the wars, his military ardour and desire for glory triumphing over his love. Years had gone by, yet he did not return, and Lorelei thought that he had perished on the field of battle, or had taken another bride and forgotten her. But she remained true to him in spite of his long silence, and spent her days in tears and prayers for his safety.

Meanwhile she was besieged by an ever-increasing band of suitors, to whom her retiring disposition and sorrowful mien but made her the more desirable. Then it began to be rumoured abroad that she was a sorceress, who won the hearts of men by magic art and with the aid of the Evil One. The rumour was spread broadcast by jealous and disappointed women who saw their menfolk succumb to the fatal charms of the Maid of Bacharach. Mothers noticed their sons grow pale and woe-begone because of her; maids their erstwhile lovers sighing out a hopeless passion for the beautiful Lorelei; so they brought against her accusations of sorcery, which in those days generally led to the death of the victim by burning. So grievously did these malign whispers add to the already heavy burden of the maid that she surrendered herself to be tried, hardly caring whether or not she were found guilty. She was summoned before the criminal court held at Rhens by the Archbishop of Cologne, and charged with practising the black art in order to ensnare men's affections.

However, when she appeared before the court her beauty so impressed the assembly, and even the old Archbishop

The Forsaken Bride

himself, that none could believe her guilty. Her lovely face bore the imprint of innocence, her grief touched every heart, and on all sides she was treated with the greatest respect and kindness. The old prelate assured her that she would not be judged harshly, but begged to hear from her own lips that she was innocent of the foul charge brought against her. This assurance she gave with artless simplicity, and a murmur of approval went up from the crowd. The sympathy of those present—for even her accusers were melted—and the kindness of the aged Churchman who was her judge moved her to confess her unhappy love-story.

"I pray thee," she concluded wearily, "I pray thee, my lord, let me die. I know, alas! that many true knights have died for love of me, and now I fain would die for the sake of one who hath forsaken me."

The prelate, moved almost to tears by the pathetic story, laid his hand on the head of the weeping maid.

"Thou shalt not die, fair maiden," he said. "I will send thee to a convent, where thou mayst live in peace." And calling to his side three trusty old knights, he bade them conduct Lorelei to the convent across the river, and charge the abbess to treat her with the greatest kindness. Having blessed the maid once more, he bade them go.

On their way to the convent they must needs pass the rock since known as the Lorelei-berg, and the girl, who had maintained a pensive silence all the way, now observed that she would fain ascend the rock and look for the last time at the castle of her betrothed knight.

Her escort would have courteously assisted her, but she, with the agility of youth, easily outstripped them, and stood alone on the summit, surveying the fair scene before her. A light barque was sailing up the river, and as she gazed on it Lorelei uttered a loud cry, for there in the bow stood her truant lover! The knight and his train heard the shriek and beheld with horror the maiden standing with outstretched arms on the very edge of the precipice. The steering of the boat was forgotten for the moment, and the frail craft ran on the rocks. Lorelei saw her lover's peril and, calling his name, leapt into the tide.

Nothing more was seen of the lovers; together they sleep the sleep of death beneath the waters of the Rhine.

A Blending of Legends

In these legends we observe how the tradition of a mere water-nymph has developed into a story concerning a hapless damsel. The first applies to the Lorelei as a water-spirit pure and simple, but legends which refer to beings originally water-spirits have a knack of becoming associated in later times with stories of distressed ladies. Indeed, one such came to the writer's knowledge only a few months ago. The mansion of Caroline Park, near Edinburgh, dating from the end of the seventeenth century, has in its vicinity a well which is reputed to be inhabited by a 'Green Lady,' who emerges from her watery dwelling at twilight and rings the great bell of the old manor-house. On visiting the vicinity for the purpose of verifying the legend information was gleaned respecting another story of a captured lady who had been incarcerated in a room in the mansion and had written some verses to her lover with her diamond ring on a window-pane. The strange thing is that these stories, though obviously of different origin, appear now to have become fused in the popular imagination: the 'Green Lady' and the verse-writing damsel become one and the

The Nixie

same, thus affording a case in point of the fusion of a mythological tale with a later and probably verifiable incident.
The Lorelei is of course a water-spirit of the siren type,
one who lures heedless mariners to their destruction. In
Scotland and the north of England we find her congener in
the water-kelpie, who lurks in pools lying in wait for
victims. But the kelpie is usually represented in the
form of a horse and not in that of a beauteous maiden.

The Nixie

Another water-spirit not unlike the Lorelei is the nixie,
which is both male and female, the male appearing like
any human being, but, as in the case of the water-spirits
of the Slavonic peoples and England, Scotland, and
Central America, being possessed of green teeth. The
male is called *nix*, the female *nixie*, the generic term for
both being *nicker*, from a root which perhaps means 'to
wash.' There is perhaps some truth in the statement
which would derive the Satanic patronymic of 'Old
Nick' from these beings, as spirits extremely familiar to
the Teutonic mind. On fine sunny days the nixies may be
seen sitting on the banks of rivers, or on the branches of
trees, combing their long golden locks. Previous to a
drowning accident the nixies can be seen dancing on the
surface of the water. Like all sea and river spirits, their
subaqueous abode is of a magnificence unparalleled
upon earth, and to this they often convey mortals, who,
however, complain that the splendours of the nixies'
palaces are altogether spoiled for them by the circumstance
that their banquets are served without salt.

> Where on the marshes boometh the bittern,
> Nicker the Soulless sits with his ghittern;
> Sits inconsolable, friendless and foeless,
> Bewailing his destiny, Nicker the Soulless.

Hero Tales & Legends of the Rhine

The Nixie of the Mummel-lake

The legend of the nixie of Seebach is one of gloom and tragedy, albeit as charming as most of the Rhine tales.

It was the custom among the young people of Seebach to assemble of an evening in the spinning-room, which on the occasion about to be dealt with was in the house of the richest and most distinguished family in the country. The girls spun and laughed and chatted, while the youths hung about their chairs and cracked jokes with them. One evening while they were thus employed there came among them a stranger, a young lady beautifully clad and carrying an ivory spinning-wheel. With becoming modesty she asked to be allowed to join the company, which permission the simple youths and maidens readily accorded. None was more eager to do honour to the new-comer than the son of their host. While the others were still gaping in awe-struck fashion, he quietly fetched her a chair and performed various little services for her. She received his attentions so graciously that a warmer feeling than courtesy sprang up in his heart for the fair spinner.

He was in truth a handsome lad, whose attentions any maid might have been proud to receive. Well-built and slender, he bore himself with a proud carriage, and the expression on his delicate features was grave and thoughtful beyond his years. When at length the fair visitor departed, he loitered disconsolate and restless, listening to the idle surmises of the peasant youths concerning the identity of the lady, but offering no opinion himself.

On the following day at the same hour she again appeared and, seeing her cavalier of the previous day, smiled and bowed to him. The young man glowed with pleasure, and diffidently renewed his attentions. Day after day

66

The Nixie of the Mummel-lake

the lady of the spinning-wheel joined the company, and it was noted that the girls were brighter and more diligent, and the young men more gentle and courteous, for her coming. It was whispered among them that she was a nixie from the Mummel-lake far under the mountains, for never mortal was so richly endowed with beauty and grace. As time went on the son of the house grew more and more melancholy as his love for the fair unknown became deeper. Only during the brief hour of her visit would he show any cheerfulness. All the rest of the day he would mope in silent wretchedness. His friends saw with distress the change which had come over him, but they were powerless to alter matters. The lady could not be persuaded to remain beyond her usual hour, nor to give any hint of her identity.

One day, thinking to prolong her visit, the young man put back the hands of the clock. When the hour drew near for her to depart, he slipped out of the house so that he might follow her and find out where she lived. When the hour struck, the lady, who seemed to have feared that she was late, walked hastily from the house in the direction of the lake. So quickly did she walk that the youth following in her path could scarcely keep pace with her. She did not pause when she reached the shore, but plunged directly into the water. A low, moaning sound rose from the waves, which boiled and bubbled furiously, and the young man, fearing that some evil had befallen the maid, sprang in after her, but the cruel currents dragged him down, and he sank out of sight.

Next day his body was found floating on the lake by some woodcutters, and the nixie of the Mummel-lake was seen no more.

Hero Tales & Legends of the Rhine

The Wild Huntsman

One of the most interesting Rhine myths is that concerning the Wild Huntsman, which is known all over Rhineland, and which is connected with many of its localities. The tale goes that on windy nights the Wild Huntsman, with his yelling pack of hounds, sweeps through the air, his prey departing souls. The huntsman is, of course, Odin, who in some of his aspects was a hunter-god. The English legend of Herne the Hunter, who haunts Windsor Park, is allied to this, and there can be little doubt that Herne is Odin. Indeed, it is here suggested that the name Herne may in some way be connected with one of Odin's titles, Hâri, the High One. It was the legend of the Wild Huntsman that inspired Sir Walter Scott to write one of his finest ballads of the mysterious. An Edinburgh friend had perused a ballad by Bürger, entitled *Lenore*, but all he could remember of it were the following four lines:

> Tramp, tramp, across the land they ride;
> Splash, splash, across the sea.
> Hurrah! the dead can ride apace,
> Dost fear to ride with me?

This verse fired Scott's imagination. He liked this sort of thing, and could do it very well himself. So on reaching home he sat down to the composition of the following ballad, of which we give the most outstanding verses:

THE WILD HUNTSMAN

> The Wildgrave winds his bugle horn:
> To horse, to horse, haloo, haloo!
> His fiery courser sniffs the morn,
> And thronging serfs their lord pursue.

The Wild Huntsman

The eager pack, from couples freed,
    Dash through the bush, the brier, the brake ;
While answering hound, and horn, and steed,
    The mountain echoes startling wake.

The beams of God's own hallowed day
    Had painted yonder spire with gold,
And, calling sinful men to pray,
    Loud, long, and deep the bell hath tolled.

But still the Wildgrave onward rides ;
    Haloo, haloo, and hark again !
When, spurring from opposing sides,
    Two stranger horsemen join the train.

Who was each stranger, left and right ?
    Well may I guess, but dare not tell.
The right-hand steed was silver-white ;
    The left, the swarthy hue of hell.

The right-hand horseman, young and fair,
    His smile was like the morn of May ;
The left, from eye of tawny glare,
    Shot midnight lightning's lurid ray.

He waved his huntsman's cap on high,
    Cried, " Welcome, welcome, noble lord !
What sport can earth, or sea, or sky,
    To match the princely chase, afford ? "

" Cease thy loud bugle's clanging knell,"
    Cried the fair youth with silver voice ;
" And for devotion's choral swell,
    Exchange the rude, unhallowed noise.

" To-day th' ill-omened chase forbear ;
    Yon bell yet summons to the fane :
To-day the warning spirit hear,
    To-morrow thou mayst mourn in vain. '

The Wildgrave spurred his ardent steed
    And, launching forward with a bound,
" Who for thy drowsy priestlike rede
    Would leave the jovial horn and hound ?

"Hence, if our manly sport offend :
　With pious fools go chant and pray.
Well hast thou spoke, my dark-brown friend,
　Haloo, haloo, and hark away ! "

The Wildgrave spurred his courser light,
　O'er moss and moor, o'er holt and hill,
And on the left and on the right
　Each stranger horseman followed still.

Up springs, from yonder tangled thorn,
　A stag more white than mountain snow ;
And louder rung the Wildgrave's horn—
　" Hark forward, forward ! holla, ho ! "

A heedless wretch has crossed the way—
　He grasps the thundering hoofs below ;
But, live who can, or die who may,
　Still forward, forward ! on they go.

See where yon simple fences meet,
　A field with autumn's blessings crowned ;
See, prostrate at the Wildgrave's feet,
　A husbandman with toil embrowned.

" Oh, mercy ! mercy ! noble lord ;
　Spare the poor's pittance," was his cry ;
" Earned by the sweat these brows have poured
　In scorching hours of fierce July."

" Away, thou hound, so basely born,
　Or dread the scourge's echoing blow ! "
Then loudly rung his bugle horn,
　" Hark forward, forward ! holla, ho ! "

So said, so done—a single bound
　Clears the poor labourer's humble pale :
Wild follows man, and horse, and hound,
　Like dark December's stormy gale.

And man, and horse, and hound, and horn
　Destructive sweep the field along,
While joying o'er the wasted corn
　Fell famine marks the madd'ning throng.

The Wild Huntsman

Full lowly did the herdsman fall:
  "Oh, spare, thou noble baron, spare
These herds, a widow's little all;
  These flocks, an orphan's fleecy care."

"Unmannered dog! To stop my sport
  Vain were thy cant and beggar whine,
Though human spirits of thy sort
  Were tenants of these carrion kine!"

Again he winds his bugle horn,
  "Hark forward, forward! holla, ho!"
And through the herd in ruthless scorn
  He cheers his furious hounds to go.

In heaps the throttled victims fall;
  Down sinks their mangled herdsman near;
The murd'rous cries the stag appal,
  Again he starts, new-nerved by fear.

With blood besmeared, and white with foam,
  While big the tears of anguish pour,
He seeks, amid the forest's gloom,
  The humble hermit's hallowed bow'r.

All mild, amid the route profane,
  The holy hermit poured his prayer:
"Forbear with blood God's house to stain:
  Revere His altar, and forbear!

"The meanest brute has rights to plead,
  Which, wronged by cruelty or pride,
Draw vengeance on the ruthless head;
  Be warned at length, and turn aside."

Still the fair horseman anxious pleads;
  The black, wild whooping, points the prey.
Alas! the Earl no warning heeds,
  But frantic keeps the forward way.

"Holy or not, or right or wrong,
  Thy altar and its rights I spurn;
Not sainted martyrs' sacred song,
  Not God Himself shall make me turn."

He spurs his horse, he winds his horn,
    " Hark forward, forward ! holla, ho ! "
But off, on whirlwind's pinions borne,
    The stag, the hut, the hermit, go.

And horse and man, and horn and hound,
    The clamour of the chase was gone ;
For hoofs, and howls, and bugle sound,
    A deadly silence reigned alone.

Wild gazed the affrighted Earl around ;
    He strove in vain to wake his horn,
In vain to call ; for not a sound
    Could from his anxious lips be borne.

High o'er the sinner's humbled head
    At length the solemn silence broke ;
And from a cloud of swarthy red
    The awful voice of thunder spoke :

" Oppressor of creation fair !
    Apostate spirits' hardened tool !
Scorner of God ! Scourge of the poor !
    The measure of thy cup is full.

" Be chased for ever through the wood,
    For ever roam the affrighted wild ;
And let thy fate instruct the proud,
    God's meanest creature is His child."

'Twas hushed : one flash of sombre glare
    With yellow tinged the forest's brown ;
Up rose the Wildgrave's bristling hair,
    And horror chilled each nerve and bone.

Earth heard the call—her entrails rend ;
    From yawning rifts, with many a yell,
Mixed with sulphureous flames, ascend
    The misbegotten dogs of hell.

What ghastly huntsman next arose,
    Well may I guess, but dare not tell :
His eye like midnight lightning glows,
    His steed the swarthy hue of hell.

Dwarfs & Gnomes

The Wildgrave flies o'er bush and thorn,
    With many a shriek of hapless woe ;
Behind him hound, and horse, and horn,
    And hark away, and holla, ho !

With wild despair's reverted eye,
    Close, close behind, he marks the throng ;
With bloody fangs, and eager cry,
    In frantic fear he scours along.

Still, still shall last the dreadful chase,
    Till time itself shall have an end ;
By day, they scour earth's caverned space;
    At midnight's witching hour, ascend.

This is the horn, and hound, and horse,
    That oft the 'lated peasant hears ;
Appalled, he signs the frequent cross,
    When the wild din invades his ears.

Dwarfs and Gnomes

Beings of the dwarf race swarmed on the banks of Rhine.
First and foremost among these are the gnomes, who
guard the subterranean treasures, but who on occasion
reveal them to mortals. We meet with these very
frequently under different guises, as, for instance, in the
case of the ' Cooper of Auerbach,' and the Yellow Dwarf
who appears in the legend of Elfeld. The *Heldenbuch*,
the ancient book in which are collected the deeds of the
German heroes of old, says that " God gave the dwarfs
being because the land on the mountains was altogether
waste and uncultivated, and there was much store of
silver and gold and precious stones and pearls still in the
mountains. Wherefore God made the dwarfs very artful
and wise, that they might know good and evil right well,
and for what everything was good. Some stones give
great strength, some make those who carry them about

them invisible. That is called a mist-cap, and therefore did God give the dwarfs skill and wisdom. Therefore they built handsome hollow-hills, and God gave them riches."

Keightley, in his celebrated *Fairy Mythology*, tells of a class of dwarfs called *Heinzelmännchen*, who used to live and perform their exploits in Cologne. These were obviously of the same class as the brownies of Scotland, Teutonic house-spirits who attached themselves to the owners of certain dwellings, and Keightley culled the following anecdote regarding them from a Cologne publication issued in 1826:

" In the time that the Heinzelmännchen were still there, there was in Cologne many a baker who kept no man, for the little people used always to make, overnight, as much black and white bread as the baker wanted for his shop. In many houses they used to wash and do all their work for the maids.

"Now, about this time, there was an expert tailor to whom they appeared to have taken a great fancy, for when he married he found in his house, on the wedding-day, the finest victuals and the most beautiful utensils, which the little folk had stolen elsewhere and brought to their favourite. When, with time, his family increased, the little ones used to give the tailor's wife considerable aid in her household affairs; they washed for her, and on holidays and festival times they scoured the copper and tin, and the house from the garret to the cellar. If at any time the tailor had a press of work, he was sure to find it all ready done for him in the morning by the Heinzelmännchen.

" But curiosity began now to torment the tailor's wife, and she was dying to get one sight of the Heinzel-

74

St. Ursula

männchen, but do what she would she could never compass it. She one time strewed peas all down the stairs that they might fall and hurt themselves, and that so she might see them next morning. But this project missed, and since that time the Heinzelmännchen have totally disappeared, as has been everywhere the case, owing to the curiosity of people, which has at all times been the destruction of so much of what was beautiful in the world. " The Heinzelmännchen, in consequence of this, went off all in a body out of the town, with music playing, but people could only hear the music, for no one could see the mannikins themselves, who forthwith got into a ship and went away, whither no one knows. The good times, however, are said to have disappeared from Cologne along with the Heinzelmännchen."

St. Ursula

One of the most interesting figures in connexion with Rhenish mythology is that of St. Ursula, whose legend is as follows :

Just two centuries after the birth of Christ, Vionest was king of Britain. Happy in his realm, his subjects were prosperous and contented, but care was in the heart of the monarch, for he was childless. At length his consort, Daria, bore him a daughter, who as she grew up in years increased in holiness, until all men regarded her as a saint, and she, devoting herself to a religious life, refused all offers of marriage, to the great grief of her parents, who were again troubled by the thought that their dynasty would fail for want of an heir. Charmed with the rumoui of her virtues, a German prince, Agrippus, asked her as a wife for his son, but the suit was declined by the maiden until an angel appeared to her in a dream and said that the nuptials ought to take place. In obedience to this heavenly mentor, St. Ursula no longer urged her former scruples, and her father hastened to make preparations of suitable magnificence for her departure to the Rhine, on whose banks her future home was to be. Eleven thousand virgins were selected from the noblest families of Britain to accompany their princess, who, marshalling them on the seashore, bade them sing a hymn to the Most High and dismiss all fears of the ocean, for she had been gifted with a divine knowledge of navigation and would guide them safely on their way.

Accordingly St. Ursula dismissed all the seamen, and standing on the deck of the principal vessel, she gave orders to her eleven thousand maiden followers, who, under the influence of inspiration, flitted over the ships dressed in virgin white, now tending the sails, now fixing the ropes, now guiding the helm, until they reached the mouth of the Rhine, up which they sailed in saintly procession to Cologne. Here they were received with great honours by the Roman governor of the place; but soon they left the city to ascend the stream to Basel on their way to Rome, to which holy city St. Ursula had determined upon making a pilgrimage. Wherever upon their journey they met the officers of state they were received as befitted their heavenly mission, and from Basel were accompanied by Pantulus, who was afterward canonized, and whose portrait is to be seen in the church of St. Ursula. Once at Rome Pope Cyriacus himself was so affected by their devoted piety that, after praying with them at the tombs of the apostles, he determined on abdicating the pontifical office to accompany them on their return down the Rhine to Cologne.

At Mayence they were joined by Prince Coman, the son

Saint or Goddess

of Agrippus, who for love of his betrothed at once forsook the errors of his pagan faith and was baptized. The eleven thousand virgins, with their sainted leader, her husband, and Pope Cyriacus, passed rapidly to Cologne, where, however, they were not long destined to live in peace. A horde of barbarians from the North invaded the place, and having gained possession of the city, they slew the virgin retinue of St. Ursula, the venerable Pope, the saint herself, and her spouse Coman, after inflicting the most horrible tortures upon them. Some were nailed living to the cross; some were burned; others stoned; but the most refined cruelties were reserved for the most distinguished victims. Look on the walls of the church of St. Ursula and you will see depicted the sufferings of the young martyr and of her youthful husband. Her chapel yet contains her effigy with a dove at her feet—fit emblem of her purity and faith and loving-kindness; while the devout may, in the same church, behold the religiously preserved bones of the eleven thousand virgins.

Saint or Goddess ?

The sainthood of St. Ursula is distinctly doubtful, and the number of her retinue, eleven thousand, has been proved to be an error in monkish calligraphy. St. Ursula is, indeed, the Teutonic goddess Ursa, or Hörsel. In many parts of Germany a custom existed during the Middle Ages of rolling about a ship on wheels, much to the scandal of the clergy, and this undoubtedly points to moon-worship, the worship of Holda, or Ursula, whom German poets of old regarded as sailing over the deep blue of the heavens in her silver boat. A great company of maidens, the stars, follow in her train. She is supposed, her nightly pilgrimage over, to enter certain hills.

Hero Tales & Legends of the Rhine

Thus in the later guise of Venus she entered the Hörsel-
berg in Thuringia, in which she imprisoned the enchanted
Tannhäuser, and there is good reason to believe that she
also presided over the Ercildoune, or Hill of Ursula, in
the south of Scotland, the modern Earlston, after which
Thomas the Rhymer took his territorial designation, and
whose story later became fused with her myth in the old
Scottish ballad of *Thomas the Rhymer*.   Thus we observe
how it is possible for a pagan myth to become an incident
in Christian hagiology.

Satan in Rhine Story

In the legends of the Rhine the picturesque figure of his
Satanic majesty is frequently presented, as in the legends
of 'The Sword-slipper of Solingen,' 'The Architect of
Cologne Cathedral,' and several other tales.   The circumstances of his appearance are distinctly Teutonic in
character, and are such as to make one doubt that the
Devil of the German peoples has evolved from the classical satyr.   May it not be that the Teutonic folk possessed
some nature-spirit from which they evolved a Satanic
figure of their own?   Against this, of course, could be
quoted the fact that the medieval conception of the Devil
was sophisticated by the Church, which in turn was strongly
influenced by classical types.

Affinity of the Rhine Legends with Romance

But on the whole the legends of the Rhine exhibit much
more affinity with medieval romance than with myth or
folklore.[1]   A large number of them are based upon plots
which can be shown to be almost universal, and which

[1] See author's *Dictionary of Medieval Romance* (London, 1913),
preface, and article 'Romance, Rise and Origin of.'

78

Venus and Tannhäuser

Ferd. Lecke

(See page 78)

The Castle of Cleves

Louis Weirter, R.B.A.

(See page 92)

occur again and again in French and British story. One of the commonest of these concerns the crusader who, rejected by his lady-love, spends hopeless years in the East, or, having married before setting out for the Orient, returns to find his bride the wife of another. The crusader exercised a strong influence upon the literature of medieval Europe, and that influence we find in a very marked degree in the legends of the Rhine. Again, a number of these tales undoubtedly consist of older materials not necessarily mythical in origin, over which a later medieval colour has been cast. Unhappily many of these beautiful old legends have been greatly marred by the absurd sentimentality of the German writers of the early nineteenth century, and their *dramatis personae*, instead of exhibiting the characteristics of sturdy medieval German folk, possess the mincing and lackadaisical manners which mark the Franco-German novel of a century ago. This contrasts most ludicrously in many cases with the simple, almost childlike, honesty which is typical of all early Teutonic literature. Had a Charles Lamb, a Leigh Hunt, or an Edgar Allan Poe recast these tales, how different would have been their treatment! Before the time of Schiller and Goethe French models prevailed in German literature. These wizards of the pen recovered the German spirit of mystery, and brought back to their haunts gnomes, kobolds, and water-sprites. But the mischief had been done ere they dawned upon the horizon, and there were other parts of Germany which appeared to them more suitable for literary presentment than the Rhine, save perhaps in drama. Moreover, the inherent sentimentality of the German character, however fitted to bring out the mysterious atmosphere which clings to these legends, has weakened them considerably.

Hero Tales & Legends of the Rhine

The Poetry of the Rhine

Robert Louis Stevenson, exiled in the South Pacific islands, used to speak with passionate fondness of the rivers of his native Scotland, the country he loved so dearly, but which the jealous fates forbade him to visit during fully half his life. Garry and Tummel, Tweed and Tay—he used to think of these as of something almost sacred; while even the name of that insignificant stream, the Water of Leith, sounded on his ear like sweet music, evoking a strangely tender and pathetic emotion. And this emotion, crystallized so beautifully by Stevenson in one of his essays in *Memories and Portraits*, must have been felt, too, by many other exiles wandering in foreign parts; for surely an analogous feeling has been experienced sometimes by every traveller of sensitive and imaginative temperament, particularly the traveller exiled irrevocably from his home and longing passionately to see it. Horatius, about to plunge into the Tiber, addressed it as his father and god, charging it to care well for his life and fortunes—fortunes in which those of all Rome were involved for the time being. *Ecce Tiber!* was the glad cry of the Romans on beholding the Tay—a cry which shows once again with what ardent devotion they thought of the river which passed by their native city; while Naaman the Syrian, told that his sickness would be cured would he but lave his leprous limbs in the Jordan, exclaimed aghast against a prescription which appeared to him nothing short of sacrilegious and insulting, and declared that there were better and nobler streams in his own land. Even the deadly complaint with which he was smitten could not shake his fidelity to these, could not alter his conviction that they were superior to alien

80

The Poetry of the Rhine

streams; and the truth is that nearly every great river—perhaps because its perpetual motion makes it seem verily a living thing—has a way of establishing itself in the hearts of those who dwell by its banks.

The Rhine is no exception to this rule; on the contrary, it is a notable illustration thereof. From time immemorial the name of the mighty stream has been sacred to the Germans, while gradually a halo of romantic glamour has wound itself about the river, a halo which appeals potently even to many who have never seen the *Vaterland. Am Rhein!*—is there not magic in the words? And how they call up dreams of robber barons, each with his strange castle built on the edge of a precipice overlooking the rushing stream; fiends of glade and dell, sprites of the river and whirlpool, weird huntsmen, and all the *dramatis personae* of legend and tradition.

The Rhine has ever held a wide fame in the domain of literature. For there is scarcely a place on the river's banks but has its legend which has been enshrined in song, and some of these songs are so old that the names of their makers have long since been forgotten. Yes, we have to go very far back indeed would we study the poetry of the Rhine adequately; we have to penetrate deeply into the Middle Ages, dim and mysterious. And looking back thus, and pondering on these legendary and anonymous writings, a poem which soon drifts into recollection is one whose scene is laid near the little town of Lorch, or Lordch. Hard by this town is a mountain, known to geographers as Kedrich, but hailed popularly as 'the Devil's Ladder.' Nor is the name altogether misplaced or undeserved, the mountain being exceeding precipitous, and its beetling, rocky sides seeming well-nigh inaccessible. This steepness, however, did not daunt the hero of the poem in question, a certain Sir Hilchen von Lorch. A saddle, said to have belonged to him, is still preserved in the town; but on what manner of steed he was wont to ride is not told explicitly, and truly it must have been a veritable Bucephalus. For the nameless poet relates that Sir Hilchen, being enamoured of a lady whom angry gnomes had carried to the top of Kedrich and imprisoned there, rode at full gallop right up the side of the mountain, and rescued the fair one!

> " Though my lady-love to a tower be ta'en,
> Whose top the eagle might fail to gain,
> Nor portal of iron nor battlement's height
> Shall bar me out from her presence bright:
> Why has Love wings but that he may fly
> Over the walls, be they never so high?"

So the tale begins, while at the end the knight is represented exulting in his doughty action:

> " Hurrah, hurrah! 'Tis gallantly done!
> The spell is broken, the bride is won!
> From the magic hold of the mountain-sprite
> Down she comes with her dauntless knight!
> Holy St. Bernard, shield us all
> From the wrath of the elves of the Whisper-Thal."

Andernach

There are several different versions of this legend, each of them just as extraordinary as the foregoing. It is evident, moreover, that matter of this sort appealed very keenly to the medieval dwellers by the Rhine, much of the further legendary lore encircling the river being concerned with deeds no less amazing than this of Sir Hilchen's; and among things which recount such events a notable instance is a poem consecrated to the castle of Andernach. Here, once upon a time, dwelt a count bearing the now famous name of Siegfried, and being of

Andernach

a religious disposition, he threw in his lot with a band of crusaders. For a long while, in consequence, he was absent from his ancestral domain; and at length, returning thither, he was told by various lying tongues that his beautiful wife, Genofeva, had been unfaithful to him in his absence, the chief bearer of the fell news being one Golo. This slanderer induced Siegfried to banish Genofeva straightway, and so the lady fled from the castle to the neighbouring forest of Laach, where a little later she gave birth to a boy. Thenceforth mother and son lived together in the wilds, and though these were infested by wild robbers, and full of wolves and other ravening beasts, the pair of exiles contrived to go unscathed year after year, while, more wonderful still, they managed to find daily sustenance. And now romance reached a happy moment; for behold, Count Siegfried went hunting one day in the remoter parts of the forest, and fortuitously he passed by the very place where the two wanderers were living—his wife and the child whom he had never seen.

'Tis in the woody vales of Laach the hunter's horn is wound,
And fairly flies the falcon, and deeply bays the hound;
But little recks Count Siegfried for hawk or quarry now:
A weight is on his noble heart, a gloom is on his brow.
Oh! he hath driven from his home—he cannot from his mind—
A lady, ah! the loveliest of all her lovely kind;
His wife, his Genofeva!—and at the word of one,
The blackest traitor ever looked upon the blessed sun.
He hath let the hunters hurry by, and turned his steed aside,
And ridden where the blue lake spreads its waters calm and wide,
And lo! beneath a linden-tree, there sits a lady fair,
But like some savage maiden clad in sylvan pageant rare.
Her kirtle's of the dappled skin of the rapid mountain roe;
A quiver at her back she bears, beside her lies a bow;
Her feet are bare, her golden hair adown her shoulders streams,
And in her lap a rosy child is smiling in its dreams.

Hero Tales & Legends of the Rhine

The count had never thought to see his wife again. He imagined that she had long since starved to death or been devoured; and now, finding her alive, his pulses quicken. He knows well that only a miracle could have preserved her during all this period of estrangement, and reflects that on behalf of the virtuous alone are miracles worked. Seeing herein ample proof of Genofeva's innocence, he welcomes her back to his arms and with beating heart bears her to the castle:

> Oh! there was joy in Andernach upon that happy night:
> The palace rang with revelry, the city blazed with light:
> And when the moon her paler beams upon the turrets shed,
> Above the Roman gate was seen the traitor Golo's head.

The Brothers

Doubtless it was the thaumaturgic element in this pretty romance which chiefly made it popular among its pristine audiences, yet it was probably the pathos with which it is coloured that granted it longevity, causing it to be handed down from generation to generation long before the advent of the printing-press.

Pathos, of course, figures largely in all folk-literature, and the story of Count Siegfried is by no means the only tale of a touching nature embodied in the early poetry of the Rhine, another similar work which belongs to this category being a poem associated with Liebenstein and Sterrenberg, two castles not far from each other. These places, so goes the tale, once belonged to a nobleman who chanced to have as his ward a young lady of singular loveliness. He had also two sons, of whom the elder was heir to Liebenstein, while the younger was destined to inherit Sterrenberg. These brothers were fast friends, and this partitioning of the paternal estates never begot

The Brothers

so much as an angry word between them; but, alas! in an evil day they both fell in love with the same woman—their father's ward. Such events have happened often, and usually they have ended in bitter strife; but the elder of the young men was of magnanimous temperament, and, convinced that the lady favoured the other's advances more than his, he left him to woo and win her, and so in due course it was announced that the younger brother and she were affianced. Anon the date fixed for their nuptials drew near, but it happened that, in the interim, the young knight of Sterrenberg had become infected with a desire to join a crusade; and now, despite the entreaties of his *fiancée* and his father, he mustered a troop of men-at-arms, led them to join the Emperor Conrad at Frankfort, and set off for the Holy Land. Year after year went by; still the warrior was absent, and betimes his friends and relations began to lose all hope of ever seeing him again, imagining that he must have fallen at the hands of the infidel. Yet this suspicion was never actually confirmed, and the elder brother, far from taking the advantage which the strange situation offered, continued to eschew paying any addresses to his brother's intended bride, and invariably treated her simply as a beloved sister. Sometimes, no doubt, it occurred to him that he might win her yet; but of a sudden his horizon was changed totally, and changed in a most unexpected fashion. The rover came back! And lo! it was not merely a tale of war that he brought with him, for it transpired that while abroad he had proved false to his vows and taken to himself a wife, a damsel of Grecian birth who was even now in his train. The knight of Liebenstein was bitterly incensed on hearing the news, and sent his brother a fierce challenge to meet him in single combat; but scarcely had they met and drawn swords ere the injured lady intervened. She reminded the young men of their sacred bond of fraternity; she implored them to desist from the crime of bloodshed. Then, having averted this, she experienced a great longing to renounce all earthly things, and took the veil in a neighbouring convent, thus shattering for ever the re-kindled hopes of her elder suitor. But he, the hero of the drama, was not the only sufferer, for his brother was not to go unpunished for his perfidy. A strange tale went forth, a scandalous tale to the effect that the Grecian damsel was unfaithful to her spouse. Sterrenberg began to rue his ill-timed marriage, and ultimately was forced to banish his wife altogether. And so, each in his wind-swept castle— for their father was now dead—the two knights lived on, brooding often on the curious events of which their lives had been composed. The elder never married, and the younger had no inclination to take that step a second time.

> They never entered court or town,
>   Nor looked on woman's face;
> But childless to the grave went down,
>   The last of all their race.
> And still upon the mountain fair
>   Are seen two castles grey,
> That, like their lords, together there
>   Sink slowly to decay.
>
> The gust that shakes the tottering stone
>   On one burg's battlement,
> Upon the other's rampart lone
>   Hath equal fury spent.
> And when through Sternberg's shattered wall
>   The misty moonbeams shine,
> Upon the crumbling walls they fall
>   Of dreary Liebenstein.

This legend is recounted here to illustrate the poetry of the Rhine. A variant of it is given on p. 171.

Argenfels

Argenfels

But the warriors who flit across the lore of Rhineland were not all so unfortunate, and one who fared better was Sir Dietrich of Schwarzenbeck. Marching by the Rhine on his way to join a band of crusaders, this Dietrich chanced to pass a few days at the castle of Argenfels, whose owner was the father of two daughters. The younger of the pair, Bertha by name, soon fell in love with the guest, while he, too, was deeply impressed by her charm; but silken dalliance was not for him at present—for was he not under a vow to try to redeem the Holy Sepulchre?—and so he resumed his journey to Palestine. Here an arduous campaign awaited him. In the course of a fierce battle he was wounded sorely, and while trying to escape from the field he was taken prisoner. This was a terrible fate, a far worse fate than death, for the Saracens usually sold their captives as slaves; and Sir Dietrich as he languished in captivity, wondering whether he was destined to spend the rest of his days serving the infidel in some menial capacity, vowed that if he should ever regain his native Germany he would build there a chapel to St. Peter. Nor did his piety go unrewarded, for shortly afterward a body of his compatriots came to his aid, worsted his foes, and set him free. A joyful day was this for the crusader, but it was not his pious vow that he thought of first; he made for Argenfels, eager to see again the bright eyes of the lady who had enchanted him. Day and night he rode, and as he drew nearer to the castle his passion grew stronger within him; but, alas! on reaching his destination his hopes were suddenly dashed to the ground. War had meantime been waged in the neighbourhood of Bertha's home; her father had been involved, his castle burnt to the ground, and the two daughters had disappeared. Peradventure they had perished, surmised the knight; but he swore he would leave nothing undone which might lead to the restoration of his beloved. Making inquiries far and near throughout the country, he heard at last from an old shepherd that two ladies of gentle birth were sequestering themselves in a disused hermitage near the summit of a mountain called Stromberg. " Is it indeed they? " thought Sir Dietrich. He clambered up the rocky steep leading to the hermitage and a wistful sound greeted his ears, the sound of maidens' voices offering up vespers. " *Ave Maria, stella maris,*" they sang, and in the coolness of the evening the notes vibrated with a new, strange loveliness, for the lover knew that he had not climbed the Stromberg in vain. He returned, bringing Bertha with him, and in due course she became his bride. Yet the fairest rose has its thorns, and the happiness of the pair was not to be wholly undimmed by clouds. For Bertha's sister, showing a curious perversity, expressed a desire to remain in the abode which had sheltered her of late, and nothing could induce her to alter this decision. Sir Dietrich pleaded with her again and again, and of a sudden, while thus engaged, he thought of the vow he had made while a captive—the vow he had not kept. Here, possibly—here in this shadow darkening the joy of his bridal—was a message from on high! So straightway he built his chapel, choosing as situation therefor a spot hard by the wind-swept hermitage, and in this shrine to St. Peter dwelt Bertha's sister to the end of her days. Was it, mayhap, jealousy and a dart from Cupid's bow which kept her there; and was she, too, enamoured of Sir Dietrich? Well, the poet who tells the story certainly thought so!

Drinking Songs of the Rhine

Drinking Songs of the Rhine

It were a lengthy matter to recount the many other poems
of Rhineland akin to those mustered above, and enough
has been said to indicate their general characteristics;
while an ancient Rhine classic of yet a different kind,
The Mouse Tower, given elsewhere, is so familiar owing
to Southey's English version that it were superfluous to
offer any synopsis or criticism of it here. Then a class
of poems of which the great river's early literature is
naturally replete are those concerned with the growing of
the vine and the making of Rhenish, prominent among
these being one consecrated to Bacharach, a town which
was a famous centre of the wine industry in the Middle
Ages. Near Bacharach there is a huge stone in the Rhine
which, known as 'the Altar of Bacchus,' is visible only
on rare occasions, when the river chances to be particularly low; and in olden times, whenever this stone was
seen, the event was hailed by the townsfolk as an omen
that their next grape harvest would be an exceptionally
successful one. It is with this 'Altar of Bacchus' that
the poem in question deals. But coming to modern
times, many of the Rhine drinking songs are also concerned to some extent with patriotism—an element which
seems to go hand in hand with the bacchanal the world
over!—and a typical item in this category is the *Rhein-
weinlied* of Georg Hervegh, a poet of the first half of
the nineteenth century. A better patriotic song of Rhineland, however, is one by a slightly earlier poet, Wolfgang
Müller, a native of Königswinter, near Bonn, who sings
with passionate devotion of the great river, dwelling
lovingly on its natural beauties, and exalting it above
all other streams. His song appears to have been

composed when the writer was undergoing a temporary period of exile from the *Vaterland*, for a somewhat pathetic and plaintive air pervades each verse, and the poet refers to the Rhine as a memory rather than as something actually before his eyes. But very different is another fine patriotic song of which it behoves to speak, the work of August Kopisch, a contemporary of Müller. This latter song treats of an incident in the Napoleonic wars, and Blücher and his forces are represented as encamped on the Rhine and as debating whether to march forward against their French foes. Nor is it necessary to add, perhaps, that they decide to do so, for otherwise no German singer would have handled the theme!

But what, asks someone, is really the brightest gem of Rhineland poetry? while someone else adds that the majority of the writers cited above are but little known, and inquires whether none of the great German authors were ever inspired to song by their beloved river. The name of Heinrich Heine naturally comes to mind in this relation—comes to mind instantly on account of what is surely his masterpiece, *Die Lorelei*—a poem already dealt with.

But Heine's version far transcends all others, and pondering on its beauty, we think first of its gentle, *andante* music, a music which steals through the senses like a subtle perfume :

> Ich weiss nicht was soll es bedeuten,
> Dass ich so traurig bin ;
> Ein Märchen aus alten Zeiten,
> Das kommt mir nicht aus dem Sinn.

There, surely, is a sound as lovely as the fateful maiden herself ever sang; and here, again, is a verse which is a

Drinking Songs of the Rhine

tour de force in the craft of landscape-painting; for not only are the externals of the scene summoned vividly before the reader's eyes, but some of the mystery and strangely wistful appeal of nature are likewise found in the lines:

> Die Luft ist kühl und es dunkelt
> Und ruhig fliesst der Rhein ;
> Der Gipfel des Berges funkelt
> Im Abendsonnenschein.

CHAPTER III : CLEVES
TO THE LÖWENBURG

Lohengrin

THE tale or myth of the Knight of the Swan who came to the succour of the youthful Duchess of Brabant is based upon motives more or less common in folklore—the enchantment of human beings into swans, and the taboo whereby, as in the case of Cupid and Psyche, the husband forbids the wife to question him as to his identity or to look upon him. The myth has been treated by both French and German romancers, but the latter attached it loosely to the Grail legend, thus turning it to mystical use.

As a purely German story it is found at the conclusion of Wolfram von Eschenbach's *Parzival*,[1] from which the following version is drawn. The name of the hero as written by Wolfram (Loherangrîn) may possibly be traced to Garin le Loherin or Garin of Lorraine. Wagner's version is taken from the same source, but the mighty master of melody altered many of the details for dramatic and other reasons.

The principal French versions of the romance are *Le Chevalier au Cygne* and *Helyas*, and there are medieval English forms of these.[2]

The Knight of the Swan

In a dungeon in the castle of Cleves lay Elsa of Brabant, languishing in captivity. Her father, the Duke of Brabant, had ere he died appointed his most powerful

[1] See my *Dictionary of Medieval Romance*, articles 'Grail,' 'Parzival,' 'Perceval,' and 'Garin.'
[2] *Op. cit.*

The Knight of the Swan

vassal, one Frederick of Telramund, to be her guardian; but he, seeking only the advancement of his own ends, shamefully abused the confidence of his lord. Using his authority as Elsa's guardian, he sought to compel her to become his wife, and threw her into prison to await the wedding-day, knowing well that none would dare to dispute his action.

An appeal was made on Elsa's behalf to the Emperor, Henry I, who decreed that she should choose a champion, so that the matter might be settled by combat. But, alas! there was not a knight who would venture to match his skill against that of Frederick, who was a giant in stature and an expert in sword-play. In accordance with the Emperor's decree Telramund sent out a herald at stated times to proclaim his readiness to do battle with any who would champion the cause of Elsa.

Time passed, yet the challenge was not accepted, and at length the day was fixed for the bridal. Behind her prison bars the lady wept ceaselessly, and called upon the Virgin to save her from the threatened fate. In her despair she beat her breast with her chaplet, whereon was hung a tiny silver bell. Now this little bell was possessed of magic properties, for when it was rung the sound, small at first as the tinkling of a fairy lure, grew in volume the further it travelled till it resembled the swelling of a mighty chorus. Rarely was its tone heard, and never save when its owner was in dire straits, as on the present occasion. When Elsa beat her breast with it, therefore, its magical qualities responded to her distress, and its faint, sweet tinkle fell on her ear.

Far away over hill and dale went the sound of the bell, growing ever richer and louder, till at length it reached the temple where Parsifal and his knights guarded the

Holy Grail. To them it seemed that the swelling notes contained an appeal for help directed to the Holy Vessel over which they kept vigil. While they debated thereon a loud and mysterious voice was heard bidding Parsifal send his son Lohengrin to the rescue of Elsa of Brabant, whom he must take for his wife, yet without revealing to her his identity.

The awed knights recognized the voice as that of the Holy Grail, and Lohengrin at once set out, bound he knew not whither. When he reached the shores of the Rhine he found awaiting him a boat drawn by a stately swan. Taking it as a sign from Heaven, he stepped into the little boat and was carried up the Rhine, to the sound of the most exquisite music.

It was the day on which Elsa was to be wedded to her tyrant. She had spent the night in tears and bitter lamentations, and now, weary and distraught, too hopeless even for tears, she looked out from the bars of her prison with dull, despairing eyes. Suddenly she heard the melodious strains and a moment later saw the approach of a swan-drawn boat, wherein lay a sleeping knight. Hope leapt within her, for she remembered the prophecy of an old nun, long since dead, that a sleeping knight would rescue her from grave peril. Directly he stepped ashore the youth made his way to the place of her confinement and, espying her face at the heavily barred window, knelt before her and begged that she would take him for her champion.

At that moment the blast of a trumpet was heard, followed by the voice of the herald as, for the last time, he challenged any knight to take up arms on behalf of Elsa of Brabant. Lohengrin boldly accepted the challenge, and Telramund, when the news reached him of the

The Knight of the Swan

unexpected opposition, on the very day he had appointed for his wedding, was surprised and enraged beyond measure, yet he dared not refuse to do battle with the stranger knight, because of the Emperor's decree. So it was arranged that the combat should take place immediately. News of it reached the people of Cleves, and a great concourse gathered to witness the spectacle, all of them secretly in sympathy with the persecuted maiden, though these feelings were carefully concealed from the ruthless Telramund.

Fierce indeed was the combat, for Lohengrin, though less powerfully built than his gigantic opponent, was nevertheless tall and strong, and well versed in the arts of war. At length he laid his enemy in the dust with a well-aimed sword-stroke, and the crowd broke into cheers. The combat was over, and Elsa was free!

Heeding not the acclamations of the people, Lohengrin strode toward Elsa and again knelt at her feet. The blushing maiden bade him name his reward, whereupon the knight begged her hand in marriage, confessing, however, that he might only remain with her so long as she did not question him with regard to his identity. It seemed a small condition to Elsa, who willingly promised to restrain any curiosity she might feel concerning his name and place of abode. The cheers of the populace were redoubled when they learned that Elsa was to bestow her hand on the Swan Knight.

In a few weeks the couple were married, and henceforth for a good many years they lived together very happily. Three sons were born to them, who grew in time to be handsome and chivalrous lads, of noble bearing and knightly disposition. Then it was that Elsa, who had hitherto faithfully kept her promise to her husband, began

to fancy that she and her sons had a grievance in that
the latter were not permitted to bear their father's
name.

For a time she brooded in silence over her grievance, but
at length it was fanned into open rebellion by a breath of
outside suspicion. Some of the people looked askance at
the knight whose name no one knew. So Elsa openly
reproached her husband with his secrecy, and begged that
for the benefit of their sons he would reveal his name and
station. Even the children of humble parents, the children
of the peasants, of their own retainers, had a right to their
father's name, and why not her sons also?

Lohengrin paled at her foolish words, for to him they were
the sign that he must leave his wife and family and betake
himself once more to the temple of the Holy Grail.

"Oh, Elsa," he said sorrowfully, "thou knowest not
what thou hast done. Thy promise is broken, and to-day
I must leave thee for ever." And with that he blew a
blast on his silver horn.

Elsa had already repented her rash words, and right
earnestly she besought him to remain by her side. But,
alas! her tears and pleadings were in vain, for, even as
her entreaties were uttered, she heard the exquisite strains
of music which had first heralded her lover's approach,
while from the window of the castle she espied the swan-
boat rapidly drawing toward the shore.

With grave tenderness Lohengrin bade farewell to his
wife and family, first, however, revealing to them his
identity, and commending them to the care of some of his
trusty followers.

Tradition tells that Elsa did not long survive the loss of
her beloved husband, but her sons became brave knights,
well worthy of the proud name they bore.

Lohengrin overcomes Telramund

Ferd. Lecke

(See page 92)

Cologne Cathedral

Louis Weirter, R.B.A.

(See page 104)

A Legend of Liége

A Legend of Liége

A legend of Liége! and is not Liége itself now almost legendary? Its venerable church, its world-famous library replete with the priceless treasures of the past, "with records stored of deeds long since forgot," where are they?—but crumbling clusters of ruins fired by the barbarian torch whose glow, we were told, was to enlighten an ignorant and uncultured Europe! But one gem remains: the wonderful Hôtel de Ville, type of the Renaissance spirit in Flanders. Liége may be laid in ruins, but the memory of what it was can never die:

> Athens in death is nobler far
> Than breathing cities of the West;

and the same may be said of those splendours in stone, those wonders of medieval architecture, even the blackened walls of which possess a dignity and beauty which will ever assist the imagination to re-create the picture of what has been.

Liége is a city of the Middle Ages. Time was when the place boasted but a single forge; and though bucklers were heaped beside the anvil, and swords and spears lay waiting for repair, the blacksmith leant against his door-post, gazing idly up the hill-side. Gradually he was aware of a figure, which seemed to have grown into shape from a furze-bush, or to have risen from behind a stone; and as it descended the slope he eyed curiously the grimy face, long beard, and squat form of what he was half unwilling to recognize as a human being. Hobbling awkwardly, and shrugging his shoulders as though cold, the man came in time to the smithy door.

"What! Jacques Perron—idle when work is to be done?

97

Idle smith! idle smith! The horse lacks the bit, and the
rider the spur.

> ' Ill fares the hide when the buckler wants mending;
>   Ill fares the plough when the coulter wants tending.'

Idle smith! idle smith!"

"Idle enough," quoth Jacques. "I'm as idle as you are
ugly; but I can't get charcoal any more than you can get
beauty, so I must stand still, and you be content with your
face, though I'd fain earn a loaf and a cup full enough for
both of us this winter morning."

Though the strange man must have known he was
horribly ugly—that is, if he ever bent to drink of the clear
bright waters of the lovely Meuse, which reflected in those
days every lily-bell and every grass-blade which grew
upon its banks, and gave a faithful portraiture in its cool
waters of every creature that leant over them—though he
was certainly the most frightful creature that had ever
met the blacksmith's sight, it was evident enough that he
did not like being called Ugly-face. But when the honest,
good-natured smith spoke of earning a draught for his
new acquaintance as well as himself, he smacked his ugly
lips and twisted out a sort of smile which made him still
more hideous.

"Ah, ah!" said he, "wine's good in winter weather,
wine's good in winter weather. Listen, listen! Jacques
Perron! listen, listen! Go you up the hill-side—yonder,
yonder!" and he pointed with a yellow finger, which
seemed to stretch out longer and longer as the smith
strained his eyes up the slope, until the digit looked quite
as long as the tallest chimney that smoked over Liége.
"Listen, listen!" and he sang in a voice like the breath
of a huge bellows:

A Legend of Liége

"'Wine's good in winter weather;
Up the hill-side near the heather
Go and gather the black earth,
It shall give your fire birth.
Ill fares the hide when the buckler wants mending;
Ill fares the plough when the coulter wants tending:
Go! Go!'

"Mind my cup of wine—mind my cup of wine!" As he ended this rude chant Jacques saw the long finger run back into the shrivelled hand, as a telescope slips back into its case, and then the hand was wrapped up in the dingy garment, and with a dreadful shiver, and a chattering of teeth as loud as the noise of the anvils now heard on the same spot, the ugly man was wafted away round the corner of the building like a thick gust of smoke from a newly fed furnace.

"Mind my cup of wine—mind my cup of wine!" rang again in the ears of the startled Jacques, and after running several times round his house in vain pursuit of the voice, he sat down on the cold anvil to scratch his head and think. It was quite certain he had work to do, and it was as certain as half a score searches could make it that he had not a single coin in his pouch to buy charcoal to do it with. He was reflecting that the old man was a very strange creature—he was more than half afraid to think who he might be—when in the midst of his cogitation he heard his three children calling out for their morning meal. Not a loaf had Jacques in store, and twisting his hide apron round his loins, he muttered, "Demon or no demon, I'll go," and strode out of the smithy and up the hill-side as fast as though he feared that if he went slowly his courage would not carry him as far up as the heather-bush which the long yellow finger had pointed out.

When the young wife of Jacques came to look for her husband, she saw him returning with his apron full of black morsels of shining stone. She smiled at him; but when he threw them on the furnace and went to get a brand to set them alight, she looked solemn enough, for she thought he had left his wits on the hill-top. Great was her surprise when *she saw the stones burn!* But her joy was greater than her surprise when she heard her husband's hammer ring merrily, and found the wage of the smith all spared for home use, instead of being set aside for the charcoal-burner. That night Jacques had two full wine-cups and, setting them on the anvil, had scarcely said to himself, " I wonder whether *He'll* come! " when in walked the Old Man and, nodding familiarly, seated himself on the head of the big hammer. Jacques was a bold and grateful as well as a good-natured fellow, and in a few minutes he and his visitor were on excellent terms. No more shivering or chattering of teeth was seen or heard in the smithy that night. The black stones burned away merrily on the hearth, and the bright flames shone on the honest face of the smith as he hobnobbed with his companion, and looked as though he really thought the stranger as handsome as he certainly had been useful. He sang his best songs and told his best stories, and when the wine had melted his soul he told his new friend how dearly he loved his wife and what charming, dear creatures his children were. " Demon or no demon," he swore the stranger was a good fellow, and though the visitor spoke but little, he seemed to enjoy his company very much. He laughed at the jokes, smiled at the songs, and once rather startled Jacques by letting out again his long telescope arm to pat him on his shoulder when, with a mouth full of praises of his wife, a tear sparkled in his eye as he told over again how dearly he loved his little ones.

Day broke before the wine was exhausted or their hearts flagged, and when the voice of the early cock woke the swan that tended her callow brood amongst the sedges of the Meuse the Old Man departed. Jacques never saw him again, although he often looked in all directions when he went to the hill for a supply of fuel; but from that day Liége grew up in industry, riches, and power. *Jacques had found coal*, and thus became the benefactor of his native country, and the hero of this favourite *Legend of the Liégeois*.

The Sword-slipper of Solingen

In Solingen, where the forges rang to the making of sword-blades, many smiths had essayed to imitate the falchions of Damascus, their trenchant keenness and their wondrous golden inlaying. But numerous as were the attempts made to recapture the ancient secret of the East, they all signally failed, and brought about the ruin of many masters of the sword-slipper's art.

Among these was old Ruthard, a smith grown grey in the practice of his trade. He had laid aside sufficient savings to permit himself a year's experiment in the manufacture of Damascus blades, but to no purpose. As the months wore on he saw his hard-earned gold melting steadily away. The wrinkles deepened on his brow, and his only daughter, Martha, watched the change coming over him in sorrowful silence.

One evening—the evening of all evenings, the holy Christmas eve—Martha entered the forge and saw the old man still hard at work. She gently remonstrated with him, asking him why he toiled on such an occasion.

"You work, my father, as if you feared that to-morrow we might not have bread," she said. "Why toil on this holy evening? Have you not sufficient for the future? You must have laid by enough for your old age. Then why fatigue yourself when others are spending the time by their own hearths in cheerful converse?"

The old smith's only reply was to shake his head in a melancholy manner, take some pieces of broken food in his hands, and leave the house. At that moment Wilhelm, the smith's head apprentice, entered the room. He seemed pale and disturbed, and related to Martha, to whom he was betrothed, that he had asked Ruthard for her hand. The old man had firmly told him that he could not consent to their union until he had discovered the secret of making Damascus blades. This he felt was hopeless to expect, and he had come to say "good-bye" ere he set out on a quest from which he might never return. At the news Martha was greatly perturbed. She rose and clung to the young man, her wild grief venting itself in heart-rending sobs. She begged him not to depart. But his mind was fully made up, and, notwithstanding her tears and caresses, he tore himself away and quitted the house and the town.

For nearly a fortnight the youth tramped over hill and valley with little in his pouch and without much hope that the slender means of which he was possessed would bring him to the land of the Saracens, where alone he could hope to learn the great art of tempering the blades of Damascus. One evening he entered the solitary mountain country of Spessart and, unacquainted with the labyrinths of the road, lost himself in an adjoining forest. By this time night had fallen, and he cast about for a place in which to lay his head. But the inhospitable forest showed

no sign of human habitation.   After wandering on, however, stumbling and falling in the darkness, he at length
saw a light burning brightly at a distance.   Quickly he
made for it and found that it came from the window of a
cottage, at the door of which he knocked loudly.   He had
not long to wait for an answer, for an old woman speedily
opened and inquired what he wanted at so late an hour.
He told her that he desired food and lodging, for which
he could pay, and he was at once admitted.   She told
him, however, that she expected another visitor.   Whilst
she cooked his supper Wilhelm detailed to her the
circumstances of his journey.   After he had eaten he
retired to rest, but, tired as he was, he could not sleep.
Later a dreadful storm arose, through the din of which he
heard a loud noise, as if someone had entered the house
by way of the chimney.   Peering through the keyhole
into the next room, he perceived a man seated at the table
opposite his hostess whose appearance filled him with
misgiving.   He had not much leisure for a detailed
examination of this person, however, for the witch—for such
she was—came to the door of his room, entered, and bade
him come and be introduced to a stranger from the East
who could tell him the secret of forging Damascus blades.
Wilhelm followed the old woman into the other room and
beheld there a swarthy man seated, wrapped in a flame-
coloured mantle.   For a long time the stranger regarded
him steadily, then demanded what he wanted from him.
Wilhelm told him the circumstances of his quest, and
when he had finished the story the man laughed and,
drawing from his pocket a document, requested the youth
to sign it.   Wilhelm perceived that it was of the nature
of a pact with Satan, by which he was to surrender his
soul in return for the coveted secret.   Nevertheless, he

set his signature to the manuscript and returned to his couch—but not to sleep. The consequences of his terrible act haunted him, and when morning came he set off on his homeward journey with a fearful heart, carefully guarding a well-sealed letter which the mysterious stranger had put into his hand.

Without further adventure he reached Solingen, and having acquainted Ruthard with what had transpired, he handed him the letter. But the good old man refused to unseal it.

"You must keep this until your own son and my grandson can open it," he said to Wilhelm, "for over his infant soul the enemy can have no power."

And so it happened. Wilhelm married Martha, and in the course of a few years a little son was born to them, who in due time found the letter, opened it, and mastered the Satanic secret, and from that time the blades of Solingen have had a world-wide renown.

The Architect of Cologne Cathedral

Travellers on the Rhine usually make a halt at Cologne to see the cathedral, and many inquire the name of its creator. Was the plan the work of a single architect? they ask; or did the cathedral, like many another in Europe, acquire its present form by slow degrees, being augmented and duly embellished in divers successive ages? These questions are perfectly reasonable and natural, yet, strange to relate, are invariably answered in evasive fashion, the truth being that the name of the artist in stone who planned Cologne Cathedral is unknown. The legend concerning him, however, is of world-wide celebrity, for the tale associated with the founding of the famous edifice is replete with that grisly element which

The Architect of Cologne Cathedral

has always delighted the Germans, and figures largely in their medieval literature, and more especially in the works of their early painters—for example, Dürer, Lucas Cranach, and Albrecht Altdörfer.

It was about the time of the last-named master that a Bishop of Cologne, Conrad von Hochsteden, formed the resolve of increasing the pecuniary value of his diocese. He was already rich, but other neighbouring bishops were richer, each of them being blest with just what Conrad lacked—a shrine sufficiently famous to attract large numbers of wealthy pilgrims able to make generous offerings. The result of his jealous musing was that the crafty bishop vowed he would build a cathedral whose like had not been seen in all Germany. By this means, he thought, he would surely contrive to bring rich men to his diocese. His first thought was to summon an architect from Italy, in those days the country where beautiful building was chiefly carried on; but he found that this would cost a far larger sum than he was capable of raising; so, hearing that a gifted young German architect had lately taken up his abode at Cologne itself, Conrad sent for him and offered him a rich reward should he accomplish the work satisfactorily. The young man was overjoyed, for as yet he had received no commissions of great importance, and he set to work at once. He made drawing after drawing, but, being in a state of feverish excitement, found that his hand had lost its cunning. None of his designs pleased him in the least; the bishop, he felt, would be equally disappointed; and thinking that a walk in the fresh air might clear his brain, he threw his drawing-board aside and repaired to the banks of the Rhine. Yet even here peace did not come to him; he was tormented by endless visions of groined arches, pediments, pilasters, and the like, and having a stick in his hand, he made an effort to trace some on the sand. But this new effort pleased him no better than any of its predecessors. Fame and fortune were within his reach, yet he was incapable of grasping them; and he groaned aloud, cursing the day he was born.

As the young man uttered his fierce malediction he was surprised to hear a loud "Amen" pronounced; he looked round, wondering from whom this insolence came, and beheld an individual whose approach he had not noticed. He, too, was engaged in drawing on the sand, and deeming that the person, whoever he was, intended to mock his attempts at a plan for the projected cathedral, the architect strode up to him with an angry expression on his face. He stopped short, however, on nearing the rival draughtsman; for he was repelled by his sinister aspect, while at the same time he was thunderstruck by the excellence of his drawing. It was indeed a thaumaturgic design, just such a one as the architect himself had dreamt of, but had been unable to execute; and while he gazed at it eagerly the stranger hailed him in an ugly, rasping voice. "A cunning device, this of mine," he said sharply; and the architect was bound to agree, despite the jealousy he felt. Surely, he thought, only the Evil One could draw in this wise. Scarcely had the thought crossed his mind ere his suspicion was confirmed, for now he marked the stranger's tail, artfully concealed hitherto. Yet he was incapable of withholding his gaze from the plan drawn so wondrously on the sand, and the foul fiend, seeing that the moment for his triumph was come, declared his identity without shame, and added that, would the architect but agree to renounce all hopes of salvation in the next world, the peerless design would be his to do with as he pleased.

The Architect of Cologne Cathedral

The young man shuddered on receiving the momentous offer, but continued to gaze fixedly at the cunning workmanship, and again the Evil One addressed him, bidding him repair that very night to a certain place on a blasted heath, where, if he would sign a document consigning his soul to everlasting damnation, he would be presented with the plan duly drawn on parchment. The architect still wavered, now eager to accept the offer, and now vowing that the stipulated price was too frightful. In the end he was given time wherein to come to a decision, and he hurried from the place at hot speed as the tempter vanished from his sight.

On reaching his dwelling the architect flung himself upon his bed and burst into a paroxysm of weeping. The good woman who tended him observed this with great surprise, for he was not given to showing his emotions thus; and wondering what terrible sorrow had come to him, she proceeded to make kindly inquiries. At first these were met with silence, but, feeling a need for sympathy, the architect eventually confessed the truth ; and the good dame, horrified at what she heard, hurried off to impart the story to her father-confessor. He, too, was shocked, but he was as anxious as Bishop Conrad that the proposed cathedral should be duly built, and he came quickly to the architect's presence. " Here," he told him, " is a piece of our Lord's cross. This will preserve you. Go, therefore, as the fiend directed you, take the drawing from him, and brandish the sacred relic in his accursed face the moment you have received it."

When evening drew near the architect hurried to the rendezvous, where he found the Devil waiting impatiently. But a leer soon spread over his visage, and he was evidently overjoyed at the prospect of wrecking a soul.

He quickly produced a weird document, commanding his victim to affix his signature at a certain place. " But the beautiful plan," whispered the young man; " I must see it first; I must be assured that the drawing on the sand has been faithfully copied." " Fear nothing." The Devil handed over the precious piece of vellum; and glancing at it swiftly, and finding it in order, the architect whipped it under his doublet. " Aha! you cannot outwit me," shrieked the fiend; but as he was laying hands upon the architect the young man brought forth the talisman he carried. " A priest has told you of this, for no one else would have thought of it," cried the Devil, breathing flame from his nostrils. But his wrath availed him naught; he was forced to retreat before the sacred relic, yet as he stepped backward he uttered a deadly curse. " You have deceived me," he hissed; "but know that fame will never come to you; your name will be forgotten for evermore."

And behold, the fiend's prophecy was fulfilled. The cathedral was scarcely completed ere the young architect's name became irrevocably forgotten, and now this grisly tale is all that is known concerning his identity.

Cologne Cathedral : Its Erection

There are several other tales to account for the belief prevalent at one time that Cologne Cathedral would never be completed. The following legend attributes the unfinished state of the edifice to the curse of a jealous architect. At the time the building was commenced a rival architect was engaged in planning an aqueduct to convey to the city a supply of water purer than that of the Rhine. He was in this difficulty, however: he had been unable to discover the exact position of the spring from which the water was to be drawn. Tidings of the proposed structure reached the ears of the builder of the cathedral, a man of strong passions and jealous disposition, and in time the other architect asked his opinion of the plans for the aqueduct.

Now it so happened that the architect of the cathedral alone had known the situation of the spring, and he had communicated it to his wife, but to no other living creature; so he replied boastfully:

"Speak not to me of your aqueduct. My cathedral, mighty as it will be, shall be completed before your little aqueduct." And he clinched his vainglorious assertion with an oath.

Indeed, it seemed as though his boast would be justified, for the building of the sacred edifice proceeded apace, while the aqueduct was not even begun, because of the difficulty of finding the spring. The second architect was in despair, for of a certainty his professional reputation was destroyed, his hopes of fame for ever dashed, were he unable to finish the task he had undertaken.

His faithful wife strove to lighten his despondency, and at last, setting her woman's wit to work, hit on a plan whereby the threatened calamity might be averted. She set out to visit the wife of the rival architect, with whom she was intimate. The hostess greeted her effusively, and the ladies had a long chat over bygone times. More and more confidential did they become under the influence of old memories and cherry wine. Skilfully the guest led the conversation round to the subject of the hidden spring, and her friend, after exacting a promise of the strictest secrecy, told her its exact situation. It lay under the great tower of the cathedral, covered by the massive stone known as the 'Devil's Stone.'

"Let me have your assurance again," said the anxious lady, "that you will never tell anyone, not even your husband. For I do not know what would become of me if my husband learnt that I had told it to you."

The other renewed her promises of secrecy and took her leave. On her return home she promptly told her husband all that had passed, and he as promptly set to work, sunk a well at the spot indicated, and found the spring. The foundations of the aqueduct were laid and the structure itself soon sprang up. The architect of the cathedral saw with dismay that his secret was discovered. As the building of the aqueduct progressed he lost all interest in his own work; envy and anger filled his thoughts and at last overcame him. It is said that he died of a broken heart, cursing with his latest breath the cathedral which he had planned.

The Wager

An alternative story is that of the Devil's wager with the architect of the cathedral. The Evil One was much irritated at the good progress made in the erection of the building and resolved, by means of a cunning artifice, to stop that progress. To this end he paid a visit to the architect, travelling incognito to avoid unpleasant attentions.

The architect was a man of wit and good sense, as courteous as he was clever; but he had one outstanding failing—a love of wagering. Satan, who ever loves to find the joints in an opponent's armour, chose this one weak spot as a point of attack. His host offered him meat and drink, which the Devil declined as not being sufficiently high-seasoned for his taste.

"I have come on a matter of business," said he briskly.

The Wager

" I have heard of you as a sporting fellow, a man who loves his wager.   Is that correct? "

The architect indicated that it was, and was all eagerness and attention in a moment.

"Well," said the other, " I have come, in a word, to make a bet with you concerning the cathedral."

"And what is your wager? "

"Why, I'll wager that I bring a stream from Treves to Cologne before you finish the cathedral, and I'll work single-handed, too."

" Done ! " said the delighted architect.   " But what's the wager? "

" If I win, your soul passes into my possession; if you win, you may have anything you choose."   And with that he was gone.

Next day the architect procured the services of all the builders that were to be had on such short notice, and set them to work in real earnest.   Very soon the whole town was in a state of excitement because of the unusual bustle.   The architect took to dreaming of the wealth, or the fame, or the honour he should ask as his due when the stakes were won.   Employing his imagination thus, he one day climbed to the top of the highest tower, which by this time was completed, and as he feasted his eyes on the beautiful landscape spread before him he happened to turn toward the town of Treves, and lo ! a shining stream was threading its way to Cologne.   In a very short time it would reach the latter city.

The Devil had won !

With a laugh of defiance the architect cast himself from the high tower and was instantly killed.   Satan, in the form of a black hound, sprang upon him, but was too late to find him alive.

But his death stopped for many years the progress of the cathedral; it long stood at the same stage of completion as when the brook first flowed from Treves to Cologne.

The Fire-bell of Cologne

In one of the grand towers of Cologne Cathedral hangs a massive bell, some 25,000 lb. in weight. No mellow call to prayer issues from its brazen throat, no joyous chimes peal forth on gala-days; only in times of disaster, of storm and stress and fire, it flings out a warning in tones so loud and clamorous, so full of dire threatenings, that the stoutest hearts quail beneath the sound. Because its awful note is only to be heard in time of terror it is known as the Fire-bell, and a weird tradition relates the story of its founding and the reason for its unearthly sound.

Long ago, when bell-founding was looked upon as an art of the highest importance, and especially so among the Germans, the civic authorities of Cologne made it known that the cathedral was in need of a new bell. There was no lack of aspirants for the honour of casting the bell, and more than one exponent of the art imagined his handiwork swinging in the grand tower of the cathedral, a lasting and melodious monument to its creator's skill.

Among those whose ambitious souls were stirred by the statement of the city fathers was one, a bell-founder named Wolf, a man of evil passions and overbearing disposition, whose heart was firmly set on achieving success. In those days, let it be said, the casting of a bell was a solemn, and even a religious, performance, attended by elaborate ceremonies and benedictions. On the day which Wolf had appointed for the operation it seemed as though the entire populace had turned out to witness the spectacle. Wolf, having prepared the mould, made ready to pour into it the

The Fire-bell of Cologne

molten metal. The silence was almost oppressive, and on it fell distinctly the solemn words of the bell-founder, as in God's name he released the metal. The bright stream gushed into the mould, and a cheer broke from the waiting crowd, who, indeed, could scarce be restrained till the bell had cooled, such was their curiosity to see the result. At last the earthy mould was removed, they surged round eagerly, and lo! from crown to rim of the mighty bell stretched a gaping crack!

Expressions of disappointment burst from the lips of the people, and to Wolf himself the failure was indeed galling. But his ambitious spirit was not yet completely crushed. "I am not beaten yet," he said boastfully. "I shall make another, and success shall yet be mine."

Another mould was made, once more the people came forth to see the casting of the bell, once more the solemn invocation of God's name fell on awed ears. The glowing metal filled the mould, cooled, and was withdrawn from its earthy prison. Once more cries of disappointment were heard from the crowd; again the massive bell was completely riven!

Wolf was beside himself. His eyes glowed with fury, and he thrust aside the consolations of his friends.

"If God will not aid me," he said fiercely, "then the Devil will!"

The crowd shrank back from the impious words; nevertheless on the third occasion they attended in even greater numbers than before.

Again was all made ready for the casting of the huge bell. The mould was fashioned as carefully as on the previous occasions, the metal was heated in the great furnace, and Wolf, pale and sullen, stood ready to release it. But when he spoke a murmur of astonishment, of horror, ran through the crowd. For the familiar words "In the name of God!" he had substituted "In the name of the Devil!" With fascinated eyes the people watched the bright, rushing metal, and, later, the removal of the mould.

And behold! the bell was flawless, perfect in shape and form, and beautiful to look upon!

Wolf, having achieved the summit of his ambition, cared little for the means by which he had ascended. From among a host of competitors he was chosen as the most successful. His bell was to hang in the belfry of Cologne Cathedral, for the envy of other bell-founders and the admiration of future generations.

The bell was borne in triumph through the streets and fixed high in the tower. Wolf requested that he might be the first to try its tone, and his request was granted. He ascended into the tower and took the rope in his hands; the mighty bell swung forth, but ah! what a sound was that! The people pressed their hands over their ears and shuddered; those in the streets hurried to their homes; all were filled with deadly fear as the diabolical bell flung its awful tones over the startled city. This, then, was the result of Wolf's invocation of the Devil.

Wolf himself, high in the cathedral tower, was overcome with the brazen horror of the sound, and, driven mad with remorse and terror, flung himself from the tower and fell, a crushed and shapeless mass, on the ground below.

Henceforth the bell was used only to convey warning in times of danger, to carry a message of terror far and wide across the city, and to remind the wicked at all times of the danger of trafficking with the Evil One.

The Archbishop's Lion

The Archbishop's Lion

In 957 Cologne was constituted an imperial free city, having as its nominal prince the archbishop of the see, but possessing the right to govern its own affairs. The good bishop of that time acquiesced in the arrangement, but his successors were not content to be princes in name only, and strove hard to obtain a real influence over the citizens. Being for the most part men of unscrupulous disposition, they did not hesitate to rouse commonalty and aristocracy against each other, hoping to step in and reap the benefits of such internecine warfare as might ensue. And, indeed, the continual strife was not conducive to the prosperity of the burghers, but rather tended to sap their independence, and one by one their civil liberties were surrendered. Thus the scheming archbishops increased their power and influence in the city of Cologne. There came a time, however, in the civic history when the limit was overstepped. In the thirteenth century Archbishop Engelbert, more daring and ambitious than any of his predecessors, demanded that the municipal treasure should be given up to him. Not content with taking away the privileges of the burghers, he wished to lay his hands on the public purse as well. This was indeed the last straw, and the sluggish blood of the burghers was at length roused to revolt.

At this time the Burgomaster of Cologne, Hermann Grein by name, was an honest, far-seeing, and diplomatic citizen, who had seen with dismay the ancient liberties of his beloved city destroyed by the cunning of the Archbishop. The latter's bold attempt at further encroachments gave him the opportunity he sought, and with the skill of a born leader Hermann Grein united nobles and commons in the determination to resist their mutual enemy. Feuds were for the time being forgotten, and with a gallant effort the galling yoke of the Archbishop-prince was thrown off, and the people of Cologne were once more free.

Grein performed his civic duties so firmly, albeit so smoothly and gently, that he won the love and respect of all sections of the populace. Old and young hailed him in their hearts as the deliverer of their city from ecclesiastical tyranny. Only Engelbert hated him with a deadly hatred, and swore to be revenged; nor was his resolve weakened when a later attempt to subdue the city was frustrated by the foresight of Grein. It became obvious to the Archbishop that force was unavailing, for the majority of all classes were on the side of liberty, and were likely to remain so while Hermann Grein was at their head. So he made up his mind to accomplish by means of strategy the death of the good old man.

Now there were in the monastery close by Cologne two canons who shared Engelbert's hatred of Grein, and who were only too willing to share in his revenge. And the plan was indeed a cunning one. Belonging to a small collection of animals attached to the monastery was a fierce lion, which had more than once proved a convenient mode of removing the Church's enemies. So it was arranged that the Burgomaster should be asked to meet the Archbishop there. The latter sent a suave message to his enemy saying that he desired to treat with him on matters connected with the civic privileges, which he was disposed to restore to the city, with a few small exceptions. This being the case, would the Burgomaster consent to dine with him at the monastery on a certain date?

116

The Archbishop's Lion

The Burgomaster consented heartily, for he was a man to whom treachery was entirely foreign, and therefore not prone to suspect that vice in others ; nevertheless he took the simple precautions of arming himself and making his destination known to his friends before he set out. When he arrived at the monastery resplendent in the rich garments countenanced by the fashion of the time, he was told that the Archbishop was in the garden.

"Will you walk in our humble garden with his Highness ?" the canons asked the Burgomaster, and he, a lover of nature, bade them lead the way.

The garden was truly a lovely spot, gay with all manner of flowers and fruit ; but Grein looked in vain for his host. "His Highness," said the wily canons, "is in the private garden, where only the heads of the Church and their most honoured guests are admitted. Ah, here we are ! Enter, noble Burgomaster ; we may go no farther."

With that they stopped before a strong iron-bound door, opened it, and thrust the old man inside. In a moment the heavy door had swung to with a crash, and Grein found himself in a narrow, paved court, with high, unscalable walls on every side. And from a dark corner there bounded forth to meet him a huge lion ! With a pious prayer for help the Burgomaster drew his sword, wrapped his rich Spanish mantle round his left arm, and prepared to defend himself against his adversary. With a roar the lion was upon him, but with wonderful agility the old man leapt to one side. Again the great beast sprang, endeavouring to get the man's head between its jaws. Again and again Grein thrust valiantly, and in one of these efforts his weapon reached the lion's heart and it rolled over, dead. Weak and exhausted from loss of blood, the Burgomaster lost consciousness.

Ere long he was roused from his swoon by the awe-inspiring tones of the alarm-bell and the sound of a multitude of voices. A moment later he recalled his terrible struggle with the lion, and uttered a devout thanksgiving for his escape from death.

Meanwhile the people, growing anxious at his prolonged absence, and fearing that some ill had befallen him, had hastened to the monastery. The two canons, seeing the approaching crowd, ran out to meet them, wringing their hands and exclaiming that the Burgomaster had strayed into the lion's den and there met his death. The angry crowd, in nowise deceived by their pretences, demanded to be shown the lion's den. Arrived there, they broke down the door and, to their great joy, found Grein alive, though wounded and much shaken. They bore him triumphantly through the town, first crowning his hastily improvised litter with flowers and laurels.

As for the monks, their priestly garb could not protect their persons from the wrath of the mob, and they were hanged at the gate of the monastery, which thereafter became known as the 'Priests' Gate.'

The White Horses

The year 1440 was a memorable one throughout Germany, for the great plague raged with fearful violence, leaving blanks in many families hitherto unvisited by death. Among the victims was Richmodis, the beloved wife of Sir Aducht of Cologne, who deeply mourned her loss.

The lady was buried with a valuable ring—her husband's gift—upon her finger; this excited the cupidity of the sextons, who, resolved to obtain possession of it, opened the tomb in the night and wrenched off the coffin-lid. Their difficulties, however, were not at an end, for when they tried to possess themselves of the ring it resolutely adhered to the finger of the corpse.

Suddenly, to their horror, the dead body gently raised itself, with a deep sigh, as though the soul of Richmodis regarded this symbol of wifely duty as sacred, and would resist the efforts of the thieves to take it from her.

The dark and hollow eyes opened and met those of the desecrators, and a threatening light seemed to come from them. At this ghastly sight the terrified sextons fled in abject panic.

Richmodis recovered by degrees, and gradually realizing where she was, she concluded that she must have been buried while alive. In her terror she cried aloud for help. But nobody could hear her; it was the lone hour of midnight, when all nature reposes.

Summoning strength, she resolved to make an effort to go to the husband who had placed the ring upon her finger, and getting out of the coffin, she made her way shivering toward their home.

The wind moaned dismally through the trees, and their foliage cast dark, spectral shadows that swayed fitfully to and fro in the weird light of the waning moon as Richmodis staggered along feebly, absorbed in the melancholy thoughts which her terrible experience suggested.

Not a sound, save the soughing of the wind, was heard within God's peaceful acre, for over the wrecks of Time Silence lay motionless in the arms of Death.

The moon's pale rays illumined the buildings when Richmodis arrived at her house in the New Market. She knocked repeatedly, but at first received no response to her summons. After a time Sir Aducht opened the window and looked out, annoyed at the disturbance at such an hour.

He was about to speak angrily when the apparition looked up at him with a tender regard of love and asked him to descend quickly and open the door to receive his wife, nearly exhausted by cold and terror. The bereaved husband refused to believe that the wife whom he had just buried had come back to him, and he declared that he would as soon expect his horses to climb upstairs as believe that his dead wife could return to him alive.

He had hardly uttered the words when the trampling of his two horses on the staircase was distinctly heard. A moment or two later he looked from the casement and saw the steeds at an upper window, and he could doubt no longer. Rushing to the door, he received his shivering wife into his arms. The ring she still wore would have removed all doubts had there been room for such.

Husband and wife spent many years together in domestic happiness, and in memory of that remarkable night Sir Aducht fixed wooden effigies of two horses' heads to the outside of the window, where they still remain for all to see.

The Magic Banquet

Another interesting tale of Cologne deals with the famous magician and alchemist, Albertus Magnus, who at one time dwelt in the convent of the Dominicans, not far from that city. It is recorded that on one occasion, in the depth of winter, Albertus invited William of Holland to a feast which was to be held in the convent garden. The recipients of the curious invitation, William and his courtiers, were naturally much amazed at the terms thereof, but decided not to lose the opportunity of attending such a novel banquet.

In due course they arrived at the monastery, where all

The Magic Banquet

was in readiness for the feast, the tables being laid amid
the snow. The guests had fortified themselves against
the severe weather by wearing their warmest clothing and
furs. No sooner had they taken their seats, however,
than Albertus, exercising the magic powers he possessed,
turned the wintry garden into a scene of summer bloom
and loveliness. The heavy furs were laid aside, and the
guests were glad to seek the shade of the spreading
foliage. Iced drinks were brought to allay their thirst,
and a sumptuous banquet was provided by their hosts;
thus the hours passed unheeded, till the *Ave Maria* was
rung by the convent-bell. Immediately the spell was
broken, and once more snow and ice dominated the scene.
The courtiers, who had rid themselves of as much of their
clothing as court etiquette would permit, shivered in the
bitter blast, and looked the very picture of blank amazement—so much so that William forgot his own suffering
and laughed heartily at the discomfiture of his train.

This story has a quaint sequel. To show his approval of
the magic feat William granted to the convent a piece
of land of considerable extent in the neighbourhood of
Cologne, and sent some of his courtiers to present the
deed of gift. The hospitable prior, anxious that the
members of the deputation should be suitably entertained,
drew from the well-furnished cellars of the monastery
some choice Rhenish, which so pleased the palates of the
courtiers that they drank and drank and did not seem to
know when to stop. At length the prior, beholding with
dismay the disappearance of his finest vintage, privately
begged the magician to put a stop to this drain on the
resources of his cellar. Albertus consented, and once
more the wine-cups were replenished. Imagine the
horror of the courtiers when each beheld ghastly flames

issuing from his cup! In their dismay they seized hold of one another and would not let go.

Only when the phenomenon had disappeared did they discover that each held his neighbour by the nose! and such was their chagrin at being seen in this unconventional pose that they quitted the monastery without a word, and never entered it again.

Truenfels

At a place called Truenfels, near the Oelberg, and not very far from Cologne, there lived at one time in the Middle Ages a knight named Sir Balther. His schloss was known as The Mount, and there dwelt with him here his only daughter, Liba, whose great beauty had won for her a vast entourage of suitors. Each was equally importunate, but only one was in any way favoured, Sir Sibert Ulenthal, and at the time the story opens this Sir Sibert had lately become affianced to Sir Balther's daughter.

Now Sir Balther felt an ardent aversion to one of his neighbours, the Bishop of Cologne, and his hatred of this prelate was shared abundantly by various other knights and nobles of the district. One evening it chanced a body of these were gathered together at The Mount; and after Rhenish had circulated freely among them and loosened their tongues, one and all began to vent wrath on the ill-starred Churchman, talking volubly of his avarice and misdeeds in general. But why, cried one of them, should they be content with so tame a thing as scurrilous speech? Were not men of the sword more doughty than men of the robe? he added; and thereupon a wild shout was raised by the revellers, and they swore that they would sally forth instantly and slay him whom they all loathed so passionately.

Truenfels

It happened that, even as they set out, the bishop was returning from a visit to a remote part of his diocese; and being wholly unprepared to cope with a gang of desperadoes like these, he fell an easy prey to their attack. But the Church in medieval days did not take acts of this sort passively, and the matter being investigated, and it transpiring that The Mount had been the rallying ground of the murderers, a band of troops was sent to raze Sir Balther's castle and slay its inmates. The news, meanwhile, reached the fair Liba's *fiancé*, Sir Sibert, and knowing well that, in the event of The Mount being stormed by the avenging party, death or an equally terrible fate might befall his betrothed, the lover felt sad indeed. He hastened to the King and implored his intervention; on this being refused, he proposed that he himself should join the besiegers, at the same time carrying with him a royal pardon for Liba, for what concern had she with her father's crimes? His Majesty was persuaded to give the requisite document to Sir Sibert, who then hied him at full speed to The Mount, there to find the siege going forward. The walls of the castle were strong, and as yet the inmates were showing a good fight; but as day after day went past their strength and resources began to wane, and anon it seemed as though they could not possibly hold out longer. Accordingly the soldiers redoubled their efforts to effect a breach, which being compassed ultimately, they rushed upon the little garrison; and now picture the consternation of Liba when she found that her own lover was among the assailants of her home! Amid the din of battle he called to her loudly, once and again, telling her that he carried a royal pardon for her, and that all she had to do was to forsake her father and follow her betrothed instead. But in the din of battle she did not hear, or mistook the tenor of his words ; and ere he could make himself understood the garrison of the castle began to yield, and a moment later the building was in flames. Many of the besieged were burnt to death, but Liba and her father hastened to a little chamber at the base of the schloss, and thence they won to a subterranean passage which was known only to themselves, and which led to a distant place in the surrounding wilds.

Gazing at the blackened ruins, Sir Sibert felt as though henceforth the world held for him no joy whatsoever. He refused to be comforted, so convinced was he that Liba had perished in the terrible fray ; but one stormy evening, wandering in the neighbourhood of the castle, he perceived two figures who seemed to him familiar. True, both were haggard and tattered, but as he drew near to them the knight's pulses quickened of a sudden, for he knew that his beloved stood before him. Would she listen to him now? he wondered ; or would she still imagine him perfidious, and scorn the aid which he offered? While he was debating with himself the storm increased, and the great peals of thunder sounding overhead made the lover's heart beat faster. He drew the all-important document from within his doublet and approached the pair. "Heart of my heart" . . . the words faltered to Sir Sibert's lips, but he got no further ; a great flash of lightning descended from on high, and lo! Sir Balther and Liba lay stricken in death.

The broken-hearted lover built a chapel on the spot where his betrothed had fallen, and here he dwelt till the end of his days. It would seem, nevertheless, that those pious exercises wherewith hermits chiefly occupy themselves were not his only occupation ; for long after the chapel itself had become a ruin its sight was marked by a great stone which bore an inscription in rude characters—the single word " Liba." Doubtless Sir Sibert had hewn this epitaph with his own hands.

Rolandseck and Nonnenwerth

The castle of Rolandseck stands opposite Drachenfels. Below them, on an island in the Rhine, is the convent of Nonnenwerth.

Roland, Charlemagne's nephew, whose fame had spread throughout the world, while riding one day on the banks of the Rhine, sought the hospitality of the Lord of Drachenfels.

Honoured at receiving such a distinguished guest, the lord of the castle hastened to welcome him.

The ladies gave the brave knight as cordial a reception as their lord, whose charming daughter seemed deeply impressed by the visitor's knightly deportment. Roland's admiring glances lingered lovingly on the fair maid, who blushed in sweet confusion, and whose tender looks alone betrayed the presence of Cupid, who but waited for an opportunity to manifest his power.

At his host's bidding Roland put off his armour, but even in his own room a vision of maidenly beauty haunted him, thereby showing how subtly the young girl's charms had wound themselves around the knight's heart.

Roland remained for some time with the Lord of Drachenfels, fascinated more and more by the grace and beauty of his winsome daughter. Besides being beautiful, she was a clever needlewoman, and he admired the dexterity with which she embroidered ornamental designs on damask.

Only when asked by her to relate some deeds of daring, or describe the wondrous countries through which he had

125

travelled, would Roland become eloquent. Then he grew enthusiastic, his cheeks glowed, his eyes sparkled, and the enamoured maid would regard her hero with admiration. She evinced a lively interest in his exploits, their eyes would meet, then with a throbbing breast she would resume her work by his side. From this blissful dream Roland was summoned to the wars again.

The brave soldier prepared to depart, but he realized the joys he must renounce. Once more he visited the favourite haunts where they had spent such happy moments. The sound of someone weeping aroused him from his reverie, and he beheld his lady-love seated in an arbour, sobbing bitterly. Each knew the grief which separation must bring. Roland consoled the maiden by promising to return soon, nevermore to part. Only her tears betrayed how deeply the arrow of the wingèd god had sunk into her heart.

A few days later they were betrothed, after which Roland departed in quest of glory. Many victories were gained by him, and soon the enemy was vanquished. Rejoicings were held to celebrate the event.

But at Drachenfels Castle sad faces and tearful eyes told a tale of sorrow, for it had been announced that Roland was dead. The maid's rosy cheeks grew pale with grief; nothing could console her; for was not her hero departed from her for ever?

In the intensity of her anguish she sought relief in prayer and found a refuge in religion. She entered the convent at Nonnenwerth, resolved to dedicate her life to Heaven, since the joys of earth had fled.

Her afflicted parents reluctantly acquiesced in this proposal. Daily they beheld their daughter waving her hand to them as she entered the chapel.

Rolandseck & Nonnenwerth

Suddenly there appeared before the gates of Drachenfels a troop of cavaliers, whose armour shone brilliantly in the sun. Roland had returned home from the wars, crowned with glory, to claim his bride. But when he heard that she had taken the veil his buoyant spirits sank. The Lord of Drachenfels told him that they had believed the report of his death to be true.

A cry of despair broke from the hero of a hundred fights. He crossed the Rhine to the castle of Rolandseck, where he remained for many weeks, abandoned to grief.

Frequently he looked toward the convent which held his beloved. One evening he heard the bells tolling and saw a funeral procession of nuns carrying a coffin to the chapel. His page told him that his love was dead, but Roland had already divined that she who had mourned his supposed death had died through grief for him who was still alive to mourn her death.

Time rolled on and Roland went again to the wars and achieved greater conquests, but at length he fell fighting against the Moors at Roncevaux, dying on the battlefield as he had wished. His valorous deeds and his glorious death were sung by minstrels throughout all Christendom, and his fame will never die.

LEGENDS OF AIX-LA-CHAPELLE

Aix-la-Chapelle was the ancient seat of the Empire of Charlemagne, and many legends cluster around it, several of which have already been noticed in connexion with its great founder. The following legends, however, deal with the town itself, and not with any circumstance connected with the mighty Karl.

The Hunchbacked Musician

In Aix-la-Chapelle dwelt two hunchbacked musicians. Friedel was a lively fellow with a pleasant face and an engaging manner. Heinz had red hair, green eyes, and a malevolent expression. Friedel was a better player than Heinz; that, combined with his agreeable looks, made him a general favourite.

Friedel loved Agathe, the daughter of a rich wine-merchant. The lovers' prospects were not encouraging, for Agathe's father sought a son-in-law from higher circles. The poor musician's plight was rendered desperate by the wine-merchant compelling his daughter to accept a rich but dissipated young man. When the hunchback approached the merchant to declare his feelings toward the maiden, he was met with derision and insult. Full of bitterness, he wandered about, till midnight found him in the fish-market, where the Witches' Sabbath was about to take place. A weird light was cast over everything, and a crowd of female figures quickly gathered. A lady who seemed to be at the head of the party offered the hunchback refreshment, and others handed him a violin, desiring him to play for them. Friedel played, and the witches danced; faster and faster, for the violin was bewitched. At last the violinist fell exhausted, and the dancing ceased. The lady now commanded him to kneel and receive the thanks of the company for his beautiful playing. Then she muttered strange words over the kneeling hunchback.

When Friedel arose his hump was gone.

Just then the clock struck one, everything vanished, and the musician found himself alone in the market-place. Next morning his looking-glass showed him that he had

Aix-la-Chapelle

Louis Weirter, R.B.A.

(See page 127)

The Kreuzberg, Bonn

Louis Weirter, R.B.A.

(See page 133)

Legend of the Cathedral of Aix-la-Chapelle

not been dreaming, and in his pocket he found a large sum of money, which made him the equal of the richest in the town. Overjoyed at the transformation, he lost no time in seeking Agathe's house. The sight of his gold turned the scale in his favour, and the wine-merchant consented to his suit.

Now Heinz was inflamed with jealousy, and tried to calumniate his companion by spreading evil stories. Friedel's strange adventure leaked abroad, and Heinz determined to try his fortune likewise. So at the next witch-meeting he hastened to the fish-market, where at the outset everything happened in exactly the same manner. Heinz was requested to play, but his avaricious gaze was fixed on the golden vessels on the table, and his thoughts were with the large reward he would ask. Consequently his playing became so discordant that the indignant dancers made him cease.

Kneeling down to receive his reward, he demanded the valuable drinking-cups, whereupon with scornful and mocking words the lady who was the leader of the band fixed on his breast the hump she had taken from Friedel. Immediately the clock struck one, and all disappeared. The poor man's rage was boundless, for he found himself now saddled with two humps. He became an object of ridicule to the townsfolk, but Friedel pitied him, and maintained him ever after.

The Legend of the Cathedral of Aix-la-Chapelle

In former times the zealous and devout inhabitants of Aix-la-Chapelle determined to build a cathedral. For six months the clang of the hammer and axe resounded with wonderful activity, but, alas! the money which had been supplied by pious Christians for this holy work became exhausted, the wages of the masons were perforce suspended, and with them their desire to hew and hammer, for, after all, men must have money wherewith to feed their families.

Thus the cathedral stood, half finished, resembling a falling ruin. Moss, grass, and wild parsley flourished in the cracks of the walls, screech-owls already discovered convenient places for their nests, and amorous sparrows hopped lovingly about where holy priests should have been teaching lessons of chastity.

The builders were confounded. They endeavoured to borrow here and there, but no rich man could be induced to advance the large sum required. The collections from house to house produced little, so that instead of the much-wished-for golden coins nothing was found in the boxes but copper. When the magistracy received this report they were out of humour, and looked with desponding countenances toward the cathedral walls, as fathers look upon the remains of favourite children.

At this moment a stranger of commanding figure and something of pride in his voice and bearing entered the council chamber and exclaimed: "*Bon Dieu!* it is said that you are out of spirits. Hem! if nothing but money is wanting, you may console yourselves, gentlemen. I possess mines of gold and silver, and both can and will most willingly supply you with a ton of them."

The astounded magistrates sat like a row of pillars, measuring the stranger from head to foot. The Burgomaster first found his tongue. "Who are you, noble lord," said he, "that thus, entirely unknown, speak of tons of gold as though they were sacks of beans? Tell us your name, your rank in this world, and whether you are sent from the regions above to assist us."

Legend of the Cathedral of Aix-la-Chapelle

"I have not the honour to reside there," replied the stranger, "and, between ourselves, I beg most particularly to be no longer troubled with questions concerning who and what I am. Suffice it to say I have gold plentiful as summer hay!" Then, drawing forth a leathern pouch, he proceeded: "This little purse contains the tenth of what I'll give. The rest shall soon be forthcoming. Now listen, my masters," continued he, clinking the coin; "all this trumpery is and shall remain yours if you promise to give me the first little soul that enters the door of the new temple when it is consecrated."

The astonished magistrates sprang from their seats as if they had been shot up by an earthquake and rushed pell-mell into the farthest corner of the room, where they rolled and clung to each other like lambs frightened at flashes of lightning. Only one of the party had not entirely lost his wits, and he collected his remaining senses and, drawing his head out of the heap, uttered boldly: "Avaunt, thou wicked spirit!"

But the stranger, who was no less a person than Master Urian, laughed at them. "What's all this outcry about?" said he at length. "Is my offence so heinous that you are all become like children? It is I that may suffer from this business, not you. With my hundreds and thousands I have not far to run to buy a score of souls. Of you I ask but one in exchange for all my money. What are you picking at straws for? One may plainly see you are a mere set of humbugs! For the good of the commonwealth (which high-sounding name is often borrowed for all sorts of purposes) many a prince would instantly conduct a whole army to be butchered, and you refuse one single man for that purpose! Fie! I am ashamed, O overwise counsellors, to hear you reason thus absurdly

and citizen-like. What, do you think to deprive yourselves of the kernel of your people by granting my
wish? Oh, no; there your wisdom is quite at fault, for,
depend on it, hypocrites are always the earliest church
birds."

By degrees, as the cunning fiend thus spoke, the magistrates took courage and whispered in each other's ears:
"What is the use of our resisting? The grim lion will
only show his teeth once. If we don't assent, we shall
infallibly be packed off ourselves. It is better, therefore,
to quiet him directly."

Scarcely had they given effect to this new disposition
and concluded the bargain when a swarm of purses flew
into the room through doors and windows. Urian now
took leave, but he stopped at the door and called out with
a grim leer: "Count it over again for fear I may have
cheated you."

The hellish gold was piously expended in finishing the
cathedral, but nevertheless, when the building was completed, splendid though it was, the whole town was filled
with fear and alarm at the sight of it. The fact was that,
although the magistrates had promised by bond and oath
not to trust the secret to anybody, one had prated to his
wife, and she had made it a market-place tale, so that one
and all declared they would never set foot within the walls.
The terrified council now consulted the clergy, but the
good priests hung their heads. At last a monk cried out:
"A thought strikes me. The wolf which has so long
ravaged the neighbourhood of our town was this morning
caught alive. This will be a well-merited punishment for
the destroyer of our flocks; let him be cast to the devil in
the fiery gulf. 'Tis possible the arch hell-hound may not
relish this breakfast, yet, *nolens volens*, he must swallow it.

A Legend of Bonn

You promised him certainly a soul, but whose was not decidedly specified."

The monk's plan was plausible, and the magistrates determined to put the cunning trick into execution. The day of consecration arrived. Orders were given to bring the wolf to the principal entrance of the cathedral, and just as the bells began to ring, the trap-door of the cage was opened and the savage beast darted out into the nave of the empty church. Master Urian from his lurking-place beheld this consecration-offering with the utmost fury; burning with choler at being thus deceived, he raged like a tempest, and finally rushed forth, slamming the brass gate so violently after him that the ring cracked in twain.

This fissure commemorates the priest's victory over the devices of the Devil, and is still exhibited to travellers who visit the cathedral.

A Legend of Bonn

The city of Bonn is one of the most beautiful of all those situated on the banks of the Rhine, and being the birth-place of no less celebrated a composer than Beethoven, it naturally attracts a goodly number of pilgrims every year, these coming from many distant lands to do homage at the shrine of genius. But Bonn and its neighbourhood have older associations than this—associations which carry the mind of the traveller far into the Middle Ages—for hard by the town is Rolandseck; while a feature of the district is the *Siebengebirge* (Seven Mountains), a fine serried range of peaks which present a very imposing appearance when viewed from any of the heights over-looking Bonn itself, and which recall a justly famous legend.

This story tells that in the thirteenth century there lived

133

at a castle in the heart of these mountains a nobleman called Wolfram Herzog von Bergendorf; and being no freebooter like most of the other German barons of the time, but a man of very pious disposition, he was moved during the prime of his life to forsake his home and join a body of crusaders. Reaching Palestine after a protracted journey, these remained there for a long time, Wolfram fighting gallantly in every fray and making his name a terror to the Saracens. But the brave crusader was wounded eventually, and now he set out for Germany, thirsting all the way for a sight of his beloved *Siebengebirge*, and dreaming of the wind-swept schloss which was his home. As he drew nearer to it he pictured the welcome which his fond Herzogin would give him, but scarcely had the drawbridge been lowered to admit him to his castle ere a fell piece of news was imparted to him. In short, it transpired that his wife Elise had been unfaithful to him during his absence and, on hearing that he was returning, had fled precipitately with her infant son. It was rumoured that she had found refuge in a convent, but Wolfram was quite unable to ascertain his wife's whereabouts, the doors of all nunneries being impassable to men; while even the joy of revenge was denied him, for, try as he might, he could not find out the name of the person who had wronged him. So the Herzog was broken-hearted, and he vowed that henceforth he would live a solitary life within his castle, spending his time in prayer and seeing only his own retainers.

For many years this vow was piously observed, and Wolfram never stirred abroad. In course of time, however, he began to chafe at the restraint, feeling it the more acutely because he was an old soldier and had known the

A Legend of Bonn

excitement of warfare; and so it came about that he revoked his decision and began to travel about the country as of old. It seemed also, to some of his henchmen, that he was gradually becoming more like his former self, and they sometimes said among themselves that he would marry again and had quite forgotten his wrongs. But the very reverse was the truth, and if Wolfram was growing more cheerful, it was because new hopes of retribution were springing up in his heart. The chance would come, he often told himself; surely the fates would one day confront him with his wife's lover! And one day, as he rode through the village of Gudesburg, these revengeful thoughts were uppermost in his mind. They engrossed him wholly, and he took little heed of the passers-by; but an unexpected stumble on the part of his horse caused him to look up, and of a sudden his eyes blazed like live coals. Here, walking only a few yards away from him, was a youth who bore an unmistakable resemblance to the unfaithful Elise; and dismounting instantly, the Herzog strode up to the stranger, hailed him loudly, and proceeded to question him concerning his identity. The youth was surprised at the anger expressed on the elder man's countenance; and being overawed, he answered all questions without hesitation, unfolding the little he knew about his parentage. Nor had Wolfram's instincts deceived him; the tale he heard confirmed his suspicions, and drawing his sword, he slew the youth in cold blood, denying him even a moment in which to repeat a paternoster.

A rude iron cross, still standing by the road at Gudesburg, is said to mark the place where the ill-starred and unoffending young man met his doom. Possibly this cross was erected by Wolfram himself because he experienced remorse, and felt that he had been unduly hasty in taking life ; but be that as it may, the story concludes by asserting that the Herzog once more vowed that he would spend the rest of his days in solitude and prayer, and that henceforth to the end his vow remained unbroken.

The Treasure-seeker

This is a picturesque tale of the consequences of wealth attained by the aid of the supernatural which hangs about the ancient village of Endenich, near Bonn, where at the end of the seventeenth century there dwelt a certain sheriff and his son, Konrad, who was a locksmith by trade. They were poor and had lost everything in the recent wars, which had also ruined Heribert, another sheriff, who with his daughter, the beautiful Gretchen, eked out a frugal but peaceful existence in the same neighbourhood. The two young people fell in love with each other, but Gretchen's father, becoming suddenly and mysteriously very rich and arrogant withal, desired a wealthy or highly placed official as his son-in-law and not a poor lad with no expectations such as Konrad, the locksmith. The lovers were therefore compelled to meet in secret, and it was on one of these occasions that Heribert, surprising them together, attacked Konrad and felled him to the ground in his rage that he should dare to approach his daughter.

Spurred by his love and knowing that he could never hope to win Gretchen without wealth, the unhappy youth decided to barter for gold the only possession left to him —his soul.

Now there lived in the churchyard a Lapp wizard who made such bargains ; so in the dead of night Konrad took his way to this dreadful and unfrequented spot and exhorted the sorcerer to come forth. At the third cry a terrible apparition appeared and demanded to know his wishes, to which the terrified Konrad could only reply : "Gold." Thereupon the sorcerer led the way deep into a forest and, pointing mysteriously to a certain spot, disappeared. At this spot Konrad found a chest full of gold and silver coins, and returning to Bonn, he bought a house the splendour of which surpassed that of Heribert, who could no longer refuse his daughter to so wealthy a suitor.

The young wife tried all her arts to solve the mystery of her husband's wealth, and he was at length about to reveal it to her when he was suddenly arrested and thrown into prison. Here he was put to torture by the authorities, who suspected him of robbery, and at length he confessed that he had found a treasure, while to his wife he confided the gruesome details, all of which were overheard by his jailers.

He was released, but almost immediately re-arrested on the suspicion that he had killed a Jew named Abraham, who had amassed great sums during the wars as a spy. Tortured again, in his extremity he confessed to the murder and named Heribert as his accomplice, where-upon both men were sentenced to be hanged. Just as this doom was about to be carried out a Jew who had arrived from a far country hurriedly forced his way through the crowd. It was Abraham, who had returned in time to save the innocent.

But his sin did not pass unpunished, for Konrad died childless ; he bequeathed his wealth to the Church and charities, in expiation of his sin of having attained wealth by the aid of an evil spirit.

The Miller's Maid of Udorf

Udorf is a little village on the left bank of the Rhine, not far from the town of Bonn, and at no great distance from it stands a lonely mill, to which attaches the following story of a woman's courage and resourcefulness.

Hännchen was the miller's servant-maid, a buxom young woman who had been in his service for a number of years, and of whose faithfulness both he and his wife were assured.

One Sunday morning the miller and his wife had gone with their elder children to attend mass at the neighbouring village of Hersel, leaving Hännchen at the mill in charge of the youngest child, a boy of about five years of age.

On the departure of the family for church Hännchen busied herself in preparing dinner, but had scarcely commenced her task ere a visitor entered the kitchen. This was no other than her sweetheart, Heinrich, whom she had not seen for some time. Indeed, he had earned so bad a reputation as a loafer and an idle good-for-nothing that the miller, as much on Hännchen's account as on his own, had forbidden him the house. Hännchen, however, received her lover with undisguised pleasure, straightway set food before him, and sat down beside him for a chat, judging that the miller's dinner was of small consequence compared with her ill-used Heinrich! The latter ate heartily, and toward the end of the meal dropped his knife, as though by accident.

"Pick that up, my girl," said he.

Hännchen protested good-humouredly, but obeyed none the less. As she stooped to the floor Heinrich seized her by the neck and held another knife to her throat.

138

The Miller's Maid of Udorf

"Now, girl, show me where your master keeps his money," he growled hoarsely. "If you value your life, make haste."

"Let me go and I'll tell you," gasped Hännchen; and when he had loosened his grip on her throat she looked at him calmly.

"Don't make such a fuss about it, Heinrich," she said pleasantly. "If you take my master's money, you must take me too, for this will be no place for me. Will you take me with you, Heinrich?"

The hulking fellow was taken completely off his guard by her apparent acquiescence, and touched by her desire to accompany him, which he attributed, with the conceit of his kind, to his own personal attractions.

"If I find the money, you shall come with me, Hännchen," he conceded graciously. "But if you play me false——"

The sentence ended with an expressive motion of his knife.

"Very well, then," said the maid. "The money is in master's room. Come and I will show you where it is concealed."

She led him to the miller's room, showed him the massive coffer in which lay her master's wealth, and gave him a piece of iron wherewith to prise it open.

"I will go to my own room," she said, "and get *my* little savings, and then we shall be ready to go."

So she slipped away, and her erstwhile sweetheart set to work on the miller's coffer.

"The villain!" said Hännchen to herself when she was outside the room. "Now I know that master was right when he said that Heinrich was no fit suitor to come courting me."

With that she slammed the door to and turned the key, shutting the thief in a room as secure as any prison-cell. He threatened and implored her, but Hännchen was deaf to oaths and entreaties alike. Outside she found the miller's son playing happily, and called him to her. "Go to father as quickly as you can," she said, putting him on the road to Hersel. "You will meet him down there. Tell him there is a thief in the mill."

The child ran as fast as his little legs would carry him, but ere he had gone many yards a shrill whistle sounded from the barred window behind which Heinrich was imprisoned.

"Diether," shouted the robber to an accomplice in hiding, "catch the child and come and stop this wench's mouth." Hännchen looked around for the person thus addressed, but no one was in sight. A moment later, however, Diether sprang up from a ditch, seized the frightened boy, and ran back toward the mill. The girl had but little time in which to decide on a course of action. If she barricaded herself in the mill, might not the ruffian slay the child? On the other hand, if she waited to meet him, she had no assurance that he would not kill them both. So she retired to the mill, locked the door, and awaited what fate had in store for her. In vain the robber threatened to kill the child and burn the mill over her head if she would not open to him at once. Seeing that his threats had no effect, he cast about for some means of entering the mill. His quick eye noted one unprotected point, an opening in the wall connected with the big mill-wheel, a by no means easy mode of ingress. But, finding no other way, he threw the frightened child on the grass and slipped through the aperture.

Meanwhile Hännchen, who from the position of her upper window could not see what was going on, was pondering how she could attract the attention of the miller or any of their neighbours. At last she hit upon a plan.

Rosebach & its Legend

It was Sunday and the mill was at rest. If she were to set the machinery in motion, the unusual sight of a mill at work on the day of rest would surely point to some untoward happening. Hardly had the idea entered her head ere the huge sails were revolving. At that very moment Diether had reached the interior of the great drum-wheel, and his surprise and horror were unbounded when it commenced to rotate. It was useless to attempt to stop the machinery; useless, also, to appeal to Hännchen. Round and round he went, till at last he fell unconscious on the bottom of the engine, and still he went on rotating. As Hännchen had anticipated, the miller and his family were vastly astonished to see the mill in motion, and hastened home from church to learn the reason for this departure from custom. Some of their neighbours accompanied them. In a few words Hännchen told them all that had occurred ; then her courage forsook her and she fainted in the arms of the miller's eldest son, who had long been in love with her, and whom she afterward married.

The robbers were taken in chains to Bonn, where for their many crimes they suffered the extreme penalty of the law.

Rosebach and its Legend

The quiet and peaceful valley of Hammerstein is one of the most beautiful in all Rhineland, yet, like many another lovely stretch of country, this valley harbours some gruesome tales, and among such there is one, its scene the village of Rosebach, which is of particular interest, as it is typical of the Middle Ages, and casts a light on the manner of life and thought common in those days. For many centuries there stood at this village of Rosebach a monastery, which no longer exists, and it was probably one of its early abbots who first wrote down the legend, for it is concerned primarily with the strange events which led to the founding and endowment of this religious house, and its whole tenor suggests the pen of a medieval cleric.

In a remote and shadowy time there lived at Schloss Rosebach a certain Otto, Count of Reuss-Marlinberg of Hammerstein; and this Count's evil deeds had made him notorious far and near, while equally ill-famed was his favourite henchman, Riguenbach by name, a man who had borne arms in the Crusades and had long since renounced all belief in religion. This ruffian was constantly in attendance on his master, Otto; and one day, when the pair were riding along the high-road together, they chanced to espy a bewitching maiden who was making her way from a neighbouring village to the convent of Walsdorf, being minded to enter the novitiate there and eventually take the veil. The Count doffed his hat to the prospective nun, less because he wished to be courteous than because it was his habit to salute every wayfarer he encountered on his domain; and Riguenbach, much amused by Otto's civility to one of low degree, burst into a loud laugh of derision and called after the maiden, telling her to come back. She obeyed his behest, and thereupon the two horsemen drew rein and asked the damsel whither she was bound. "To Walsdorf," she replied; and though Otto himself would have let her go forward as she pleased, the crafty Riguenbach was not so minded. "There are many dangers in the way," he said to the girl; "if you push on now that evening is drawing near you may fall a prey to robbers or wolves, so you had better come to the castle with us, spend the night there, and continue your journey on the morrow." Pleased by the apparently friendly offer, and never dreaming of the fate in store for her, the girl willingly accepted the invitation. That night the people around Schloss Rosebach heard piercing screams and wondered what new villainy was on foot. But the massive stone walls kept their secret, and the luckless maiden never again emerged from the castle.

For a time the Count's crime went unpunished, and about a year later he commenced paying his addresses to Eldegarda, a lady of noble birth. In due course the nuptials of the pair were celebrated. The bride had little idea what manner of man she had espoused, but she was destined to learn this shortly; for on the very night of their marriage an apparition rose between the two.

"Otto," cried the ghost in weird, sepulchral tones, "I alone am thy lawful spouse; through thee I lost all hopes of Heaven, and now I am come to reward thee for thy evil deeds." The Count turned livid with fear, and the blush on Eldegarda's cheek faded to an ashen hue; but the spectre remained with them throughout the night. And night after night she came to them thus, till at last Otto grew desperate and summoned to his aid a Churchman who happened to be in the neighbourhood, the Abbot Bernard of Clairvaux.

Now this Bernard enjoyed no small fame as a worker of miracles, but when Otto unfolded his case to him the Abbot declared straightway that no miracle would be justifiable in the present instance, and that only by repentance and by complete renunciation of the world might the Count be released from his nightly menace. Otto hung his head on hearing this verdict, and as he stood hesitating, pondering whether it were possible for him to forgo all earthly joys, his old henchman, Riguenbach, chanced to enter, and learning his master's quandary, he laughed loudly and advised the Count to eject Bernard forcibly. The Abbot met the retainer's mirth with a look of great severity, and on Riguenbach showing that he was still bent on insolence, the Churchman cried to him : "Get thee behind me, Satan"; whereupon a flame of lightning darted suddenly across the chamber, and the man who had long aided and abetted the Count's wicked-ness was consumed to ashes.

For a moment Otto stood aghast at the awful fate of his retainer; and now, beholding how terrible a thing is divine vengeance, he began at last to feel truly repentant. He consented to have his marriage annulled without delay, and even declared that he himself would become a monk. At the same time he counselled his wife to take the veil, and they parted, thinking never to see each other again. But one night, ere either of them had taken the irrevocable vows, the Virgin Mary appeared to Abbot Bernard and told him he had acted unwisely in parting the bride and bridegroom in this wise, for was not Eldegarda wholly innocent? The Churchman instantly returned to Otto's presence, and on the following day the Count and his wife were duly remarried. The newly found piety of the penitent found expression in the building and endowment of a religious edifice upon his domains.

So it was, then, that the Abbey of Rosebach was founded, and though the ruthless hand of time has levelled its walls, the strange events to which they owed their being long ago are still remembered and recited in the lovely vale of Hammerstein ; for, though all human things must needs perish, a good story long outlives them all.

The Dancers of Ramersdorf

The Dancers of Ramersdorf

At Ramersdorf every Sunday afternoon the lads and lasses
of the hamlet gathered on the village green and danced
gaily through the sunny hours. But wild prophecies of
the coming end of the world, when the year 1000
should break, were spreading throughout the countryside,
and the spirit of fear haunted the people, so that music
died away from their hearts and there was no more dancing
on the village green. Instead they spent the hours praying
in the church for divine mercy, and the Abbot of Löwenburg was well pleased.

The dreaded year came and went, yet the world had not
ceased; the sun still rose and set, life went on just the
same. So fear passed from the hearts of the people, and
because they were happy again the young folk once more
assembled to dance the Sundays away on the village green.
But the abbot was wroth at this. When the music began
he appeared among the villagers, commanding them to
cease from their revels and bethink themselves of the
House of God. But the lads and lasses laughed, and the
music went on as they footed it gaily. Then the abbot
was angered; he raised his hands to heaven and cursed
the thoughtless crowd, condemning the villagers to dance
there unceasingly for a year and a day.

As they heard the dreadful words the young folk tried to
stop, but their feet must needs go on to the endless music.
Faster and faster in giddy round they went, day and night,
rain and shine, throughout the changing seasons, until the
last hours of the extra day, when they fell in a senseless
heap in the hollow worn by their unresting feet. When
they awoke to consciousness all reason had passed from
them. To the day of their death they remained helpless

145

idiots. Henceforth the village green was deserted; no more were seen the lads and lasses dancing there on the Sabbath day.

The Löwenburg

Tradition asserts that on the summit of this mountain once stood a castle, of which, however, not the slightest trace can be found at the present day. There is also a story of the lord who dwelt there, Hermann von Heinsberg, with whom, for his sins, the direct line of the family became extinct.

Graf Hermann was possessed by one overmastering passion, that of the chase. The greater part of his life was spent in the dense forests which clothed the valleys and mountains about his castle. Every other interest must, perforce, stand aside. The cornfields, vineyards, and gardens of his vassals were oftentimes devastated in his sport, to the utter ruin of many. If any dared complain he laughed at or reviled them; but if he were in angry mood he set his hounds on them and hunted his vassals as quarry, either killing them outright or leaving them terribly injured. Needless to say, he was well hated by these people, also by his own class, for his character was too fierce and overbearing even for their tolerance. To crown his unpopularity, he was under the ban of the all-powerful Church, for saints' days and Lord's Day alike he hunted to his heart's content, and once, on receiving a remonstrance, had threatened to hunt the Abbot of Heisterbach himself. So he lived, isolated, except for his troop of jägers, from the rest of mankind. The forest was his world, his only friends the hounds.

Once, on the eve of a holy festival, Hermann set out to

The Löwenburg

hunt in the ancient forest about the base of the Löwenburg
In the excitement of the chase he outstripped his followers,
his quarry disappeared, and, overtaken by night, his surroundings, in the dim light, took on such an unfamiliar
aspect that he completely lost all sense of direction.   Up
and down he paced in unrestrained yet impotent anger,
feeling that he was under some evil spell.   Maddened by
this idea, he endeavoured to hack his way through the
thick undergrowth, but the matted boughs and dense
foliage were as effectual as prison bars.   He was trapped,
he told himself, in some enchanted forest, for the place
seemed more and more unfamiliar.   He strove to bring
back some recollection of the spot, which surely he must
have passed a thousand times.   But no—he could not dis-
tinguish any feature that seemed familiar.   His spirits
sank lower and lower, his strength seemed on the point of
failing, his brain seemed to be on fire.   Round and round
he went like some trapped animal ; then he threw himself
madly upon a mass of tangled underwood and succeeded
in breaking through to a more open space.   This also
seemed unfamiliar, and in the dim light of the stars the
tall trees shut him in as if with towers of impenetrable
shadow ; silence seemed to lay everything under a spell
of terror, ominous of coming evil.

Wearied in body and mind, Hermann flung himself down
on the sward and quickly fell asleep.   But suddenly a
plunging in the brushwood aroused him, and with the
instinct of the huntsman he sprang up instantly, seizing
his spear and whistling to his dogs, which, however,
crouched nearer to the earth, their hair bristling and eyes
red with fear.   Again their master called, but they refused
to stir, whining, with eyes strained and fixed on the undergrowth.   Then Graf Hermann went forward alone to the

spot whence proceeded the ominous sound, his spear poised, ready to strike.

He was about to penetrate into the brushwood when suddenly there emerged from it a majestic-looking man, who seemed as if hotly pursued. He was dressed in ancient garb, carrying a large crossbow in his right hand. A curved hunting-horn hung at his side, and an old-fashioned hunting-knife was stuck in his girdle.

With a stately motion of the hand he waved Hermann aside, then he raised the horn to his lips and blew upon it a terrible blast so unearthly in sound that the forest and mountains sent back echoes like the cry of the lost, to which the hounds gave tongue with a howl of fear. As if in answer to the echoes, there suddenly appeared hundreds of skeleton stags, of enormous size, each bestridden by a skeleton hunter. With one accord the ghostly riders spurred on their steeds, which with lowered antlers advanced upon the stranger, who, with a scream for mercy, sought frenziedly for some means of evading his grisly pursuers.

For the space of an hour the dreadful chase went on, Graf Hermann rooted to the spot with horror, overcome by a sense of helplessness. There in the centre he stood, the pivot round which circled the infernal hunt, unable to stay the relentless riders as with bony hands rattling against their skeleton steeds they encouraged them to charge, gore, and trample the hapless stranger, whose cries of agony were drowned by shrieks of fiendish glee and the incessant cracking of whips. Overcome at last by terror, the count fell senseless, his eyes dazed by the still whirling spectres and their flying quarry.

When at last he slowly awaked from his swoon he looked around, fearing to see again the hideous spectacle. All but the stranger, however, had vanished. Graf Hermann shuddered as he looked upon him, and only with difficulty could he summon sufficient courage to address him. Indeed, it was only after the unwonted action of crossing himself that he could speak.

"Who and what are you?" he asked in a hushed tone. But the stranger made no reply, except to sigh mournfully. Again the count asked the question, and again received but a sigh for answer.

"Then in the name of the Most High God I conjure you, speak!" he said the third time,

The stranger turned to him, as if suddenly released from bonds.

"By the power of God's holy name the spell is broken at last. Listen now to me!"

He beckoned Hermann to his side and in strange, stern tones he related the following:

"I am your ancestor. Like you, I loved the chase beyond everything in life—beyond our holy faith or the welfare of any human being, man, woman, or child. To all that stood in my path I showed no mercy. There came a time when famine visited the land. The harvest was destroyed by blight and the people starved. In their extremity they broke into my forests; famished with hunger, they destroyed and carried off the game. Beside myself with rage, I swore that they should suffer for it—that for every head of game destroyed I would exact a human life. I kept my oath. Arming my retainers, servants, and huntsmen, I seized my presumptuous vassals in the dead of night, and dragging them to the castle, I flung them into the deepest dungeons. There for three days I let them starve—for three days also I kept my hounds without food. Meantime my huntsmen had caught a great number of the largest and strongest deer in the forests. At the end of three days the unfortunate wretches were brought out, diminished now by a full hundred. My ready retainers bound them naked to the stags. My best steeds were saddled. Then the kennels were thrown open and the famished hounds rushed forth like a host of demons. Off went the deer like the wind, each with his human burden, the dogs following, and then the horsemen, shouting with glee at the new sport. By nightfall not a stag or his rider was left alive. The hounds in their fury worried and tore at both man and beast, and the last unfortunate wretch met a hideous death on this spot where we now stand."

He paused as if overcome by the memory of his crime.

" God avenged that dreadful deed. That night I died, and I am now suffering the tortures of the damned. Every night I am hunted by my victims, as you have seen. I am now the quarry, hunted from the castle court, on through the forest, to this hidden and haunted spot. Thousands and thousands of times I have suffered this : I endure all the agonies I made them suffer. I am doomed to undergo this to the last day, when I shall be hunted over the wastes of hell by legions of demons."

Again he paused, his eyes terrible with the anguish of a lost soul. He resumed in a sterner tone:

" Take warning by my fate. Providence, kinder to you than to me, has guided you hither to-night that you might learn of my punishment. While you still have time repent of your crimes and endeavour to make amends for the suffering you have inflicted. Remember —the wages of sin is death. Remember me—and my fate ! "

The next moment the phantom had faded from view.

The Löwenburg

Only the hounds were crouching near the count, panting fearfully. All else was silent gloom and night. After a terrible vigil the morning came, and Graf Hermann, now a changed man, returned to his castle in silence, and henceforth endeavoured to profit by the warning and follow the advice of his unhappy ancestor.

CHAPTER IV : DRACHENFELS TO RHEINSTEIN

The Dragon's Rock

AMONG the many legends invented by the early Christian monks to advance their faith, there are few more beautiful than that attached to the *Drachenfels*, the Dragon's Rock, a rugged and picturesque mass of volcanic porphyry rising above the Rhine on its right bank. Half-way up one of its pointed crags is a dark cavern known as the ' Dragon's Cave,' which was at one time, in that misty past to which all legends belong, the habitation of a hideous monster, half-beast and half-reptile. The peasants of the surrounding district held the creature in superstitious awe, worshipped him, and offered up sacrifices of human beings at the instigation of their pagan priests. Foremost among the worshippers of the dragon were two warrior princes, Rinbod and Horsrik, who frequently made an onslaught on the Christian people dwelling on the opposite bank of the Rhine, carrying off many captives to be offered as sacrifices to the dragon.

On one such occasion, while, according to their custom, they were dividing their prisoners, the pagan princes quarrelled over one of their captives, a Christian maiden, whose beauty and helpless innocence won the hearts of her fierce captors, so that each desired to possess her, and neither was inclined to renounce his claim. The quarrel became so bitter at length that the princes seized their weapons and were about to fight for the fair spoil. But at this juncture their priests intervened.

"It is not meet," said they, "that two noble princes should come to blows over a mere Christian maid. To-morrow she shall be offered to the dragon, in thanks-

The Drachenfels

Louis Weirter, R.B.A.

(See page 152)

Schloss Lahneck

Louis Weirter, R.B.A.

(See page 159)

The Dragon's Rock

giving for your victory." And they felt that they had done well, for had they not averted the impending quarrel, and at the same time gained a victim for their cruel rites? But the heart of Rinbod was heavy indeed, for he truly loved the young Christian maid, and would have given his life to save her from the horrible fate that awaited her. However, the decree of the priests was irrevocable, and no pleadings of his could avail. The girl was informed of the cruel destiny that was to befall her on the morrow, and with a calm mind she sought consolation from Heaven to enable her to meet her fate with courage befitting a Christian.

Early on the following morning she was led with much ceremony to a spot before the Dragon's Cave and there bound to an oak, to await the approach of the monster, whose custom it was to sally forth at sunrise in search of prey. The procession of priests, warriors, and peasants who had followed the victim to the place of sacrifice now climbed to the summit of the crag and watched eagerly for the coming of the dragon. Rinbod watched also, but it was with eyes full of anguish and apprehension. The Christian maid seemed to him more like a spirit than a human being, so calmly, so steadfastly did she bear herself.

Suddenly a stifled cry broke from the lips of the watchers —the hideous monster was seen dragging its heavy coils from the cavern, fire issuing from its mouth and nostrils. At its mighty roar even the bravest trembled. But the Christian maid alone showed no sign of fear; she awaited the oncoming of the dreadful creature with a hymn of praise on her lips. Nearer and nearer came the dragon, and at length, with a horrible roar, it sprang at its prey. But even as it did so the maiden held out her crucifix before her, and the dragon was checked in its onrush. A moment later it turned aside and plunged into the Rhine. The people on the crag were filled with awe at the miraculous power of the strange symbol which had overcome their idol and, descending, hastened to free the young girl from her bonds. When they learned the significance of the cross they begged that she would send them teachers that they might learn about the new religion. In vain their priests endeavoured to dissuade them. They had seen the power of the crucifix, and their renunciation of their pagan creed was complete.

Among the first to adopt the Christian religion was Rinbod; he married the beautiful captive and built a castle for her on the Drachenfels, whose ruins remain to this day.

It seems a pity that such a beautiful legend should have doubts cast upon its authenticity, but it has been conjectured that the word Drachenfels has a geological rather than a romantic significance—being, in fact, derived from *Trachyt-fels*, meaning 'Trachyte-rock.' This view is supported by the fact that there is another Drachenfels near Mannheim of a similar geological construction, but without the legend. However, it is unlikely that the people of antiquity would bestow a geological name upon any locality.

Okkenfels: A Rash Oath

On a rugged crag overlooking the Rhine above the town of Linz stands the ruined stronghold of Okkenfels. History tells us little or nothing concerning this ancient fortress, but legend covers the deficiency with the tale of the Baron's Rash Oath.

Rheinhard von Renneberg, according to the story,

Okkenfels : A Rash Oath

flourished about the beginning of the eleventh century, when the Schloss Okkenfels was a favourite rendezvous with the rude nobility of the surrounding district. Though they were none of them distinguished for their manners, by far the most rugged and uncouth was the Baron von Renneberg himself. Rough in appearance, abrupt in conversation, and inclined to harshness in all his dealings, he inspired in the breast of his only daughter a feeling more akin to awe than affection.

The gentle Etelina grew up to be a maiden of singular beauty, of delicate form and feature, and under the careful tutelage of the castle chaplain she became as good as she was beautiful. Lovers she had in plenty, for the charms of Etelina and the wealth of her noble father, whose sole heiress she was, formed a combination quite irresistible in the eyes of the young gallants who frequented the castle. But none loved her more sincerely than one of the baron's retainers, a young knight of Linz, Rudolph by name.

On one occasion Rheinhard was obliged to set out with his troop to join the wars in Italy, and ere he departed he confided his daughter to the care of the venerable chaplain, while his castle and lands he left in charge of Sir Rudolph. As may be supposed, the knight and the maiden frequently met, and ere long it became evident that Rudolph's passion was returned. The worthy chaplain, who loved the youth as a son, did not seek to interfere with the course of his wooing, and so in due time the lovers were betrothed.

At the end of a year the alarming news reached them that the baron was returning from the wars, bringing in his train a noble bridegroom for Etelina. In despair the lovers sought the old chaplain and begged his advice.

155

They knew only too well that the baron would not brook resistance to his will; for he had ever dealt ruthlessly with opposition. Yet both were determined that nothing should part them.

"I would rather die with Rudolph than marry another," cried the grief-stricken maiden. And indeed it seemed that one or other of these alternatives would soon fall to her lot.

But the wise old priest was planning a way of escape. "Ye were meant for one another, my children," he said philosophically; "therefore it is not for man to separate you. I will marry you at once, and I know a place where you may safely hide for a season."

It was nearing midnight on the eve of the day fixed for Rheinhard's return, so there was no time to be lost. The three repaired to the chapel, where the marriage was at once solemnized. Taking a basket of bread, meat, and wine, a lamp, and some other necessaries, the old man conducted the newly married pair through a subterranean passage to a cavern in the rock whereon the castle stood, a place known only to himself. Then, having blessed them, he withdrew.

Early on the following morning came the baron and his train, with the noble knight chosen as a husband for Etelina.

Rheinhard looked in vain for his daughter among the crowd of retainers who waited to welcome him. "Where is my little maid?" he asked.

The chaplain answered evasively. The damsel was ill abed, he replied. When the noble lord had refreshed himself he should see her.

Directly the repast was over he hastened to his daughter's apartment, only to find her flown! Dismayed and angry, he rushed to the chaplain and demanded an explanation. The good old man, after a vain attempt to soothe his irate patron, revealed all—all, that is, save the place where the fugitives were concealed, and that he firmly refused to divulge. The priest was committed to the lowest dungeon, a vile den to which access could only be got by means of a trap-door and a rope.

With his own hands the baron swung to the massive trap, swearing a deep oath.

" If I forgive my daughter, or any of her accomplices, may I die suddenly where I now stand, and may my soul perish for ever ! "

The disappointed bridegroom soon returned to his own land, and the baron, whose increasing moroseness made him cordially hated by his attendants, was left to the bitterness of his thoughts.

Meanwhile Rudolph and his bride had escaped unseen from the castle rock and now dwelt in the forests skirting the Seven Mountains. While the summer lasted all went well with them; they, and the little son who was born to them, were content with the sustenance the forest afforded. But in the winter all was changed. Starvation stared them in the face. More and more pitiful became their condition, till at length Rudolph resolved to seek the baron, and give his life, if need be, to save his wife and child.

That very day Rheinhard was out hunting in the forest. Imagine his surprise when a gaunt figure, clad in a bear-skin, stepped from the undergrowth and bade him follow, if he wished to see his daughter alive. The startled old man obeyed the summons, and arrived at length before a spacious cavern, which his guide motioned him to enter. Within, on a pile of damp leaves, lay Etelina and her child, both half-dead with starvation. Rheinhard's anger speedily melted at the pathetic sight, and he freely forgave his daughter and Rudolph, his hitherto unrecognized guide, and bade them return with him to Okkenfels.

Etelina's first request was for a pardon for the old chaplain, and Rheinhard himself went to raise the heavy trap-door. While peering into the gloom, however, he stumbled and fell headlong into the dungeon below. " A judgment!" he shrieked as he fell, then all was silence.

The bruised remains of the proud baron were interred in the parish church of Linz, and henceforth Etelina and her husband lived happily at Okkenfels. But both they and the old chaplain offered many a pious prayer for the soul of the unhappy Baron Rheinhard.

Oberwörth

In the middle of the Rhine, a little above Coblentz, lies the island of Oberwörth, where at one time stood a famous nunnery. Included in the traditional lore of the neighbourhood is a tragic tale of the beautiful Ida, daughter of the Freiherr von Metternich, who died within its walls in the fourteenth century.

Von Metternich, who dwelt at Coblentz, was a wealthy and powerful noble, exceedingly proud of his fair daughter, and firmly convinced that none but the highest in the land was fit mate for her. But Ida had other views, and had already bestowed her heart on a young squire in her father's train. It is true that Gerbert was a high-born youth, of stainless life, pleasing appearance, and gentle manners, and, moreover, one who was likely at no distant date to win his spurs. Nevertheless the lovers instinctively concealed their mutual affection from von Metternich, and plighted their troth in secret.

But so ardent an affection could not long remain hidden.

Oberwörth

The time came when the nobleman discovered how matters stood between his daughter and Gerbert, and with angry frowns and muttered oaths he resolved to exercise his paternal authority. " My daughter shall go to a nunnery," he said to himself. " And as for that jackanapes, he must be got rid of at once." He pondered how he might conveniently rid himself of the audacious squire.

That night he dispatched Gerbert on a mission to the grand prior of the Knights-Templars, who had his abode at the neighbouring castle of Lahneck. The unsuspecting squire took the sealed missive and set out, thinking as he rode along how rich he was in possessing so sweet a love as Ida, and dreaming of the time when his valour and prowess should have made their marriage possible. . But his dreams would have been rudely disturbed had he seen what was passing at Coblentz. For his betrothed, in spite of her tears and pleadings, was being secretly conveyed to the nunnery of Oberwörth, there to remain until she should have forgotten her lover—as though the stone walls of a convent could shut out the imaginings of a maid ! However, Gerbert knew nothing of this, and he rode along in leisurely fashion, until at length he came to the Schloss Lahneck, where he was at once conducted into the presence of the grand prior of the Knights-Templars.

The grand prior was a man of middle age, with an expression of settled melancholy on his swarthy features. Gerbert approached him with becoming reverence, bent his knee, and presented the missive.

The prior turned his gaze so earnestly on the young man's face that Gerbert dropped his eyes in confusion. A moment later the prior broke the seal and hastily scanned the letter.

"Who mayest thou be, youth?" he asked abruptly.

"Gerbert von Isenburg, sir."

"And thy mother?"

"Guba von Isenburg," was the astonished Gerbert's reply.

The prior seemed to be struggling with deep emotion.

"Knowest thou the purport of this missive?" he said at last.

"It concerns me not," answered Gerbert simply.

"Nay, my son," said the prior, "it doth concern thee, and deeply, too. Know that it is thy death-warrant, boy! The Freiherr has requested me to send thee to the wars in Palestine, and so to place thee that death will be a certainty. This he asks in the name of our ancient friendship and for the sake of our order, to which he has ever shown himself well disposed."

Seeing the dismay and incredulity which were depicted in his listener's face, the prior hastened to read aloud a passage describing von Metternich's discovery of his daughter's love for the humble squire, and Gerbert could no longer doubt that his fate was sealed.

The prior looked at him kindly.

"Gerbert," he said, "I am not going to put the cruel order into execution. Though I lose friendship, the honour of our order, life itself, the son of Guba von Isenburg shall not suffer at my hands. I sympathize with thy passion for the fair Ida. I myself loved thy mother."

The impetuous Gerbert started to his feet, hand on sword, at the mention of his mother, whose good name he set before all else; but with a dignified gesture the prior motioned him to his seat.

Then in terse, passionate phrases the elder man told how he had loved the gentle Guba for years, always hesitating to declare his passion lest the lady should scorn him. At length he could bear it no longer, and made up his mind to reveal his love to her. With this intent he rode toward her home, only to learn from a passing page that Guba, his mistress, was to be married that very day to von Isenburg. He gave to the page a ring, bidding him carry it to his mistress with the message that it was from one who loved her greatly, and who for her sake renounced the world.

"The ring," he concluded, "is on thy finger, and in thy face and voice are thy mother's likeness. Canst thou wonder that I would spare thy life?"

Gerbert listened in respectful silence. His love for Ida enabled him to sympathize with the pathetic tale unfolded by the prior. Tears fell unchecked from the eyes of both.

"And now," said the prior at last, "we must look to thy safety."

"I would not bring misfortune on thee," said Gerbert. "May I not go to Palestine and win my way through with my sword?"

"It is impossible," said the elder man. "Von Metternich would see to it that thou wert slain. Thou must go to Swabia, where a prior of our order will look after thy safety in the meantime."

The same day Gerbert was conveyed to Swabia, where, for a time at least, he was safe from persecution.

The Dance of Death

In the nunnery of Oberwörth, on a pallet in a humble cell, Ida lay dying. A year had gone past since she had been separated from her lover, and every day had seen her grow weaker and more despondent. Forget Gerbert? That would she never while life remained to her. Wearily she tossed on her pallet, her only companion a sister of

161

the convent. Willingly now would the Freiherr give his dearest possessions to save his daughter, but already she was beyond assistance, her only hope the peace of the grave.

"I am dying, sister," she said to her attendant. "Nevermore shall I see my dear Gerbert—ah! nevermore."

"Hush," murmured the nun gently, "stranger things have happened. All may yet be well." And to divert the dying maid's attention from her grief she recited tales of lovers who had been reunited after many difficulties.

But Ida refused to be pacified.

"Alas!" she said, "I am betrothed, yet I must die unwed."

"Heaven forbid!" cried the pious nun in alarm. "For then must thou join in the dance of death."

It was a popular belief in that district that a betrothed maiden who died before her wedding was celebrated must, after her death, dance on a spot in the centre of the island whereon no grass or herb ever grew—that is, unless in the interval she took the veil. Every night at twelve o'clock a band of such hapless maidens may be seen dancing in the moonlight, doomed to continue their nocturnal revels till they meet with a lover. And woe betide the knight who ventures within their reach! They dance round and round him and with him till he falls dead, whereupon the youngest maid claims him for her lover. Henceforth she rests quietly in her grave and joins no more in the ghostly frolic.

This weird tradition Ida now heard from the lips of the nun, who herself claimed to have witnessed the scenes she described.

"I beseech thee," said the sister, "do but join our convent, and all will yet be well."

"I die," murmured Ida, heeding not the words of her companion. "Gerbert—we shall meet again!"

The Dance of Death

Gerbert, her lover, heard the sad news in his dwelling-place on the shores of Lake Constance, and returned to Oberwörth with all speed. A week had elapsed ere he arrived, and Ida's body was already interred in the vaults of the convent.

It was a night of storm and darkness. No boatman would venture on the Rhine, but Gerbert, anxious to pay the last respects to the body of his beloved, was not to be deterred. With his own hands he unmoored a vessel and sailed across to Oberwörth. Having landed at that part of the island furthest from the convent, he was obliged to pass the haunted spot on his way thither. The circular patch of barren earth was said to be a spot accursed, by reason of sacrilege and suicide committed there. But such things were far from the thoughts of the distraught knight.

Suddenly he heard a strange sound, like the whisper of a familiar voice—a sound which, despite its quietness, seemed to make itself heard above the fury of the storm. Looking up, he beheld a band of white-robed maidens dancing in the charmed circle. One of them, a little apart from the others, seemed to him to be his lost Ida. The familiar figure, the grace of mien, the very gesture with which she beckoned him, were hers, and he rushed forward to clasp her to his heart. Adroitly she eluded his grasp and mingled with the throng. Gerbert followed with bursting heart, seized her in his arms, and found that the other phantoms had surrounded them. Something in the unearthly music fascinated him; he felt impelled to dance round and round, till his head reeled. And still he danced with his phantom bride, and still the maidens whirled about them. On the stroke of one the dancers vanished and the knight sank to the ground, all but dead with fatigue. In the morning he was found by the kindly nuns, who tended him carefully. But all their skill and attention were in vain; for Gerbert lived only long enough to tell of his adventure to the sisterhood. This done, he expired with the name of his beloved spirit-bride upon his lips.

Stolzenfels : The Alchemist

Alchemy was a common pursuit in the Middle Ages. The poor followed it eagerly in the vain desire for gold; the rich spent their wealth in useless experiments, or showered it on worthless charlatans.

Thus it came about that Archbishop Werner of Falkenstein, owner of the grim fortress of Stolzenfels and a wealthy and powerful Churchman, was an amateur of the hermetic art, while his Treasurer, who was by no means rich, was also by way of being an alchemist. To indulge his passion for the bizarre science the latter had extracted many a golden piece from the coffers of his reverend master, always meaning, of course, to pay them back when the weary experiments should have crystallized into the coveted philosopher's stone. He had in his daughter Elizabeth a treasure which might well have outweighed the whole of the Archbishop's coffers, but the lust for gold had blinded the covetous Treasurer to all else.

One night—a wild, stormy night, when the wind tore shrieking round the battlements of Stolzenfels—there came to the gate a pilgrim, sombre of feature as of garb, with wicked, glinting eyes. The Archbishop was not at that time resident in the castle, but his Treasurer, hearing that the new-comer was learned in alchemical mysteries, bade him enter without delay. A room was made ready in one of the highest towers, and there the Treasurer and his pilgrim friend spent many days and nights. Elizabeth saw with dismay that a change was coming over her

164

Stolzenfels
Louis Weirter, R.B.A.

(See page 164)

Schloss Sooneck

J. Jack

(See page 192)

Stolzenfels : The Alchemist

father. He was no longer gentle and kind, but morose and reserved, and he passed less time in her company than he was wont.

At length a courier arrived with tidings of the approach of the Archbishop, who was bringing some noble guests to the castle. To the dismay of his daughter, the Treasurer suddenly turned pale and, brushing aside her solicitous inquiries, fled to the mysterious chamber. Elizabeth followed, convinced that something had occurred to upset her father seriously. She was too late—the door was locked ere she reached it ; but she could hear angry voices within, the voices of her father and the pilgrim. The Treasurer seemed to be uttering bitter reproaches, while ever and anon the deep, level voice of his companion could be heard.

" Bring hither a virgin," he said. " The heart's blood of a virgin is necessary to our schemes, as I have told thee many times. How can I give thee gold, and thou wilt not obey my instructions ? "

"Villain!" cried the Treasurer, beside himself. "Thou hast taken my gold, thou hast made me take the gold of my master also for thy schemes. Wouldst thou have me shed innocent blood ? "

" I tell thee again, without it our experiments are vain."

At that moment the door was flung open and the Treasurer emerged, too immersed in his anxious thoughts to perceive the shrinking form of Elizabeth. She, when he had gone from sight, entered the chamber where stood the pilgrim.

"I have heard thy conversation," she said, "and I am ready to give my life for my father's welfare. Tell me what I must do and I will slay me with mine own hand."

With covetous glance the pilgrim advanced and strove to take her hand, but she shrank back in loathing.

"Touch me not," she said, shuddering.

A look of malice overspread the pilgrim's averted face.

"Come hither at midnight, and at sunrise thy father will be rich and honoured," he said.

"Wilt thou swear it on the cross?"

"I swear it," he returned, drawing a little crucifix from his bosom, and speaking in solemn tones.

"Very well, I promise." And with that she withdrew.

When she had gone the alchemist pressed a spring in the crucifix, when a dagger fell out.

"Thou hast served me well," he said, chuckling. Then, replacing the crucifix in his breast, he entered the adjoining room, prised up a stone from the floor, and drew forth a leathern bag full of gold. This, then, was the crucible into which the Archbishop's pieces had gone. "I have found the secret of making gold," pursued the pilgrim. "To-morrow my wealth and I will be far away in safety. The fools, to seek gold in a crucible!"

Meanwhile preparations were afoot for the reception of the Archbishop. Elizabeth, full of grief and determination, supervised the work of the serving-maids, while her father anxiously wondered how he should account to his master for the stolen pieces of gold.

The Archbishop was loudly hailed on his arrival. He greeted his Treasurer kindly and asked after the pretty Elizabeth. When her father presented her he in turn introduced her to his guests, and many a glance of admiration was directed at the gentle maid. One young knight, in particular, was so smitten with her charms that he was dumb the whole evening.

Stolzenfels: The Alchemist

When Elizabeth retired to her chamber her father bade her good-night. Hope had again arisen in his breast.

"To-morrow," he said, "my troubles will be over."

Elizabeth sighed.

At length the hour of midnight arrived. Taking a lamp, the girl crossed the courtyard to where the alchemist awaited her coming. She was not unseen, however; the young knight had been watching her window, and he observed her pass through the courtyard with surprise. Fearing he knew not what harm to the maid he loved, he followed her to the pilgrim's apartment, and there watched her through a crack in the door.

The alchemist was bending over a crucible when Elizabeth entered.

"Ah, thou hast come," he said. "I hope thou art prepared to do as I bid thee? If that is so, I will restore the gold to thy father—his own gold and his master's. If thou art willing to sacrifice thine honour, thy father's honour shall be restored; if thy life, he shall have the money he needs."

"Away, wretch!" cried Elizabeth indignantly. "I will give my life for my father, but I will not suffer insult."

With a shrug of his shoulders the alchemist turned to his crucible.

"As thou wilt," he said. "Prepare for the sacrifice."

Suddenly the kneeling maid caught up the alchemist's dagger and would have plunged it into her heart; but ere she could carry out her purpose the knight burst open the door, rushed into the room, and seized the weapon. Elizabeth, overcome with the relief which his opportune arrival afforded her, fainted in his arms.

While the young man frantically sought means to restore her the pilgrim seized the opportunity to escape, and when the maid came to herself it was to find the wretch gone and herself supported by a handsome young knight, who was pouring impassioned speeches into her ear. His love and tenderness awakened an answering emotion in her heart, and that very night they were betrothed.

When the maiden's father was apprised of her recent peril he, too, was grateful to her deliverer, and yet more grateful when his future son-in-law pressed him to make use of his ample fortune.

The pilgrim was found drowned in the Rhine, and the bag of gold, which he had carried away in his belt, was handed over to the Archbishop, to whom the Treasurer confessed all.

And the good Archbishop, by way of confirming his forgiveness, gave a handsome present to Elizabeth on her marriage with the knight.

The Legend of Boppard

Maidens had curious ways of revenging themselves on unfaithful lovers in medieval times, as the following legend of Boppard would show.

Toward the end of the twelfth century there dwelt in Boppard a knight named Sir Conrad Bayer, brave, generous, and a good comrade, but not without his faults, as will be seen hereafter.

At that time many brave knights and nobles were fighting in the Third Crusade under Frederick the First and Richard Cœur-de-Lion; but Sir Conrad still remained at Boppard. He gave out that the reason for his remaining at home was to protect his stronghold against a horde of robbers who infested the neighbourhood. But there were those who ascribed his reluctance to depart to another cause. In a neighbouring fortress there lived a beautiful maiden,

The Legend of Boppard

Maria by name, who received a great deal of attention from Sir Conrad. So frequent were his visits to her home that rumour had it that the fair lady had won his heart. This indeed was the case, and she in return had given her love unreservedly into his keeping. But as her passion grew stronger his seemed to cool, and at length he began to make preparations to join the wars in Palestine, leaving the lady to lament his changed demeanour. In vain she pleaded, in vain she sent letters to him. At last he intimated plainly that he loved her no longer. He did not intend to marry, he said, adding cruelly that if he did she should not be the bride of his choice. The lady was completely crushed by the blow. Her affection for Sir Conrad perished, and in its place arose a desire to be revenged on the unfaithful knight. The fickle lover had completed his arrangements for his journey to the Holy Land, and all was ready for his departure. As he rode gaily down from his castle to where his men-at-arms waited on the shores of the Rhine, he was suddenly confronted by an armed knight, who reined in his steed and bade Sir Conrad halt.

"Hold, Sir Conrad Bayer," he cried. "Thou goest not hence till thou hast answered for thy misdeeds—thou false knight—thou traitor!"

Sir Conrad listened in astonishment. A moment later his attendants had surrounded the bold youth, and would have slain him had not Sir Conrad interfered.

"Back!" he said. "Let me face this braggart myself. Who art thou?" he added, addressing the young knight who had thus boldly challenged him.

"One who would have thy life!" was the fierce reply.

"Why should I slay thee, bold youth?" said Conrad, amused.

"I am the brother of Maria, whom thou hast betrayed," was the response. "I have come hither from Palestine to seek thy life. Have at thee, traitor!"

Conrad, somewhat sobered, and unwilling to do battle with such a boy, asked for further proof of his identity. The young knight thereupon displayed, blazoned on his shield, the arms of his house—a golden lion on an azure field.

Sir Conrad had no longer excuse for refusing to do battle with the youth, so with a muttered "Thy blood be upon thy head!" he laid his lance in rest and drew back a few paces. The stranger did likewise; then they rushed toward each other, and such was the force of their impact that both were unhorsed. Drawing their swords—for neither was injured—the knights resumed the conflict on foot. Conrad felt disgraced at having been unhorsed by a mere youth, and he was now further incensed by receiving a deep wound in his arm. Henceforth he fought in good earnest, showering blows on his antagonist, who fell at last, mortally wounded.

In obedience to the rules of chivalry, Sir Conrad hastened to assist his vanquished foe. What was his surprise, his horror, when, on raising the head and unlacing the helm of the knight, he found that his adversary was none other than Maria!

"Conrad," she said in failing tones, "I also am to blame. Without thy love life was nothing to me, and I resolved to die by thy hand. Forget my folly, remember only that I loved thee. Farewell!" And with these words she expired. Conrad flung himself down by her side, convulsed with grief and remorse. From that hour a change came over him. Ere he set out to the Holy Land he caused the body of Maria to be interred on the summit of the Kreuzberg, and bestowed the greater part of his estates on a pious brotherhood, enjoining them to raise a nunnery over the tomb. Thus was the convent of Marienberg founded, and in time it came to be one of the richest and most celebrated on the Rhine.

Arrived in Palestine, Conrad became a Knight-Templar, fighting bravely and utterly oblivious to all danger. It was not until Acre had been won, however, that death met him. An arrow dispatched by an unknown hand found its quarry as he was walking the ramparts at night meditating on the lady he had slain and whose death had restored her to a place in his affections.

Liebenstein and Sterrenberg

Near the famous monastery of Bornhofen, and not far from the town of Camp, supposed to be an ancient Roman site, are the celebrated castles of Liebenstein and Sterrenberg, called 'the Brothers,' perhaps because of their contiguity to each other rather than through the legend connected with the name. History is practically silent concerning these towers, which occupy two steep crags united by a small isthmus which has partially been cut through. Sterrenberg lies nearest the north, Liebenstein to the south. A wooden bridge leads from one to the other, but a high wall called the Schildmauer was in the old days reared between them, obviously with the intention of cutting off communication. The legend has undoubtedly become sophisticated by literary influences, and was so altered by one Joseph Kugelgen as to change its purport entirely. It is the modern version of the legend we give here, in contradistinction to that given in the chapter on the Folklore and Literature of the Rhine (see pp. 84 *et seq.*).

Hero Tales & Legends of the Rhine

The Brothers

Heinrich and Conrad were the sons of Kurt, a brave knight who had retired from the wars, and now dwelt in his ancestral castle Liebenstein. The brothers were alike in all matters pertaining to arms and chivalry. But otherwise they differed, for Heinrich, the elder, was quiet and more given to the arts of peace; whereas Conrad was gay, and inclined to like fighting for fighting's sake.

Brought up along with them was Hildegarde, a relative and an orphan, whom the brothers believed to be their sister. On reaching manhood, however, their father told them the truth concerning her, expressing the wish that one of them should marry the maiden.

Nothing loath, both brothers wooed Hildegarde, but Conrad's ardent, impulsive nature triumphed over Heinrich's reserved and more steadfast affection. In due course preparations were made for the marriage festival, and a new castle, Sterrenberg, was raised for the young couple adjacent to Liebenstein. Heinrich found it hard to be a constant witness of his brother's happiness, so he set out for the Holy Land. Soon after his departure the old knight became ill, and died on the day that the new castle was completed. This delayed the marriage for a year, and as the months passed Conrad became associated with loose companions, and his love for Hildegarde weakened.

Meantime news came that Heinrich had performed marvellous deeds in the Holy Land, and the tidings inflamed Conrad's zeal. He, too, determined to join the Crusades, and was soon on the way to Palestine.

However, he did not, like his brother, gain renown—for

he had not the same incentive to reckless bravery—and he soon returned. He was again to prove himself more successful in love than in war, for at Constantinople, having fallen passionately in love with a beautiful Greek lady, he married her.

One day Hildegarde was sitting sorrowful in her chamber, when she beheld travellers with baggage moving into the empty Sterrenberg. Greatly astonished, she sent her waiting-maid to make inquiries, and learned to her sorrow that it was the returning Conrad, who came bringing with him a Greek wife. Conrad avoided Liebenstein, and Sterrenberg became gay with feasting and music.

Late one evening a knight demanded lodging at Lieben-stein and was admitted. The stranger was Heinrich, who, hearing about his brother's shameful marriage, had returned to the grief-stricken Hildegarde.

After he had rested Heinrich sent a message to his brother reproaching him with unknightly behaviour, and challenging him to mortal combat. The challenge was accepted and the combatants met on the passage separating the two castles. But as they faced each other, sword in hand, a veiled female figure stepped between them and bade them desist.

It was Hildegarde, who had recognized Heinrich and learned his intention. In impassioned tones she urged the young men not to be guilty of the folly of shedding each other's blood in such a cause, and declared that it was her firm intention to spend her remaining days in a convent. The brothers submitted themselves to her persuasion and became reconciled. Some time afterward Conrad's wife proved her unworthiness by eloping with a young knight, thus killing her husband's love for her, and at the same time opening his eyes to his own base conduct. Bitterly now did he reproach himself for his unfaithfulness to Hildegarde, who, alas! was now lost to him for ever.

Hildegarde remained faithful to her vows, and Heinrich and Conrad lived together till at last death separated them.

St. Goar

Near the town of St. Goar, at the foot of the Rheinfels, there stands a little cell, once the habitation of a pious hermit known as St. Goar, and many are the local traditions which tell of the miracles wrought by this good man, and the marvellous virtues retained by his shrine after his death. He settled on Rhenish shores, we are told, about the middle of the sixth century, and thenceforward devoted his life to the service of the rude people among whom his lot was cast. His first care was to instruct them in the Christian faith, but he was also mindful of their welfare in temporal matters, and gave his services freely to the sick and sorrowful, so that ere long he came to be regarded as a saint. When he was not employed in prayer and ministrations he watched the currents of the Rhine, and was ever willing to lend his aid to distressed mariners who had been caught by the *Sand Gewirr*, a dangerous eddy which was too often the death of unwary boatmen in these parts.

Thus he spent an active and cheerful life, far from the envy and strife of the world, for which he had no taste whatever. Nevertheless the fame of his good deeds had reached the high places of the earth. Sigebert, who at that time held his court at Andernach, heard of the piety and noble life of the hermit, and invited him to his palace. St. Goar accepted the invitation—or, rather, obeyed the command—and made his way to Andernach. He was well received by the monarch, whom his genuine holiness and single-mindedness greatly impressed. But pure as he was, the worthy Goar was not destined to escape calumny. There were at the court of Sigebert other ecclesiastics of a less exalted type, and these were filled with envy and indignation when they beheld the favours bestowed upon the erstwhile recluse. Foremost among his persecutors was the Archbishop of Treves, and with him Sigebert dealt in summary fashion, depriving him of his archbishopric and offering the see to St. Goar. The latter, however, was sick of the perpetual intrigues and squabblings of the court, and longed to return to the shelter of his mossy cell and the sincere friendship of the poor fishermen among whom his mission lay. So he refused the proffered dignity and informed the monarch of his desire to return home. As he stood in the hall of the palace preparing to take his leave, he threw his cloak over a sunbeam, and, strange to say, the garment was suspended as though the shaft of light were solid. This, we are told, was not a mere piece of bravado, but was done to show that the saint's action in refusing the see was prompted by divine inspiration.

When St. Goar died Sigebert caused a chapel to be erected over his grave, choosing from among his disciples two worthy monks to officiate. Other hermits took up their abode near the spot, and all were subsequently gathered together in a monastery. The grave of the solitary became a favourite shrine, to which pilgrims travelled from all quarters, and St. Goar became the patron saint of hospitality, not so much personally as through the monastery of which he was the patron, and one of whose rules was that no stranger should be denied hospitality for a certain period.

A goodly number of stories are told of his somewhat drastic treatment of those who passed by his shrine without bringing an offering—stories which may be traced to the monks who dwelt there, and who reaped the benefit of these offerings.

Charlemagne at the Shrine of St. Goar

Here is one of those tales concerning the great Karl. On one occasion while he was travelling from Ingelheim to Aix-la-Chapelle, by way of Coblentz, he passed the shrine of St. Goar without so much as a single thought. Nor did those who accompanied him give the saint more attention. It was the height of summer, everything was bright and beautiful, and as the Emperor's flotilla drifted lazily down the Rhine the sound of laughter and light jesting could be heard.

No sooner had the Emperor and his courtiers passed St. Goar, however, than the smiling sky became overcast, heavy clouds gathered, and the distant sound of thunder was heard. A moment more and they were in the midst of a raging storm; water surged and boiled all around, and darkness fell so thickly that scarce could one see another's face. Panic reigned supreme where all had been gaiety and merriment.

In vain the sailors strove to reach the shore; in vain the ladies shrieked and the Emperor and his nobles lent their aid to the seamen. All the exertions of the sailors would not suffice to move the vessels one foot nearer the shore. At length an old boatman who had spent the greater part of a lifetime on the Rhine approached the Emperor and addressed him thus:

"Sire, our labours are useless. We have offended God and St. Goar."

The Reconciliation

The words were repeated by the Emperor's panic-stricken train, who now saw that the storm was of miraculous origin. "Let us go ashore," said Charlemagne in an awed voice. " In the name of God and St. Goar, let us go ashore. We will pray at the shrine of the saint that he may help us make peace with Heaven."

Scarcely had he uttered the words ere the sky began to clear, the boiling water subsided to its former glassy smoothness, and the storm was over. The illustrious company landed and sought the shrine of the holy man, where they spent the rest of the day in prayer.

Ere they departed on the following morning Charlemagne and his court presented rich offerings at the shrine, and the Emperor afterward endowed the monastery with lands of great extent, by which means it is to be hoped that he succeeded in propitiating the jealous saint.

The Reconciliation

One more tale of St. Goar may be added, dealing this time with Charlemagne's sons, Pepin and Karloman. These two, brave knights both, had had a serious quarrel over the sovereignty of their father's vast Empire. Gradually the breach widened to a deadly feud, and the brothers, once the best of friends, became the bitterest enemies.

In 806 Charlemagne held an Imperial Diet at Thionville, and thither he summoned his three sons, Karloman, Pepin, and Ludwig, intending to divide the Empire, by testament, among them. Karloman was at that time in Germany, and Pepin in Italy, where, with the aid of his sword, he had won for himself broad lands. In order to reach Thionville both were obliged to take the same path—that is, the Rhine, the broad waterway of their father's dominions. Pepin was the first to come, and as he sailed up the river with his train he caught sight of the shrine of St. Goar, and bethought him that there he and his brother had last met as friends. As he pondered on the strange fate that had made enemies of them, once so full of kindness toward each other, he felt curiously moved, and decided to put ashore and kneel by the shrine of the saint.

Ere long Karloman and his train moved up the Rhine, and this prince also, when he beheld the shrine of St. Goar, was touched with a feeling of tenderness for his absent brother. Recollections of the time when Pepin and he had been inseparable surged over him, and he too stepped ashore and made his way through the wood to the sacred spot.

Meanwhile Pepin still knelt before the shrine, and great indeed was Karloman's astonishment when he beheld his brother. But when he heard Pepin pray aloud that they might be reconciled his joy and surprise knew no bounds. All armed as he was, he strode up to his kneeling brother and embraced him with tears, entreating his forgiveness for past harshnesses. When Pepin raised the prince's visor and beheld the beloved features of Karloman, his happiness was complete. Together the brothers made for their ships; not, however, till they had left valuable gifts at the shrine of the saint whose good offices had brought about their reconciliation. Together they proceeded to the court of Charlemagne, who partitioned his Empire between his three sons, making each a regent of his portion during his father's lifetime.

From that time onward the brothers were fast friends. Karloman and Pepin, however, had not long to live, for the former died in 810 and the latter in the following year.

Gutenfels

Gutenfels, a Romance

A very charming story, and one entirely lacking in the element of gloom and tragedy which is so marked a feature of most Rhenish tales, is that which tradition assigns to the castle of Gutenfels. Its ancient name of Caub, or Chaube, still clings to the town above which it towers majestically.

In the thirteenth century Caub was the habitation of Sir Philip of Falkenstein and his sister Guta, the latter justly acclaimed as the most beautiful woman in Germany. She was reputed as proud as she was beautiful, and of the many suitors who flocked to Caub to seek her hand in marriage none could win from her a word of encouragement or even a tender glance.

On one occasion she and her brother were present at a great tourney held at Cologne, where the flower of knightly chivalry and maidenly beauty were gathered in a brilliant assembly. Many an ardent glance was directed to the fair maid of Caub, but she, accustomed to such homage, was not moved thereby from her wonted composure.

At length a commotion passed through the assembly. A knight had entered the lists whose name was not announced by the herald. It was whispered that his identity was known only to the Archbishop, whose guest he was. Of fine stature and handsome features, clad in splendid armour and mounted on a richly caparisoned steed, he attracted not a little attention, especially from the feminine portion of the assemblage. But for none of the high-born ladies had he eyes, save for Guta, to whom his glance was ever and anon directed, as though he looked to her to bring him victory. The blushing looks of Guta showed that she was not indifferent to the gallantry of the noble stranger, and, truly, in her heart she wished him well. With clasped hands she watched the combatants couch their lances and charge. Ah! victory had fallen to the unknown knight. Soon it became evident that the mysterious stranger was to carry off the prize of the tourney, for there was none to match him in skill and prowess. As he rode past the place where Guta sat he lowered his lance, and she, in her pleasure and confusion at this mark of especial courtesy, dropped her glove, which the knight instantly picked up, desiring to be allowed to keep it as a guerdon.

At the grand ball which followed the tourney the victor remained all the evening at Guta's side, and would dance with no other maiden. Young Falkenstein, pleased with the homage paid to his sister by the distinguished stranger, invited him to visit them at Caub, an invitation which the gentle Guta seconded, and which the mysterious knight accepted with alacrity.

True to his promise, ere a week had elapsed he arrived at Caub, accompanied by two attendants. His visit covered three days, during which time his host and hostess did all in their power to make his stay a pleasant one. Ere he took his departure he sought out Guta and made known his love. The lady acknowledged that his affection was returned.

"Dearest Guta," said the knight, "I may not yet reveal to thee my name, but if thou wilt await my coming, in three months I shall return to claim my bride, and thou shalt know all."

"I will be true to thee," exclaimed Guta passionately. "Though a king should woo me, I will be true to thee." And with that assurance from his betrothed the knight rode away.

Three months came and went, and still Guta heard

nothing of her absent lover. She grew paler and sadder as time advanced, not because she doubted the honour of her knight, but because she feared he had been slain in battle. It was indeed a time of wars and dissensions. On the death of Conrad IV several claimants to the imperial throne of Germany made their appearance, of whom the principal were Adolph, Duke of Holland, Richard, Earl of Cornwall, brother to the English king Henry III, and Alfonso X, King of Castile. Of these three the most popular was Richard of Cornwall, who was finally chosen by the Electors, more on account of his knightly qualities than because of his fabulous wealth. Among his most ardent followers was Philip of Falkenstein, who was naturally much elated at his master's success. Now, however, the conflict was over, and Philip had returned to Caub.

One morning, about six months after the departure of Guta's lover, a gay cavalcade appeared at the gates of Caub, and a herald demanded admission for Richard, Emperor of Germany. Philip himself, scarcely concealing his joy and pride at the honour done him by his sovereign, ran out to greet him, and the castle was full of stir and bustle. The Emperor praised Philip heartily for his part in the recent wars, yet he seemed absent and uneasy.

" Sir Philip," he said at length, " I have come hither to beg the hand of thy fair sister ; why is she not with us ? "

Falkenstein was filled with amazement.

" Sire," he stammered, " I fear me thou wilt find my sister an unwilling bride. She has refused many nobles of high estate, and I doubt whether even a crown will tempt her. However, I will plead with her for thy sake."

He left the room to seek Guta's bower, but soon returned with dejected mien.

"It is as I thought, sire," he said. "She will not be moved. Methinks some heedless knight hath stolen her heart, for she hath grown pale and drooping as a gathered blossom."

Richard raised his visor.

"Knowest thou me, sir knight?" he said.

"Thou art—the knight of the tourney," cried Philip in amaze.

"The same," answered Richard, smiling. "And I am the knight who has won thy fair sister's heart. We plighted our troth after the tourney of Cologne. State affairs of the gravest import have kept me from her side, where I would fain have been these six months past. Take this token"—drawing from his breast the glove Guta had given him—"and tell her that a poor knight in Richard's train sends her this."

In a little while Philip returned with his sister. The maiden looked pale and agitated, but when she beheld Richard she rushed to him and was clasped in his arms.

"My own Guta," he whispered fondly. "And wouldst thou refuse an emperor to marry me?"

"Yea, truly," answered the maid, "a hundred emperors. I feared thou hadst forsaken me altogether," she added naively.

Richard laughed.

"Would I be a worthy Emperor an I did not keep my troth with such as thou?" he asked.

"The Emperor—thou?" cried Guta, starting back.

"Yea, the Emperor, and none other," said her brother reverently. And once more Guta hid her face on Richard's breast.

Within a week they were married, and Guta accompanied her husband to the court as Empress of Germany.

The Story of Schönburg

To the castle where his bride had passed her maidenhood
Richard gave the name of Gutenfels—'Rock of Guta'—
which name it has retained to this day.

The Story of Schönburg

The castle of Schönburg, not far from the town of Bacharach, is now in ruins, but was once a place of extraordinary
fame, for here dwelt at one time seven sisters of transcen-
dent beauty, who were courted the more assiduously
because their father, the Graf von Schönburg, was reputed
a man of great wealth. This wealth was no myth, but
an actuality, and in truth it had been mainly acquired in
predatory forays; but the nobles of Rhineland recked
little of this, and scores of them flitted around and pressed
their suit on the young ladies. None of these, however,
felt inclined toward marriage just yet, each vowing its
yoke too galling; and so the gallants came in vain to the
castle, their respective addresses being invariably dallied
with and then dismissed. Suitor after suitor retired in
despair, pondering on the strange ways of womankind;
but one evening a large party of noblemen chanced to be
assembled at the schloss, and putting their heads together,
they decided to press matters to a conclusion. They
agreed that all of them, in gorgeous raiment, should
gather in the banqueting-hall of the castle; the seven
sisters should be summoned and called upon in peremptory
fashion to have done with silken dalliance and to end
matters by selecting seven husbands from among them.
The young ladies received the summons with some amusement, all of them being blessed with the saving grace of
humour, and they bade the knight who had brought the
message return to his fellows and tell them that the
suggested interview would be held. "Only give us time,"

said the sisters, "for the donning of our most becoming dresses."

So now the band of suitors mustered, and a brave display they made, each of them thinking himself more handsome and gorgeous than his neighbours and boasting that he would be among the chosen seven. But as time sped on and the ladies still tarried, the young men began to grow anxious; many of them spoke aloud of female vanity, and made derisive comments on the coiffing and the like, which they imagined was the cause of the delay; eventually one of their number, tired of strutting before a mirror, happened to go to look out of the window toward the Rhine. Suddenly he uttered a loud imprecation, and his companions, thronging to the window, were all fiercely incensed at the sight which greeted their eyes. For the famous seven sisters were perpetrating something of a practical joke; they were leaving the castle in a boat, and on perceiving the men's faces at the windows they gave vent to a loud laugh of disdain. Hardly had the angry suitors realized that they were the butt of the ladies' ridicule when they were seized with consternation. For one of the sisters, in the attempt to shake her fist at the men she affected to despise, tried to stand up on one of the thwarts of the boat, which, being a light craft, was upset at once. The girls' taunts were now changed to loud cries for help, none being able to swim; but ere another boat could be launched the Rhine had claimed its prey, and the perfidious damsels were drowned in the swift tide.

But their memory was not destined to be erased from the traditions of the locality. Near the place where the tragedy occurred there are seven rocks, visible only on rare occasions when the river is very low, and till lately

The Legend of Pfalz

it was a popular superstition that these rocks were placed there by Providence, anxious to impart a moral to young women addicted to coquetry and practical jests. To this day many boatmen on the Rhine regard these rocks with awe, and it is told that now and then seven wraiths are to be seen there; it is even asserted that sometimes these apparitions sing in strains as delectable as those of the Lorelei herself.

The Legend of Pfalz

Musing on the legendary lore of the Rhine, we cannot but be struck by the sadness pervading these stories, and we are inclined to believe that every one of them culminates in tragedy. But there are a few exceptions to this rule, and among them is a tale associated with the island of Pfalz, near Bacharach, which concludes in fairly happy fashion, if in the main concerned with suffering.

This island of Pfalz still contains the ruins of a castle, known as Pfalzgrafenstein. It belonged in medieval days to the Palatine Princes, and at the time our story opens one of these, named Hermann, having suspected his wife, the Princess Guba, of infidelity, had lately caused her to be incarcerated within it. Its governor, Count von Roth, was charged to watch the prisoner's movements carefully; but, being sure she was innocent, his measures with her were generally lenient, while his countess soon formed a deep friendship for the Princess. Thus it seemed to Guba that her captivity was not destined to be so terrible as she had anticipated, but she was soon disillusioned, as will appear presently. It should be explained that as yet the Princess had borne no children to her husband, whose heir-apparent was consequently his brother Ludwig; and this person naturally tried to prevent a reconciliation

185

between the Palatine Prince and his wife, for should they be united again, Ludwig's hope to succeed his brother might be frustrated. So he was a frequent visitor to the Pfalz-grafenstein, constantly telling von Roth that he allowed the Princess too much liberty. Worse still, Ludwig some-times remained at the island castle for a long time, and at these periods the prisoner underwent constant ill-treatment, which the Governor was powerless to alleviate.

The people of the neighbourhood felt kindly toward Guba, but their sympathy was of little avail; and at length during one of Ludwig's visits to Pfalzgrafenstein it seemed as though he was about to triumph and effect a final separa-tion between the Princess and Hermann. For it transpired one evening that Guba was not within the castle. A hue and cry was instantly raised, and the island was searched by Ludwig and von Roth. "I wager," said Ludwig, "that at this very moment Guba is with her paramour. Let my brother the Prince hear of this, and your life will answer for it. Often have I urged you to be stricter; you see now the result of your leniency."

Von Roth protested that the Princess was taking the air alone; but while they argued the pair espied Guba, and it was as Ludwig had said—she was attended by a man.

"The bird is snared," shouted Ludwig; and as he and von Roth ran toward the offending couple they separated instantly, the man making for a boat moored hard by. But ere he could reach it he was caught by his pursuers, and recognized for a certain young gallant of the district. He was dragged to the castle, where after a brief trial he was condemned to be hanged. He blanched on hearing the sentence, but faced his fate manfully, and when the rope was about his neck he declared loudly that Guba had always discouraged his addresses and was innocent of the sin wherewith she was charged.

Guba's movements thenceforth were watched more strictly for a while, yet she seemed to grow more cheerful, while one day she even asserted that she would soon be reconciled to her husband, from whom she had now been estranged for six months. In short, she announced that she was soon to be a mother; while she was confident that the child would resemble the Palatine Prince, and that the latter's delight on finding himself a father would result in the ending of all her troubles. The Governor and his lady were both doubtful as to the parentage of the child, remembering the recent circumstances which had seemed to cast some shadow upon the Princess herself; yet they held their peace, awaiting until in due course the Princess was delivered of a boy. But, alack! the child bore no resemblance to Hermann; and so von Roth and his wife, meaning to be kind, enjoined silence and sent the child away—all of which was the more easily accomplished as the spiteful Ludwig chanced to be far distant at the time.

At first the mother was broken-hearted, but the Governor and his wife comforted her by saying that the child was no farther off than a castle on the opposite banks of the Rhine. Here, they assured her, he would be well nurtured; moreover, they had arranged that, so long as her son was alive and thriving, the fact was to be signified to her by the display of a small white flag on the battlements of his lodging. And so, day after day, the anxious mother paced her island prison, looking constantly toward the signal which meant so much to her.

Many years went by in this fashion, and in course of time Hermann was gathered to his fathers, and Ludwig ascended the Palatine throne. But scarcely was his rule begun ere it was noised abroad that he was a usurper, for a young man appeared who claimed to be the son of Hermann, and therefore the rightful heir.   Now, most of the people detested Ludwig, and when they marked the claimant's resemblance to the deceased Prince a number of them banded themselves together to set him upon the throne. A fierce civil war ensued, many of the nobles forsaking Ludwig for his rival, who, like the late Prince, bore the name of Hermann; and though at first it seemed doubtful which party was to triumph, eventually Ludwig was worsted, and was hanged for his perfidy.   The tidings spread throughout the Rhineland, and one day a body of men-at-arms came to Pfalzgrafenstein and informed von Roth that his prisoner was to be freed at once and was to repair to the Palatine court, there to take up her rightful position as Queen-Dowager.   Guba was amazed on hearing this news, for she had long since ceased to hope that her present mode of life would be altered, and asking to be presented to the chief messenger that she might question him, she suddenly experienced a yet greater surprise. . . . Yes! her son had come in person to liberate her; and von Roth and his wife, as they witnessed the glad union, were convinced at last of Guba's innocence, for the young man who clasped her to his bosom had changed wondrously since his childhood, and was now indeed the living image of his father.   For some minutes the mother wept with joy, but when her son bade her make ready for instant departure she replied that she had lost all desire for the stately life of a court.   Pfalzgrafenstein, she declared, had become truly a part of her life, so here she would end her days.   She had not long to live, she added, and what greater pleasure could she have than the knowledge that her son was alive and well, and was ruling his people wisely?

A Legend of Fürstenberg

And so Guba remained at the island, a prison no longer; and daily she paced by the swirling stream, often gazing toward the castle where her son had been nurtured, and meditating on the time when she was wont to look there for the white flag which meant so much to her anxious heart.

A Legend of Fürstenberg

High above the Rhine tower the ruins of Fürstenberg, and more than one legend clings to the ancient pile, linking it with stirring medieval times.

Perhaps the most popular of these traditions is that which tells of the Phantom Mother of Fürstenberg, a tale full of pathos and tragedy.

In the thirteenth century there dwelt in the castle a nobleman, Franz von Fürst by name, who, after a wild and licentious youth, settled down to a more sober and serious manhood. His friends, surprised at the change which had taken place in him, and anxious that this new mode of life should be maintained, urged him to take a virtuous maiden to wife. Such a bride as they desired for him was found in Kunigunda von Flörsheim, a maiden who was as beautiful as she was high-born.

For a time after their marriage all went well, and Franz and his young wife seemed quite happy. Moreover, in time a son was born to them, of whom his father seemed to be very proud. The Baron's reformation, said his friends, was complete.

One evening there came to Kunigunda a young lady friend. The girl, whose name was Amina, was the daughter of a robber-baron who dwelt in a neighbouring castle. But his predatory acts had at last forced him to flee for his life, and no one knew whither he had gone. His household was broken up, and Amina, finding herself without a home, had now repaired to Fürstenberg to seek refuge. Kunigunda, ever willing to aid those in distress, extended a hearty welcome to the damsel, and Amina was henceforth an inmate of the schloss.

Now, though Amina was fully as lovely in face and form as her young hostess, she yet lacked the moral beauty of Kunigunda. Of a subtle and crafty disposition, she showed the gratitude of the serpent by stinging the hand extended to help her; in a word, she set herself to win the unlawful affections of the Lord of Fürstenberg. He, weak creature as he was, allowed the latent baseness of his nature to be stirred by her youth and beauty. He listened when she whispered that Kunigunda had grown cold toward him; at her suggestion he interpreted his wife's modest demeanour as indifference, and already he began to feel the yoke of matrimony heavy upon him.

Poor Kunigunda was in despair when she realized that her husband had transferred his affections; but what was worse, she learned that the pair were plotting against her life. At length their cruel scheming succeeded, and one morning Kunigunda was found dead in her bed. Franz made it known that she had been stifled by a fit of coughing, and her remains were hastily conveyed to the family vault. Within a week the false Amina was the bride of the Baron von Fürstenberg.

Little Hugo, the son of Kunigunda, was to suffer much at the hands of his stepmother and her dependents. The new mistress of the Schloss Fürstenberg hated the child as she had hated his mother, and Hugo was given into the charge of an ill-natured old nurse, who frequently beat him in the night because he awakened her with his cries. One night the old hag was roused from her sleep by a strange sound, the sound of a cradle being rocked. She imagined herself dreaming. Who would come to this distant tower to rock the little Hugo? Not Amina, of that she was sure! Again the sound was heard, unmistakably the creaking of the cradle. Drawing aside her bed-curtains, the crone beheld a strange sight. Over the cradle a woman was bending, clad in long, white garments, and singing a low lullaby, and as she raised her pale face, behold! it was that of the dead Kunigunda. The nurse could neither shriek nor faint; as though fascinated, she watched the wraith nursing her child, until at cockcrow Kunigunda vanished.

In trembling tones the nurse related what she had seen to Franz and Amina. The Baron was scornful, and ridiculed the whole affair as a dream. But the cunning Amina, though she did not believe that a ghost had visited the child, thought that perhaps her rival was not really dead, and her old hatred and jealousy were reawakened. So she told her husband that she intended to see for herself whether there was any truth in the fantastic story, and would sleep that night in the nurse's bed. She did not mention her suspicions, nor the fact that she carried a sharp dagger. She was roused in the night, as the old woman had been, by the sound of a cradle being rocked. Stealthily drawing the curtains, she saw the white-robed form of the dead, the black mould clinging to her hair, the hue of death in her face. With a wild cry Amina flung herself upon Kunigunda, only to find that she was stabbing at a thing of air, an impalpable apparition which vanished at a touch. Overcome with rage and fear, she sank to the ground. The wraith moved to the door, turning with a warning gesture ere she vanished from sight, and Amina lost consciousness.

In the morning the Baron sought his wife in vain. He found instead a missive telling of her ghastly experience, intimating her intention of retiring to a nunnery, and closing with an earnest appeal to her husband to repent of his crimes.

The Baron, moved with remorse and terror, followed Amina's example; he sought in the mountain solitudes a hermitage where he might end his days in peace, and having found such a cell, he confided his little son to the care of the pastor of Wedenschied, and retired from the world in which he had played so sorry a part.

The Blind Archer

Another legend connected with the ruined stronghold of Fürstenberg is the following. Long ago, in the days when bitter feuds and rivalries existed between the owners of neighbouring fortresses, there dwelt in Fürstenberg a good old knight, Sir Oswald by name, well versed in the arts of war, and particularly proficient in archery. He had one son, Edwin, a handsome young man who bade fair to equal his father in skill and renown.

Sir Oswald had a sworn foe in a neighbouring baron, Wilm von Sooneck, a rich, unscrupulous nobleman who sought by every possible means to get the knight into his power. At length his cunning schemes met with success; an ambush was laid for the unsuspecting Oswald as he rode past Sooneck Castle, attended only by a groom, and both he and his servant were flung into a tower, there to await the pleasure of their captor.

And what that nobleman's pleasure was soon became evident. Ere many days had elapsed Oswald was informed that his eyes were to be put out, and soon the cruel decree was carried into execution.

The Blind Archer

Meanwhile Edwin awaited the coming of his father; and when he came not it was at first concluded that he had been captured or slain by robbers. But there were no evidences forthcoming to show that Sir Oswald had met with such a fate, and his son began to suspect that his father had fallen into the hands of Baron Wilm, for he knew of the bitter hatred which he bore toward the knight of Fürstenberg and of his cunning and malice. He therefore cast about for a means of verifying his suspicions, and eventually disguised himself as a wandering minstrel, took his harp—for he had great skill as a musician—and set off in the direction of Sooneck. There he seated himself under a tree and played and sang sweetly, directing his gaze the while toward a strong tower which seemed to him a likely place for the incarceration of prisoners. The plaintive charm of the melody attracted the attention of a passing peasant, who drew near to listen ; when the last note of the song had died away, he seated himself beside the minstrel and entered into conversation with him.

" Methinks thou hast an interest in yonder tower," he said.

" In truth it interests me," responded Edwin, nevertheless veiling his concern as much as possible by a seeming indifference. " Is it a prison, think you ? "

" Ay, that it is," replied the peasant with a laugh. " 'Tis the cage where my lord of Sooneck keeps the birds whose feathers he has plucked."

Edwin, still with a show of indifference, questioned him further, and elicited the fact that the peasant had witnessed the capture and incarceration in the tower of a knight and his servant on the very day when Sir Oswald and his groom had disappeared. Nothing more could

193

Edwin glean, save that a few days hence Baron Wilm was to give a grand banquet, when many nobles and knights were to be present.

The young man, his suspicions thus fully confirmed, felt that his next move must be to gain entrance to the castle, and he decided to take advantage of the excitement and bustle attendant on the banquet to achieve this end. Accordingly, on the day fixed for the feast he again donned his minstrel's garb, and repaired to the Schloss Sooneck. Here, as he had anticipated, all was excitement and gaiety. Wine flowed freely, tongues were loosened, and the minstrel was welcomed uproariously and bidden to sing his best songs in return for a beaker of Rhenish. Soon the greater part of the company were tipsy, and Edwin moved among them, noting their conversation, coming at length to the seat of the host.

" It is said," remarked a knight, " that you have captured Sir Oswald of Fürstenberg."

Wilm, to whom the remark was addressed, smiled knowingly and did not deny the charge.

" I have even heard," pursued his companion, " that you have had his eyes put out."

The Baron laughed outright, as at an excellent jest.

" Then you have heard truly," he said.

At this point another knight broke into the conversation. " It is a pity," said he. " There are but few archers to match Oswald of Fürstenberg."

" I wager he can still hit a mark if it be set up," said he who had first spoken.

" Done ! " cried Sooneck, and when the terms of the wager had been fixed the Baron directed that Oswald should be brought from the tower.

Edwin had overheard the conversation with a breaking

heart, and grief and shame almost overwhelmed him when he saw his father, pitifully quiet and dignified, led into the banquet-hall to provide sport for a company of drunken revellers. Oswald was informed of the wager, and bow and arrows were placed in his hands.

" Baron von Sooneck," he cried, " where is the mark ? "

" This cup I place upon the table," came the reply.

The arrow was fitted to the bow, released, and lo ! it was not the cup which was hit, but the Lord of Sooneck, who fell forward heavily, struck to the heart and mortally wounded.

In a moment a loud outcry was raised, but ere action could be taken the minstrel had sprung in front of Oswald, and boldly faced the assembly.

" This knight," he cried, " shamefully maltreated by yonder villain, is my father. Whoso thinks he has acted wrongly in forfeiting the life of his torturer shall answer to me. With my sword I shall teach him better judgment."

The astonished knights, completely sobered by the tragic occurrence, could not but admire the courage of the lad who thus boldly championed his father, and with one voice they declared that Sir Oswald was a true knight and had done justly.

So the blind knight, once more free, returned to his castle of Fürstenberg, compensated in part for the loss of his sight by the loving devotion of his son.

Rheinstein and Reichenstein

Centuries ago the castles of Rheinstein and Reichenstein frowned at each other from neighbouring eminences. But far from being hostile, they were the residences of two lovers. Kuno of Reichenstein loved the fair Gerda of Rheinstein with a consuming passion, and, as is so common with lovers in all ages, doubted whether his love were returned. In his devotion for the maiden he showered on her many gifts, and although his purse was light and he was master of only a single tower, he did not spare his gold if only he could make her happy and gain from her one look of approval.

On one occasion he presented to her a beauteous horse of the Limousin strain, bred under the shadow of his own castle. Deep-chested, with arched neck and eye of fire, the noble steed aroused the liveliest interest in the breast of Gerda, and she was eloquent in her thanks to the giver until, observing his ardent glances, her cheeks suffused with blushes. Taking her soft hand between his sunburnt palms, Kuno poured into her ear the story of his love.

"Gerda," he whispered, "I am a poor man. I have nothing but my sword, my ruined tower yonder, and honour. But they are yours. Will you take them with my heart?"

She lifted her blue eyes to his, full of truth and trust. "I will be yours," she murmured; "yours and none other's till death."

Young Kuno left Rheinstein that afternoon, his heart beating high with hope and happiness. The blood coursing through his veins at a gallop made him spur his charger to a like pace. But though he rode fast his brain was as busy as his hand and his heart. He must, in conformity with Rhenish custom, send as an embassy to Gerda's father one of his most distinguised relations. To whom was he to turn? There was no one but old Kurt, his wealthy uncle, whom he could send as an emissary, and although the old man had an unsavoury reputation, he decided to confide the mission to him. Kurt undertook the task in no kindly spirit, for he

Rheinstein & Reichenstein

disliked Kuno because of his virtuous life and the circumstance that he was his heir, whom he felt was waiting to step into his shoes. However, he waited next day upon Gerda's father, the Lord of Rheinstein, and was received with all the dignity suitable to his rank and age. But when his glance rested upon the fair and innocent Gerda, such a fierce desire to make her his arose in his withered breast that when she had withdrawn he demanded her hand for himself. To her father he drew an alluring picture of his rank, his possessions, his castles, his gold, until the old man, with whom avarice was a passion, gave a hearty consent to his suit, and dismissed him with the assurance that Gerda would be his within the week.

The clatter of hoofs had hardly died away when the Lord of Rheinstein sought his daughter's bower, where she sat dreaming of Kuno. In honeyed words the old man described the enviable position she would occupy as the spouse of a wealthy man, and then conveyed to her the information that Kurt had asked him for her hand. Gerda, insulted at the mere thought of becoming the bride of such a man, refused to listen to the proposal, even from the lips of her father, and she acquainted him with her love for Kuno, whom, she declared, she had fully resolved to marry. At this avowal her father worked himself into a furious passion, and assured her that she should never be the bride of such a penniless adventurer. After further insulting the absent Kuno, and alluding in a most offensive manner to his daughter's lack of discernment and good taste, he quitted her bower, assuring her as he went that she should become the bride of Kurt on the morrow.

Gerda spent a miserable night sitting by the dying fire in her chamber, planning how she might escape from the detested Kurt, until at last her wearied brain refused to work and she fell into a troubled slumber. In the morning she was awakened by her handmaiden, who, greatly concerned for her mistress, had spent the night in prayer. But Gerda's tears had fled with the morning, and she resolved, come what might, to refuse to the last to wed with the hateful Kurt. She learned that Kuno had attempted to assault the castle during the night with the object of carrying her off, but that he had been repulsed with some loss to his small force. This made her only the more determined to persist in her resistance to his uncle. Meantime the vassals and retainers of the house of Rheinstein had been summoned to the castle to attend the approaching ceremony, and their gay apparel now shone and glittered in the sunshine. The sound of pipe, tabour, and psaltery in melodious combination arose from the valley, and all hearts, save one, were happy. The gates were thrown open, and the bridal procession formed up to proceed to the ancient church where the unhappy Gerda was to be sacrificed to Kurt. First came a crowd of serfs, men, women, and children, all shouting in joyful anticipation of the wedding feast. Then followed the vassals and retainers of the Lord of Rheinstein, according to their several degrees, and, last, the principal actors in the shameful ceremony, Kurt, surrounded by his retainers, and the Lord of Rheinstein with the luckless Gerda. The mellow tones of the bell of St. Clement mingled sweetly with the sound of the flute and the pipe and the merry voices of the wedding throng. Gerda, mounted upon her spirited Limousin steed, the gift of Kuno, shuddered as she felt Kurt's eyes resting upon her, and she cast a despairing glance at the tower of Kuno's castle, where, disconsolate and heavy of heart, he watched the bridal procession from the highest turret.

Rheinstein

Louis Weirter, R.B.A.

(See page 195)

The Mouse Tower, near Bingen

Louis Weirter, R.B.A.

(See page 206)

Rheinstein & Reichenstein

The procession halted at the portal of the church, and all dismounted save Gerda. She was approached by the bridegroom, who with an air of leering gallantry offered her his assistance in alighting. At this moment swarms of gadflies rested on the flanks of the Limousin steed, and the spirited beast, stung to madness by the flies, reared, plunged, and broke away in a gallop, scattering the spectators to right and left, and flying like the wind along the river-bank.

"To horse, to horse!" cried Kurt and the Lord of Rheinstein, and speedily as many mounted, the bridegroom, for all his age, was first in the saddle.

With the clattering of a hundred hoofs the wedding party galloped madly along Rhineside, Kurt leading on a fleet and powerful charger.

"Halt!" he cried. "Draw rein—draw rein!" But notwithstanding their shouts, cries, and entreaties, Gerda spurred on the already maddened Limousin, which thundered along the familiar road to Kuno's castle of Reichenstein. The noble steed's direction was quickly espied by Kuno, who hastened to the principal entrance of his stronghold.

"Throw open the gates," he shouted. "Down with the drawbridge. Bravo, gallant steed!"

But Kurt was close behind. Gerda could feel the breath of his charger on the hands which held her rein. Close he rode by her, but might never snatch her from the saddle. Like the wind they sped. Now she was a pace in front, now they careered onward neck and neck.

Suddenly he leaned over to seize her rein, but at that instant his horse stumbled, fell, and threw the ancient gallant heavily. Down he came on a great boulder and lay motionless.

Another moment, and the hoof-beat of the breathless steed sounded on the drawbridge of Reichenstein. The vassals of Kuno hastened to the gate to resist the expected attack, but there was none. For the wretched Kurt lay dead, killed by the fall, and his vassals were now eager to acclaim Kuno as their lord, while the Lord of Rheinstein, shrewdly observing the direction of affairs, took advantage of the tumultuous moment to make his peace with Kuno.

The lovers were wedded next day amid the acclamations of their friends and retainers, and Kuno and Gerda dwelt in Rheinstein for many a year, loving and beloved.

CHAPTER V : FALKENBURG TO AUERBACH

The Legend of Falkenburg

I N the imperial fortress of Falkenburg dwelt the beautiful Liba, the most charming and accomplished of maidens, with her widowed mother. Many were the suitors who climbed the hill to Falkenburg to seek the hand of Liba, for besides being beautiful she was gentle and virtuous, and withal possessed of a modest fortune left her by her father. But to all their pleadings she turned a deaf ear, for she was already betrothed to a young knight named Guntram whom she had known since childhood, and they only waited until Guntram should have received his fief from the Palsgrave to marry and settle down.

One May morning, while Liba was seated at a window of the castle watching the ships pass to and fro on the glassy bosom of the Rhine, she beheld Guntram riding up the approach to Falkenburg, and hastened to meet him. The gallant knight informed his betrothed that he was on his way to the Palsgrave to receive his fief, and had but turned aside in his journey in order to greet his beloved. She led him into the castle, where her mother received him graciously enough, well pleased at her daughter's choice.

"And now, farewell," said Guntram. "I must hasten. When I return we two shall wed; see to it that all is in readiness."

With that he mounted his horse and rode out of the courtyard, turning to wave a gay farewell to Liba. The maiden watched him disappear round a turn in the winding path, then slowly re-entered the castle.

Meanwhile Guntram went on his way, and was at length invested with his fief. The Palsgrave, pleased with the manners and appearance of the young knight, appointed him to be his ambassador in Burgundy, which honour Guntram, though with much reluctance, felt it necessary to accept. He dispatched a messenger to his faithful Liba, informing her of his appointment, which admitted of no delay, and regretting the consequent postponement of their marriage. She, indeed, was ill-pleased with the tidings and felt instinctively that some calamity was about to befall. After a time her foreboding affected her health and spirits, her former pursuits and pleasures were neglected, and day after day she sat listlessly at her casement, awaiting the return of her lover.

Guntram, having successfully achieved his mission, set out on the homeward journey. On the way he had to pass through a forest, and, having taken a wrong path, lost his way. He wandered on without meeting a living creature, and came at last to an old dilapidated castle, into the courtyard of which he entered, thankful to have reached a human habitation. He gave his horse to a staring boy, who looked at him as though he were a ghost. "Where is your master?" queried Guntram.

The boy indicated an ivy-grown tower, to which the knight made his way. The whole place struck him as strangely sombre and weird, a castle of shadows and vague horror. He was shown into a gloomy chamber by an aged attendant, and there awaited the coming of the lord. Opposite him was hung a veiled picture, and half hoping that he might solve the mystery which pervaded the place, he drew aside the curtain. From the canvas there looked out at him a lady of surpassing beauty, and the young knight started back in awe and admiration.

The Legend of Falkenburg

In a short time the attendant returned with a thin, tall old man, the lord of the castle, who welcomed the guest with grave courtesy, and offered the hospitality of his castle. Guntram gratefully accepted his host's invitation, and when he had supped he conversed with the old man, whom he found well-informed and cultured.

"You appear to be fond of music," said the knight, indicating a harp which lay in a corner of the room.

He had observed, however, that the strings of the harp were broken, and that the instrument seemed to have been long out of use, and thought that it possibly had some connexion with the original of the veiled portrait. Whatever recollections his remark aroused must have been painful indeed, for the host sighed heavily.

"It has long been silent," he said. "My happiness has fled with its music. Good night, and sleep well." And ere the astonished guest could utter a word the old man abruptly withdrew from the room.

Shortly afterward the old attendant entered, bearing profuse apologies from his master, and begging that the knight would continue to accept his hospitality. Guntram followed the old man to his chamber. As they passed through the adjoining apartment he stopped before the veiled portrait.

"Tell me," he said, "why is so lovely a picture hidden?"

"Then you have seen it?" asked the old keeper. "That is my master's daughter. When she was alive she was even more beautiful than her portrait, but she was a very capricious maid, and demanded that her lovers should perform well-nigh impossible feats. At last only one of these lovers remained, and of him she asked that he should descend into the family vault and bring her a golden crown from the head of one of her ancestors. He did as he was bidden, but his profanation was punished with death. A stone fell from the roof and killed him. The young man's mother died soon after, cursing the foolish maid, who herself died in the following year. But ere she was buried she disappeared from her coffin and was seen no more."

When the story was ended they had arrived at the door of the knight's chamber, and in bidding him good night the attendant counselled him to say his paternoster should anything untoward happen.

Guntram wondered at his words, but at length fell asleep. Some hours later he was awakened suddenly by the rustling of a woman's gown and the soft strains of a harp, which seemed to come from the adjoining room. The knight rose quietly and looked through a chink in the door, when he beheld a lady dressed in white and bending over a harp of gold. He recognized in her the original of the veiled portrait, and saw that even the lovely picture had done her less than justice. For a moment he stood with hands clasped in silent admiration. Then with a low sound, half cry, half sob, she cast the harp from her and sank down in an attitude of utter despondency. The knight could bear it no longer and (quite forgetting his paternoster) he flung open the door and knelt at her feet, raising her hand to his lips. Gradually she became composed. "Do you love me, knight?" she said. Guntram swore that he did, with many passionate avowals, and the lady slipped a ring on his finger. Even as he embraced her the cry of a screech-owl rang through the night air, and the maiden became a corpse in his arms. Overcome with terror, he staggered through the darkness to his room, where he sank down unconscious.

The Legend of Falkenburg

On coming to himself again, he thought for a moment that the experience must have been a dream, but the ring on his hand assured him that the vision was a ghastly reality. He attempted to remove the gruesome token, but he found to his horror that it seemed to have grown to his finger.

In the morning he related his experience to the attendant. "Alas, alas!" said the old man, "in three times nine days you must die."

Guntram was quite overcome by the horror of his situation, and seemed for a time bereft of his senses. Then he had his horse saddled, and galloped as hard as he was able to Falkenburg. Liba greeted him solicitously. She could see that he was sorely troubled, but forbore to question him, preferring to wait until he should confide in her of his own accord. He was anxious that their wedding should be hastened, for he thought that his union with the virtuous Liba might break the dreadful spell.

When at length the wedding day arrived everything seemed propitious, and there was nothing to indicate the misfortune which threatened the bridegroom. The couple approached the altar and the priest joined their hands. Suddenly Guntram fell to the ground, foaming and gasping, and was carried thence to his home. The faithful Liba stayed by his side, and when he had partially recovered the knight told her the story of the spectre, and added that when the priest had joined their hands he had imagined that the ghost had put her cold hand in his. Liba attempted to soothe her repentant lover, and sent for a priest to finish the interrupted wedding ceremony. This concluded, Guntram embraced his wife, received absolution, and expired.

Liba entered a convent, and a few years later she herself passed away, and was buried by the side of her husband.

The Mouse Tower

Bishop Hatto is a figure equally well known to history and tradition, though, curiously enough, receiving a much rougher handling from the latter than the former. History relates that Hatto was Archbishop of Mainz in the tenth century, being the second of his name to occupy that see. As a ruler he was firm, zealous, and upright, if somewhat ambitious and high-handed, and his term of office was marked by a civic peace not always experienced in those times. So much for history. According to tradition, Hatto was a stony-hearted oppressor of the poor, permitting nothing to stand in the way of the attainment of his own selfish ends, and several wild legends exhibit him in a peculiarly unfavourable light.

By far the most popular of these traditions is that which deals with the *Mäuseturm*, or 'Mouse Tower,' situated on a small island in the Rhine near Bingen. It has never been quite decided whether the name was bestowed because of the legend, or whether the legend arose on account of the name, and it seems at least probable that the tale is of considerably later date than the tenth century. Some authorities regard the word *Mäuseturm* as a corruption of *Mauth-turm*, a 'toll-tower,' a probable but prosaic interpretation. Much more interesting is the name 'Mouse Tower,' which gives point to the tragic tale of Bishop Hatto's fate. The story cannot be better told than in the words of Southey, who has immortalized it in the following ballad :

The Mouse Tower

THE TRADITION OF BISHOP HATTO

The summer and autumn had been so wet,
That in winter the corn was growing yet;
'Twas a piteous sight to see all around
The grain lie rotting on the ground.

Every day the starving poor
Crowded around Bishop Hatto's door,
For he had a plentiful last-year's store,
And all the neighbourhood could tell
His granaries were furnished well.

At last Bishop Hatto appointed a day
To quiet the poor without delay;
He bade them to his great barn repair,
And they should have food for the winter there.

Rejoiced such tidings good to hear,
The poor folk flocked from far and near;
The great barn was full as it could hold
Of women and children, and young and old.

Then when he saw it could hold no more,
Bishop Hatto he made fast the door;
And while for mercy on Christ they call,
He set fire to the barn and burnt them all.

"I' faith, 'tis an excellent bonfire!" quoth he,
"And the country is greatly obliged to me
For ridding it in these times forlorn
Of rats that only consume the corn."

So then to his palace returnèd he,
And he sat down to supper merrily;
And he slept that night like an innocent man,
But Bishop Hatto never slept again.

In the morning as he enter'd the hall
Where his picture hung against the wall,
A sweat like death all over him came,
For the rats had eaten it out of the frame.

As he looked there came a man from his farm,
He had a countenance white with alarm;
"My lord, I opened your granaries this morn,
And the rats had eaten all your corn."

Another came running presently,
And he was pale as pale could be ;
" Fly, my Lord Bishop, fly ! " quoth he,
" Ten thousand rats are coming this way—
The Lord forgive you for yesterday ! "

" I'll go to my tower on the Rhine," replied he,
" 'Tis the safest place in Germany ;
The walls are high and the shores are steep,
And the stream is strong and the water deep."

Bishop Hatto fearfully hastened away,
And he crossed the Rhine without delay,
And reached his tower, and barred with care
All windows, doors, and loop-holes there.

He laid him down and closed his eyes ;—
But soon a scream made him arise,
He started and saw two eyes of flame
On his pillow from whence the screaming came.

He listened and looked—it was only the cat ;
But the Bishop he grew more fearful for that,
For she sat screaming, mad with fear,
At the army of rats that were drawing near.

For they have swum over the river so deep,
And they have climbed the shores so steep,
And up the tower their way is bent,
To do the work for which they were sent.

They are not to be told by the dozen or score,
By thousands they come, and by myriads and more,
Such numbers had never been heard of before,
Such a judgment had never been witnessed of yore.

Down on his knees the Bishop fell,
And faster and faster his beads did he tell,
As louder and louder, drawing near,
The gnawing of their teeth he could hear.

And in at the windows and in at the door,
And through the walls helter-skelter they pour,
And down through the ceiling, and up through the floor,
From the right and the left, from behind and before,
From within and without, from above and below,
And all at once to the Bishop they go.

A Legend of Ehrenfels

They have whetted their teeth against the stones,
And now they pick the Bishop's bones;
They gnawed the flesh from every limb,
For they were sent to do judgment on him.

A Legend of Ehrenfels

Many other tales are told to illustrate Hatto's cruelty and
treachery. Facing the Mouse Tower, on the opposite
bank of the Rhine, stands the castle of Ehrenfels, the
scene of another of his ignoble deeds.

Conrad, brother of the Emperor Ludwig, had, it is said,
been seized and imprisoned in Ehrenfels by the Franconian
lord of that tower, Adalbert by name. It was the fortune
of war, and Ludwig in turn gathered a small force and
hastened to his brother's assistance. His attempts to
storm the castle, however, were vain; the stronghold and
its garrison stood firm. Ludwig was minded to give up
the struggle for the time being, and would have done so,
indeed, but for the intervention of his friend and adviser,
Bishop Hatto.

"Leave him to me," said the crafty Churchman. "I
know how to deal with him."

Ludwig was curious to know how his adviser proposed to
get the better of Adalbert, whom he knew of old to be a
man of courage and resource, but ill-disposed toward the
reigning monarch. So the Bishop unfolded his scheme,
to which Ludwig, with whom honour was not an outstanding feature, gave his entire approval.

In pursuance of his design Hatto sallied forth unattended,
and made his way to the beleaguered fortress. Adalbert,
himself a stranger to cunning and trickery, hastened to
admit the messenger, whose garb showed him to be a
priest, thinking him bound on an errand of peace. Hatto

professed the deepest sorrow at the quarrel between Ludwig and Adalbert.

"My son," said he solemnly, "it is not meet that you and the Emperor, who once were friends, should treat each other as enemies. Our sire is ready to forgive you for the sake of old friendship; will you not give him the opportunity and come with me?"

Adalbert was entirely deceived by the seeming sincerity of the Bishop, and so touched by the clemency of the sovereign that he promised to go in person and make submission if Hatto would but guarantee his safety.

The conversation was held in the Count's oratory, and the Churchman knelt before the crucifix and swore in the most solemn manner that he would bring Adalbert safely back to his castle.

In a very short time they were riding together on the road to Mainz, where Ludwig held court. When they were a mile or two from Ehrenfels Hatto burst into a loud laugh, and in answer to the Count's questioning glance he said merrily:

"What a perfect host you are! You let your guest depart without even asking him whether he has breakfasted. And I am famishing, I assure you!"

The courteous Adalbert was stricken with remorse, and murmured profuse apologies to his guest. "You must think but poorly of my hospitality," said he; "in my loyalty I forgot my duty as a host."

"It is no matter," said Hatto, still laughing. "But since we have come but a little way, would it not be better to return to Ehrenfels and breakfast? You are young and strong, but I——"

"With pleasure," replied the Count, and soon they were again within the castle enjoying a hearty meal. With her own hands the young Countess presented a beaker of wine to the guest, and he, ere quaffing it, cried gaily to Adalbert:

"Your health! May you have the reward I wish for you!"

Once again they set out on their journey, and reached Mainz about nightfall. That very night Adalbert was seized ignominiously and dragged before the Emperor. By Ludwig's side stood the false Bishop.

"What means this outrage?" cried the Count, looking from one to the other.

"Thou art a traitor," said Ludwig, "and must suffer the death of a traitor."

Adalbert addressed himself to the Bishop.

"And thou," he said, "thou gavest me thine oath that thou wouldst bring me in safety to Ehrenfels."

"And did I not do so, fool?" replied Hatto contemptuously. "Was it my fault if thou didst not exact a pledge ere we set out for the second time?"

Adalbert saw now the trap into which he had fallen, and his fettered limbs trembled with anger against the crafty priest. But he was impotent.

"Away with him to the block!" said the Emperor.

"Amen," sneered Hatto, still chuckling over the success of his strategy.

And so Adalbert went forth to his doom, the victim of the cruel Churchman's treachery.

Rheingrafenstein

Rheingrafenstein, perched upon its sable foundations of porphyry, is the scene of a legend which tells of a terrible bargain with Satan—that theme so frequent in German folk-tale.

A certain nobleman, regarding the site as impregnable

and therefore highly desirable, resolved to raise a castle upon the lofty eminence. But the more he considered the plan the more numerous appeared the difficulties in the way of its consummation.

Every pro and con was carefully argued, but to no avail. At last in desperation the nobleman implored assistance from the Enemy of Mankind, who, hearing his name invoked, and scenting the possibility of gaining a recruit to the hosts of Tartarus, speedily manifested his presence, promising to build the castle in one night if the nobleman would grant him the first living creature who should look from its windows. To this the nobleman agreed, and upon the following day found the castle awaiting his possession. He did not dare to enter it, however. But he had communicated his secret to his wife, who decided to circumvent the Evil One by the exercise of her woman's wit. Mounting her donkey, she rode into the castle, bidding all her men follow her. Satan waited on the alert. But the Countess amid great laughter pinned a kerchief upon the ass's head, covered it with a cap, and, leading it to the window, made it thrust its head outside.

Satan immediately pounced upon what he believed to be his lawful prey, and with joy in his heart seized upon and carried off the struggling beast of burden. But the donkey emitted such a bray that, recognizing the nature of his prize, the Fiend in sheer disgust dropped it and vanished in a sulphurous cloud, to the accompaniment of inextinguishable laughter from Rheingrafenstein.

Rüdesheim and its Legends

The town of Rüdesheim is a place famous in song and story, and some of the legends connected with it date from almost prehistoric times. Passing by in the steamer, the

Rheingrafenstein

Louis Weirter, R.B.A.

(See page 211)

Eppstein

Louis Weirter, R.B.A.

(See page 242)

traveller who cares for architecture will doubtless be surprised to mark an old church which would seem to be at least partly of Norman origin; but this is not the only French association which Rüdesheim boasts, for Charlemagne, it is said, loved the place and frequently resided there, while tradition even asserts that he it was who instituted the vine-growing industry on the adjacent hills. He perceived that whenever snow fell there it melted with amazing rapidity; and, judging from this that the soil was eminently suitable for bringing forth a specially fine quality of grape, he sent to France for a few young vine plants. Soon these were thriving in a manner which fully justified expectations. The wines of Rüdesheim became exceptionally famous; and, till comparatively recent times, one of the finest blends was always known as *Wein von Orleans*, for it was thence that the pristine cuttings had been imported.

But it need scarcely be said, perhaps, that most of the legends current at Rüdesheim are not concerned with so essentially pacific an affair as the production of Rhenish. Another story of the place relates how one of its medieval noblemen, Hans, Graf von Brauser, having gone to Palestine with a band of Crusaders, was taken prisoner by the Saracens; and during the period of his captivity he vowed that, should he ever regain his liberty, he would signify his pious gratitude by causing his only daughter, Minna, to take the veil. Rather a selfish kind of piety this appears! Yet mayhap Hans was really devoted to his daughter, and his resolution to part with her possibly entailed a heart-rending sacrifice; while, be that as it may, he had the reward he sought, for now his prison was stormed and he himself released, whereupon he hastened back to his home at Rüdesheim with intent to fulfil his promise to God. On reaching his schloss, however, Graf Hans was confronted by a state of affairs which had not entered into his calculations, the fact being that in the interim his daughter had conceived an affection for a young nobleman called Walther, and had promised to marry him at an early date. Here, then, was a complication indeed, and Hans was sorely puzzled to know how to act, while the unfortunate Minna was equally perplexed, and for many weeks she endured literal torment, her heart being racked by a constant storm of emotions. She was deeply attached to Walther, and she felt that she would never be able to forgive herself if she broke her promise to him and failed to bring him the happiness which both were confident their marriage would produce; but, on the other hand, being of a religious disposition, she perforce respected the vow her father had made, and thought that if it were broken he and all his household would be doomed to eternal damnation, while even Walther might be involved in their ruin. "Shall I make him happy in this world only that he may lose his soul in the next?" she argued; while again and again her father reminded her that a promise to God was of more moment than a promise to man, and he implored her to hasten to the nearest convent and retire behind its walls. Still she wavered, however, and still her father pleaded with her, sometimes actually threatening to exert his parental authority. One evening, driven to despair, Minna sought to cool her throbbing pulses by a walk on the wind-swept heights overlooking the Rhine at Rüdesheim. Possibly she would be able to come to a decision there, she thought; but no! she could not bring herself to renounce her lover, and with a cry of despair she flung herself over the steep rocks into the swirling stream.

Gisela

A hideous death it was. The maiden was immolated on the altar of superstition, and the people of Rüdesheim were awestruck as they thought of the pathetic form drifting down the river. Nor did posterity fail to remember the story, and down to recent times the boatmen of the neighbourhood, when seeing the Rhine wax stormy at the place where Minna was drowned, were wont to whisper that her soul was walking abroad, and that the maiden was once again wrestling with the conflicting emotions which had broken her heart long ago.

Gisela

Knight Brömser of Rüdesheim was one of those who renounced comfort and home ties to throw in his lot with the Crusaders. He was a widower, and possessed a beautiful daughter, Gisela. In the holy wars in Palestine Brömser soon became distinguished for his bravery, and enterprises requiring wit and prowess often were entrusted to him.

Now it befell that the Christian camp was thrown into consternation by the appearance of a huge dragon which took up its abode in the mountainous country, the only locality whence water could be procured, and the increasing scarcity of the supply necessitated the extirpation of the monster. The Crusaders were powerless through fear ; many of them regarded the dragon as a punishment sent from Heaven because of the discord and rivalry which divided them.

At last the brave Brömser offered to attempt the dragon's destruction, and after a valiant struggle he succeeded in slaying it. On his way back to the camp he was surprised by a party of Saracens, and after various hardships was cast into a dungeon. Here he remained in misery for a long while, and during his solitary confinement he made a vow that if he ever returned to his native land he would found a convent and dedicate his daughter as its first nun.

Some time later the Saracens' stronghold was attacked by Christians and the knight set free. In due course he returned to Rüdesheim, where he was welcomed by Gisela, and the day after his arrival a young knight named Kurt of Falkenstein begged him for her hand. Gisela avowed her love for Kurt, and Brömser sadly replied that he would willingly accede to the young people's wishes, for Falkenstein's father was his companion-in-arms, were he not bound by a solemn vow to dedicate his daughter to the Church. When Falkenstein at last understood that the knight's decision was irrevocable he galloped off as if crazed. The knight's vow, however, was not to be fulfilled; Gisela's reason became unhinged, she wandered aimlessly through the corridors of the castle, and one dark and stormy night cast herself into the Rhine and was drowned. Brömser built the convent, but in vain did he strive to free his conscience from remorse. Many were his benefactions, and he built a church on the spot where one of his servants found a wooden figure of the Crucified, which was credited with miraculous powers of healing. But all to no purpose. Haunted by the accusing spirit of his unfortunate daughter, he gradually languished and at last died in the same year that the church was completed.

Further up the river is Oestrich, adjacent to which stood the famous convent of Gottesthal, not a vestige of which remains to mark its former site. Its memory is preserved, however, in the following appalling legend, the noble referred to being the head of one of the ancient families of the neighbourhood.

The Nun of Oestrich

The Nun of Oestrich

Among the inmates of Gottesthal was a nun of surpassing
loveliness, whose beauty had aroused the wild passion of
a certain noble.   Undeterred by the fact of the lady being
a cloistered nun, he found a way of communicating his
passion to her, and at last met her face to face, despite
bars and bolts.   Eloquently he pleaded his love, swearing
to free her from her bonds, to devote his life to her if
only she would listen to his entreaties.   He ended his
asseverations by kneeling before the statue of the Virgin,
vowing in her name and that of the Holy Babe to be
true, and renouncing his hopes of Heaven if he should fail
in the least of his promises.   The nun listened and in the
end, overcome by his fervour, consented to his wishes.

So one night, under cover of the darkness, she stole from
the sheltering convent, forgetting her vows in the arms of
her lover.   Then for a while she knew a guilty happiness,
but even this was of short duration, for the knight soon
tired and grew cold toward her.   At length she was left
alone, scorned and sorrowful, a prey to misery, while her
betrayer rode off in search of other loves and gaieties,
spreading abroad as he went the story of his conquest and
his desertion.

When the injured woman learned the true character of
her lover her love changed to a frenzied hate.   Her
whole being became absorbed in a desire for revenge,
her thoughts by day being occupied by schemes for com-
passing his death, her dreams by night being reddened
by his blood.   At last she plotted with a band of ruffians,
promising them great rewards if they would assassinate
her enemy.   They agreed and, waylaying the noble,
stabbed him fatally in the name of the woman he had

wronged and slighted, then, carrying the hacked body into the village church, they flung it at the foot of the altar.

That night the nun, in a passion of insensate fury, stole into the holy place. Down the length of the church she dragged her lover's corpse, and out into the graveyard, tearing open his body and plucking his heart therefrom with a fell purpose that never wavered. With a shriek she flung it on the ground and trampled upon it in a ruthlessness of hate terrible to contemplate.

And the legend goes on to tell that after her death she still pursued her lover with unquenchable hatred. It is said that when the midnight bell is tolling she may yet be seen seeking his tomb, from which she lifts a bloody heart. She gazes on it with eyes aflame, then, laughing with hellish glee, flings it three times toward the skies, only to let it fall to earth, where she treads it beneath her feet, while from her thick white veil runnels of blood pour down and all around dreary death-lights burn and shed a ghastly glow upon the awful spectre.

Ingelheim : Charlemagne the Robber

Among the multitude of legends which surround the name of Charlemagne there can hardly be found a quainter or more interesting one than that which has for a background the old town of Ingelheim (Angel's Home), where at one time the Emperor held his court.

It is said that one night when Charlemagne had retired to rest he was disturbed by a curious dream. In his vision he saw an angel descend on broad white pinions to his bedside, and the heavenly visitant bade him in the name of the Lord go forth and steal some of his neighbour's goods. The angel warned him ere he departed that the

speedy forfeiture of throne and life would be the penalty
for disregarding the divine injunction.

The astonished Emperor pondered the strange message,
but finally decided that it was but a dream, and he turned
on his side to finish his interrupted slumbers. Scarcely
had he closed his eyelids, however, ere the divine messenger was again at his side, exhorting him in still
stronger terms to go forth and steal ere the night passed,
and threatening him this time with the loss of his soul
if he failed to obey.

When the angel again disappeared the trembling monarch
raised himself in bed, sorely troubled at the difficulty of
his situation. That he, so rich, so powerful that he
wanted for nothing, should be asked to go out in the dead
of night and steal his neighbour's goods, like any of the
common robbers whom he was wont to punish so severely!
No! the thing was preposterous. Some fiend had appeared
in angelic form to tempt him. And again his weary head
sank in his pillow. Rest, however, was denied him. For
a third time the majestic being appeared, and in tones
still more stern demanded his obedience.

"If thou be not a thief," said he, "ere yonder moon
sinks in the west, then art thou lost, body and soul, for
ever."

The Emperor could no longer disbelieve the divine nature
of the message, and he arose sadly, dressed himself in
full armour, and took up his sword and shield, his spear
and hunting-knife. Stealthily he quitted his chamber,
fearing every moment to be discovered. He imagined himself being detected by his own court in the act of privily
leaving his own palace, as though he were a robber,
and the thought was intolerable. But his fears were
unfounded; all—warders, porters, pages, grooms, yea,

the very dogs and horses—were wrapped in a profound slumber. Confirmed in his determination by this miracle —for it could be nothing less—the Emperor saddled his favourite horse, which alone remained awake, and set out on his quest.

It was a beautiful night in late autumn. The moon hung like a silver shield in the deep blue arch of the sky, casting weird shadows on the slopes and lighting the gloom of the ancient forests. But Charlemagne had no eye for scenery at the moment. He was filled with grief and shame when he thought of his mission, yet he dared not turn aside from it. To add to his misery, he was unacquainted with the technicalities of the profession thus thrust upon him, and did not quite know how to set about it.

For the first time in his life, too, he began to sympathize with the robbers he had outlawed and persecuted, and to understand the risks and perils of their life. Nevermore, he vowed, would he hang a man for a trifling inroad upon his neighbour's property.

As he thus pursued his reflections a knight, clad from head to foot in coal-black armour and mounted on a black steed, issued silently from a clump of trees and rode unseen beside him.

Charlemagne continued to meditate upon the dangers and misfortunes of a robber's life.

"There is Elbegast," said he to himself; "for a small offence I have deprived him of land and fee, and have hunted him like an animal. He and his knights risk their lives for every meal. He respects not the cloth of the Church, it is true, yet methinks he is a noble fellow, for he robs not the poor or the pilgrim, but rather enriches them with part of his plunder. Would he were with me now!"

Ingelheim: Charlemagne the Robber

His reflections were suddenly stopped, for he now observed the black knight riding by his side.

"It may be the Fiend," said Charlemagne to himself, spurring his steed.

But though he rode faster and faster, his strange companion kept pace with him. At length the Emperor reined in his steed, and demanded to know who the stranger might be. The black knight refused to answer his questions, and the two thereupon engaged in furious combat. Again and again the onslaught was renewed, till at last Charlemagne succeeded in cleaving his opponent's blade.

"My life is yours," said the black knight.

"Nay," replied the monarch, "what would I with your life? Tell me who you are, for you have fought gallantly this night."

The stranger drew himself up and replied with simple dignity, "I am Elbegast."

Charlemagne was delighted at thus having his wish fulfilled. He refused to divulge his name, but intimated that he, too, was a robber, and proposed that they should join forces for the night.

"I have it," said he. "We will rob the Emperor's treasury. I think I could show you the way."

The black knight paused. "Never yet," he said, "have I wronged the Emperor, and I shall not do so now. But at no great distance stands the castle of Eggerich von Eggermond, brother-in-law to the Emperor. He has persecuted the poor and betrayed the innocent to death. If he could, he would take the life of the Emperor himself, to whom he owes all. Let us repair thither."

Near their destination they tied their horses to a tree and strode across the fields. On the way Charlemagne wrenched off the iron share from a plough, remarking that it would be an excellent tool wherewith to bore a hole in the castle wall—a remark which his comrade received in silence, though not without surprise. When they arrived at the castle Elbegast seemed anxious to see the ploughshare at work, for he begged Charlemagne to begin operations.

" I know not how to find entrance," said the latter.

" Let us make a hole in the wall," the robber-knight suggested, producing a boring instrument of great strength. The Emperor gallantly set to work with his ploughshare, though, as the wall was ten feet thick, it is hardly surprising that he was not successful. The robber, laughing at his comrade's inexperience, showed him a wide chasm which his boring instrument had made, and bade him remain there while he fetched the spoil. In a very short time he returned with as much plunder as he could carry.

" Let us get away," said the Emperor. " We can carry no more."

" Nay," said Elbegast, " but I would return, with your permission. In the chamber occupied by Eggerich and his wife there is a wonderful caparison, made of gold and covered with little bells. I want to prove my skill by carrying it off."

" As you will," was Charlemagne's laughing response.

Without a sound Elbegast reached the bedchamber of his victim, and was about to raise the caparison when he suddenly stumbled and all the bells rang out clearly.

" My sword, my sword!" cried Eggerich, springing up, while Elbegast sank back into the shadows.

" Nay," said the lady, trying to calm her husband. " You did but hear the wind, or perhaps it was an evil dream. Thou hast had many evil dreams of late, Eggerich;

Ingelheim: Charlemagne the Robber

methinks there is something lies heavily on thy mind. Wilt thou not tell thy wife?"

Elbegast listened intently while with soft words and caresses the lady strove to win her husband's secret.

"Well," said Eggerich at last in sullen tones, "we have laid a plot, my comrades and I. To-morrow we go to Ingelheim, and ere noon Charlemagne shall be slain and his lands divided among us."

"What!" shrieked the lady. "Murder my brother! That will you never while I have strength to warn him." But the villain, with a brutal oath, struck her so fiercely in the face that the blood gushed out, and she sank back unconscious.

The robber was not in a position to avenge the cruel act, but he crawled nearer the couch and caught some of the blood in his gauntlet, for a sign to the Emperor. When he was once more outside the castle he told his companion all that had passed and made as though to return. "I will strike off his head," said he. "The Emperor is no friend of mine, but I love him still."

"What is the Emperor to us?" cried Charlemagne. "Are you mad that you risk our lives for the Emperor?" The black knight looked at him solemnly.

"An we had not sworn friendship," said he, "your life should pay for these words. Long live the Emperor!" Charlemagne, secretly delighted with the loyalty of the outlawed knight, recommended him to seek the Emperor on the morrow and warn him of his danger. But Elbegast, fearing the gallows, would not consent to this; so his companion promised to do it in his stead and meet him afterward in the forest. With that they parted, the Emperor returning to his palace, where he found all as he had left it.

In the morning he hastily summoned his council, told them of his dream and subsequent adventures, and of the plot against his life. The paladins were filled with horror and indignation, and Charlemagne's secretary suggested that it was time preparations were being made for the reception of the assassins. Each band of traitors as they arrived was seized and cast into a dungeon. Though apparently clad as peaceful citizens, they were all found to be armed. The last band to arrive was led by Eggerich himself. Great was his dismay when he saw his followers led off in chains, and angrily he demanded to know the reason for such treatment.

Charlemagne thereupon charged him with treason, and Eggerich flung down the gauntlet in defiance. It was finally arranged that the Emperor should provide a champion to do battle with the traitor, the combat to take place at sunrise on the following morning.

A messenger rode to summon Elbegast, but he had much difficulty in convincing the black knight that it was not a plot to secure his undoing.

"And what would the Emperor with me?" he demanded of the messenger, as at length they rode toward Ingelheim.

"To do battle to the death with a deadly foe of our lord the Emperor—Eggerich von Eggermond."

"God bless the Emperor!" exclaimed Elbegast fervently, raising his helmet. "My life is at his service."

Charlemagne greeted the knight affectionately and asked what he had to tell concerning the conspiracy, whereupon Sir Elbegast fearlessly denounced the villainous Eggerich, and said he, "I am ready to prove my assertions upon his body." The challenge was accepted, and at daybreak the following morning a fierce combat took place. The issue, however, was never in doubt: Sir Elbegast was victorious, the false Eggerich was slain, and his body hanged on a gibbet fifty feet high. The emperor now revealed himself to the black knight both as his companion-robber and as the messenger who had brought him the summons to attend his Emperor.

Charlemagne's sister, the widow of Eggerich, he gave to Sir Elbegast in marriage, and with her the broad lands which had belonged to the vanquished traitor. Thenceforward the erstwhile robber and his sovereign were fast friends.

The place where these strange happenings befell was called *Ingelheim*, in memory of the celestial visitor, and Ingelheim it remains to this day.

The Knight and the Yellow Dwarf

Elfeld is the principal town of the Rheingau, and in ancient times was a Roman station called Alta Villa. In the fourteenth century it was raised to the rank of a town by Ludwig of Bavaria, and placed under the stewardship of the Counts of Elz.

These Counts of Elz dwelt in the castle by the river's edge, and of one of them, Ferdinand, the following tale is told. This knight loved pleasure and wild living, and would indulge his whims and passions without regard to cost. Before long he found that as a result of his extravagance his possessions had dwindled away almost to nothing. He knew himself a poor man, yet his desire for pleasure was still unsatisfied. Mortified and angry, he hid himself in the castle of Elz and spent his time lamenting his poverty and cursing his fate. While in this frame of mind the news reached him of a tournament that the Emperor purposed holding in celebration of his wedding. To this were summoned the chivalry and beauty of

Germany from far and near, and soon knights and ladies were journeying to take their part in the tourney, the feasting and dancing.

Ferdinand realized that he was precluded from joining his brother nobles and was inconsolable. He became the prey of rage and shame, and at last resolved to end a life condemned to ignominy. So one day he sought a height from which to hurl himself, but ere he could carry out his purpose there appeared before him a dwarf, clad in yellow from top to toe. With a leer and a laugh he looked up at the frantic knight, and asked why the richest noble in the land should be seeking death. Something in the dwarf's tone caused Ferdinand to listen and suddenly to hope for he knew not what miracle. His eyes gleamed as the dwarf went on to speak of sacks of gold, and when the little creature asked for but a single hair in return he laughed aloud and offered him a hundred. But the dwarf smiled and shook his head. The noble bowed with a polite gesture, and as he bent his head the little man reached up and plucked out but one hair, and, lo! a sack of gold straightway appeared. At this Ferdinand thought that he must be dreaming, but the sack and gold pieces were real enough to the touch, albeit the dwarf had vanished. Then, in great haste, Ferdinand bought rich and costly clothing and armour, also a snow-white steed caparisoned with steel and purple trappings, spending on these more than twenty sacks of gold, for the dwarf returned to the noble many times and on each occasion gave a sack of gold in exchange for one hair. At last Ferdinand set out for the tournament, where, besides carrying off the richest prizes and winning the heart of many a fair lady, he attracted the notice of the Emperor, who invited him to stay at his court.

Mainz

And there the knight resumed his former passions and pleasures, living the wildest of lives and thinking no price too
high for careless enjoyment. And each night, ere the hour
of twelve finished striking, the yellow dwarf appeared with
a sack of gold, taking his usual payment of only one hair.
This wild life now began to tell upon Ferdinand. He fell
an easy prey to disease, which the doctors could not cure,
and to the pricks of a late-roused conscience, which no
priests could soothe. All his wasted past rose before him.
Day and night his manifold sins appeared before him
like avenging furies, until at last, frenzied by this double
torture of mind and body, he called upon the Devil to aid
him in putting an end to his miserable existence, for so
helpless was he, he could neither reach nor use a weapon.
Then at his side appeared once more the dwarf, smiling
and obliging as usual. He proffered, not a sack of gold this
time, but a rope of woven hair, the hair which he had taken
from Ferdinand in exchange for his gold. In the morning
the miserable noble was found hanging by that rope.

Mainz

Mainz, the old Maguntiacum, was the principal fortress
on the Upper Rhine in Roman times. It was here that
Crescentius, one of the first preachers of the Christian
faith on the Rhine, regarded by local tradition as
the pupil of St. Peter and first Archbishop of Mainz,
suffered martyrdom in the reign of Trajan in A.D. 103.
He was a centurion in the Twenty-second Legion,
which had been engaged under Titus in the destruction
of Jerusalem, and it is supposed that he preached the
Gospel in Mainz for thirty-three years before his execution. Here also it was that the famous vision of Constantine, the cross in the sky, was vouchsafed to the

Christian conqueror as he went forth to meet the forces of Mainz. The field of the Holy Cross in the vicinity of Mainz is still pointed out as the spot where this miracle took place. The city flourished under the Carlovingians, and was in a high state of prosperity at the time of Bishop Hatto, whose name, as we have seen, has been held up to obloquy in many legends.

During the fourteenth century Mainz shared the power and glory of the other cities of the Rhenish Confederation, then in the full flush of its heyday. Its cathedral witnesses to its aforetime civic splendour. This magnificent building took upward of four hundred years to complete, and its wondrous brazen doors and sumptuous chapels are among the finest ecclesiastical treasures of Germany.

The Fiddler

In the cathedral of Mainz was an image of the Virgin, on whose feet were golden slippers, the gift of some wealthy votary. Of this image the following legend is told:

A poor ragged fiddler had spent the whole of one bitter winter morning playing through the dreary streets without any taking pity upon his plight. As he came to the cathedral he felt an overmastering desire to enter and pour out his distress in the presence of his Maker. So he crept in, a tattered and forlorn figure. He prayed aloud, chanting his woes in the same tones which he used in the street to touch the hearts of the passers-by.

As he prayed a sense of solitude came upon him, and he realized that the shadowy aisles were empty. A sudden whim seized him. He would play to the golden-shod Virgin and sing her one of his sweetest songs. And drawing nearer he lifted his old fiddle to his shoulder, and into his playing he put all his longing and pain; his

228

The Fiddler

quavering voice grew stronger beneath the stress of his fervour. It was as if the springtime had come about him ; life was before him, gay and joyful, sorrow and pain were unknown. He sank to his knees before the image, and as he knelt, suddenly the Virgin lifted her foot and, loosening her golden slipper, cast it into the old man's ragged bosom, as if giving alms for his music.

The poor old man, astounded at the miracle, told himself that the Blessed Virgin knew how to pay a poor devil who amused her. Overcome by gratitude, he thanked the giver with all his heart.

He would fain have kept the treasure, but he was starving, and it seemed to have been given him to relieve his distress. He hurried out to the market and went into a goldsmith's shop to offer his prize. But the man recognized it at once. Then was the poor old fiddler worse off than before, for now he was charged with the dreadful crime of sacrilege. The old man told the story of the miracle over and over again, but he was laughed at for an impudent liar. He must not hope, they told him, for anything but death, and in the short space of one hour he was tried and condemned and on his way to execution.

The place of death was just opposite the great bronze doors of the cathedral which sheltered the Virgin. " If I must die," said the fiddler, " I would sing one song to my old fiddle at the feet of the Virgin and pray one prayer before her. I ask this in her blessed name, and you cannot refuse me."

They could not deny the prisoner a dying prayer, and, closely guarded, the tattered figure once more entered the cathedral which had been so disastrous to him. He approached the altar of the Virgin, his eyes filling with tears as again he held his old fiddle in his hands. Then he

229

played and sang as before, and again a breath as of spring-time stole into the shadowy cathedral and life seemed glad and beautiful. When the music ceased, again the Virgin lifted a foot and softly she flung her other slipper into the fiddler's bosom, before the astonished gaze of the guards. Everyone there saw the miracle and could not but testify to the truth of the old man's former statement; he was at once freed from his bonds and carried before the city fathers, who ordered his release.

And it is said that, in memory of the miracle of the Virgin, the priests provided for the old fiddler for the rest of his days. In return for this the old man surrendered the golden slippers, which, it is also said, the reverend fathers carefully locked away in the treasure-chest, lest the Virgin should again be tempted to such extravagant almsgiving.

The Maiden's Leap

Once in the Hardt mountains there dwelt a giant whose fortress commanded a wide view of the surrounding country. Near by, a lovely lady, as daring in the hunt as she was skilful at spinning, inhabited an abandoned castle. One day the twain chanced to meet, and the giant thereupon resolved to possess the beauteous damsel.

So he sent his servant to win her with jewels, but the deceitful fellow intended to hide the treasures in a forest.

There he met a young man musing in a disconsolate attitude, who confided that poverty alone kept him from avowing how passionately he adored his sweetheart.

The shrewd messenger realized that this rustic's charmer was the same fair lady who had beguiled his master's soul. He solicited the youth's aid in burying the treasures

The Maiden's Leap

promising him a share in the spoil sufficient to enable him to wed his beloved.

In a solitary spot they dug a deep hole, when suddenly the robber assailed his companion, who thrust him aside with great violence. In his rage the youth was about to stab the wretch, when he craved pardon, promising to reveal a secret of more value than the jewels he had intended to conceal.

The youth stayed his hand, and the servant related how his master, for love of the pretty mistress of the castle, had sent him to gain her favour.

Conscious of his worth, the ardent youth scornfully declared that he feared no rival, then, seizing half of the treasure, he left the wretch to his own devices.

Meanwhile the giant impatiently awaited his servant's return. At length, tired of waiting, he decided to visit the lady and declare in person his passion for her. Upon his arrival at the castle the maid announced him, and it was with a secret feeling of dread that the lady went to meet her unwelcome visitor. More than ever captivated by her charms, the giant asked the fair maid to become his wife. On being refused, he threatened to kill her and demolish the castle.

The poor lady was terrified and she tearfully implored the giant's mercy, promising to bestow all her treasure upon him. Her maids, too, begged him to spare their mistress's life, but he only laughed as they knelt before him. Ultimately the hapless maiden consented to marry her inexorable wooer, but she attached a novel condition : she would ride a race with her relentless suitor, and should he overtake her she would accompany him to his castle.

But the resolute maiden had secretly vowed to die rather than submit to such degradation. Choosing her fleetest steed, she vaulted nimbly into the saddle and galloped away. Her persecutor pursued close behind, straining every nerve to come up with her. Shuddering at the very thought of becoming his bride, she chose death as the only alternative. So she spurred her horse onward to the edge of a deep chasm.

The noble animal neighed loudly as though conscious of impending danger. The pursuer laughed grimly as he thought to seize his prize, but his laughter was turned to rage when the horse with its fair burden bounded lightly across the chasm, landing safely on the other side.

The enraged tyrant now beheld his intended victim kneeling in prayer and her steed calmly grazing among the green verdure by her side. He strode furiously hither and thither, searching for a crossing, and suddenly a shout of joy told the affrighted maid that he had discovered some passage.

His satisfaction, however, was short-lived, for just then a strange knight with drawn sword rushed upon the giant. The maid watched the contest with breathless fear, and many times she thought that the tyrant would slay her protector. At last in one such moment the giant stooped to clutch a huge boulder with which he meant to overwhelm his adversary, when, overreaching himself, he slipped and fell headlong down the steep rocks.

Then the maid hastened to thank her rescuer, and great was her surprise to discover in the gallant knight the youth whose former poverty had kept him from wooing her. They returned to the castle together, and it was not long ere they celebrated their wedding.

Both lived long and happily, and their union was blessed with many children. The rock is still known as "The Maiden's Leap."

The Wonderful Road

The Wonderful Road

Near Homburg, on the pinnacle of a lofty mountain, are the ruins of Falkenstein Castle, access to which is gained by a steep, winding path.

Within the castle walls there once dwelt a maiden of surpassing beauty. Many suitors climbed the stern acclivity to woo this charming damsel, but her stern father repelled one and all. Only Kuno of Sayn was firm enough to persevere in his suit against the rebuffs of the stubborn Lord of Falkenstein, and in the end he was rewarded with the smiles and kind looks of the fair maid.

One evening, as they watched the sun set, Kuno pointed out to the maiden where his own castle was situated. The beauty of the landscape beneath them made its appeal to their souls, their hands touched and clasped, and their hearts throbbed with the passion felt by both. A few days later Kuno climbed the steep path, resolved to declare his love to the damsel's father. Fatigued with the ascent, he rested for a brief space at the entrance to the castle ere mounting to the tower.

The Lord of Falkenstein and his daughter had beheld Kuno's journey up the rugged path from the windows of the tower, and the father demanded for what purpose he had come thither. With a passionate glance at the blushing maid, the knight of Sayn declared that he had come to ask the noble lord for his daughter's hand in marriage. After meditating on the knight's proposal for some time, the Lord of Falkenstein pretended to be willing to give his consent—but he attached a condition. "I desire a carriage-drive to be made from the lowland beneath to the gate of my castle, and if you can accomplish this my daughter's hand is yours—but the feat must be *achieved by to-morrow morning!* "

The knight protested that such a task was utterly impossible for anyone to perform, even in a month, but all to no purpose. He then resolved to seek some way whereby he could outwit the stubborn lord, for he would not willingly resign his lady-love. He left the tower, vowing to do his utmost to perform the seemingly impossible task, and as he descended the rocky declivity his beloved waved her handkerchief to encourage him.

Now Kuno of Sayn possessed both copper and silver mines, and arriving at his castle he summoned his overseer. The knight explained the nature of the task which he desired to be undertaken, but the overseer declared that all his miners, working day and night, could not make the roadway within many months.

Dismayed, Kuno left his castle and wandered into a dense forest, driven thither by his perturbed condition. Night cast dusky shadows over the foliage, and the perplexed lover cursed the obstinate Lord of Falkenstein as he forced his way through the undergrowth.

Suddenly an old man of strange and wild appearance stood in his path. Kuno at once knew him for an earth-spirit, one of those mysterious guardians of the treasures of the soil who are jealous of the incursion of mankind into their domain.

"Kuno of Sayn," he said, "do you desire to outwit the Lord of Falkenstein and win his beauteous daughter?"

Although startled and taken aback by the strange apparition, Kuno hearkened eagerly to its words as showing an avenue of escape from the dilemma in which he found himself.

The Wonderful Road

"Assuredly I do," he replied, "but how do you propose I should accomplish it?"

"Cease to persecute me and my brethren, Kuno, and we shall help you to realize your wishes," was the reply.

"Persecute you!" exclaimed Kuno. "In what manner do I trouble you at all, strange being?"

"You have opened up a silver mine in our domain," said the earth-spirit, "and as you work it both morning and afternoon we have but little opportunity for repose. How, I ask you, can we slumber when your men keep knocking on the partitions of our house with their picks?"

"What, then, would you have, my worthy friend?" asked Kuno, scarcely able to suppress a smile at the wistful way in which the gnome made his complaint. "Tell me, I pray you, how I can oblige you."

"By instructing your miners to work in the mine during the hours of morning only," replied the gnome. "By so doing I and my brothers will obtain the rest we so much require."

"It shall be as you say," said Kuno; "you have my word for it, good friend."

"In that case," said the earth-spirit, "we shall assist you in turn. Go to the castle of Falkenstein after dawn to-morrow morning, and you shall witness the result of our friendship and gratitude."

Next morning the sun had scarcely risen when Kuno saddled his steed and hied him to the heights of Falkenstein. The gnome had kept his word. There, above and in front of him, he beheld a wide and lofty roadway leading to the castle-gate from the thoroughfare below. With joy in his heart he set spurs to his horse and dashed up the steep but smooth acclivity. At the gate he encountered the old Lord of Falkenstein and his daughter, who had

been apprised of the miracle that had happened and had
come out to view the new roadway. The knight of Sayn
related his adventure with the earth-spirit, upon which the
Lord of Falkenstein told him how a terrible thunderstorm
mingled with unearthly noises had raged throughout the
night. Terrified, he and his daughter had spent the hours
of darkness in prayer, until with the approach of dawn
some of the servitors had plucked up courage and
ventured forth, when the wonderful avenue up the side
of the mountain met their startled gaze.

Kuno and his lady-love were duly united. Indeed, so
terrified was the old lord by the supernatural manifesta-
tions of the dreadful night he had just passed through
that he was incapable of further resistance to the wishes
of the young people. The wonderful road is still to be
seen, and is marvelled at by all who pass that way.

Osric the Lion

Other tales besides the foregoing have their scene laid in
the castle of Falkenstein, notable among them being the
legend of Osric the Lion, embodied in the following weird
ballad from the pen of Monk Lewis:

> Swift roll the Rhine's billows, and water the plains,
> Where Falkenstein Castle's majestic remains
>   Their moss-covered turrets still rear:
> Oft loves the gaunt wolf 'midst the ruins to prowl,
> What time from the battlements pours the lone owl
>   Her plaints in the passenger's ear.
>
> No longer resound through the vaults of yon hall
> The song of the minstrel, and mirth of the ball;
>   Those pleasures for ever are fled:
> There now dwells the bat with her light-shunning brood,
> There ravens and vultures now clamour for food,
>   And all is dark, silent, and dread!

Osric the Lion

Ha! dost thou not see, by the moon's trembling light
Directing his steps, where advances a knight,
   His eye big with vengeance and fate?
'Tis Osric the Lion his nephew who leads,
And swift up the crackling old staircase proceeds,
   Gains the hall, and quick closes the gate.

Now round him young Carloman, casting his eyes,
Surveys the sad scene with dismay and surprise,
   And fear steals the rose from his cheeks.
His spirits forsake him, his courage is flown;
The hand of Sir Osric he clasps in his own,
   And while his voice falters he speaks.

"Dear uncle," he murmurs, "why linger we here?
'Tis late, and these chambers are damp and are drear,
   Keen blows through the ruins the blast!
Oh! let us away and our journey pursue:
Fair Blumenberg's Castle will rise on our view,
   Soon as Falkenstein forest be passed.

"Why roll thus your eyeballs? why glare they so wild?
Oh! chide not my weakness, nor frown, that a child
   Should view these apartments with dread;
For know that full oft have I heard from my nurse,
There still on this castle has rested a curse,
   Since innocent blood here was shed.

"She said, too, bad spirits, and ghosts all in white,
Here used to resort at the dead time of night,
   Nor vanish till breaking of day;
And still at their coming is heard the deep tone
Of a bell loud and awful—hark! hark! 'twas a groan!
   Good uncle, oh! let us away!"

"Peace, serpent!" thus Osric the Lion replies,
While rage and malignity gleam in his eyes;
   "Thy journey and life here must close:
Thy castle's proud turrets no more shalt thou see;
No more betwixt Blumenberg's lordship and me
   Shalt thou stand, and my greatness oppose.

"My brother lies breathless on Palestine's plains,
And thou once removed, to his noble domains
   My right can no rival deny:
Then, stripling, prepare on my dagger to bleed;
No succour is near, and thy fate is decreed,
   Commend thee to Jesus and die!"

Thus saying, he seizes the boy by the arm,
Whose grief rends the vaulted hall's roof, while alarm
   His heart of all fortitude robs;
His limbs sink beneath him; distracted with fears,
He falls at his uncle's feet, bathes them with tears,
   And "Spare me! oh, spare me!" he sobs.

But vainly the miscreant he tries to appease;
And vainly he clings in despair round his knees,
   And sues in soft accents for life;
Unmoved by his sorrow, unmoved by his prayer,
Fierce Osric has twisted his hand in his hair,
   And aims at his bosom a knife.

But ere the steel blushes with blood, strange to tell!
Self-struck, does the tongue of the hollow-toned bell
   The presence of midnight declare:
And while with amazement his hair bristles high,
Hears Osric a voice, loud and terrible, cry,
   In sounds heart-appalling, "Forbear!"

Straight curses and shrieks through the chamber resound,
Shrieks mingled with laughter; the walls shake around;
   The groaning roof threatens to fall;
Loud bellows the thunder, blue lightnings still flash;
The casements they clatter; chains rattle; doors clash,
   And flames spread their waves through the hall.

The clamour increases, the portals expand!
O'er the pavement's black marble now rushes a band
   Of demons, all dropping with gore,
In visage so grim, and so monstrous in height,
That Carloman screams, as they burst on his sight,
   And sinks without sense on the floor.

Not so his fell uncle:—he sees that the throng
Impels, wildly shrieking, a female along,
   And well the sad spectre he knows!
The demons with curses her steps onwards urge;
Her shoulders, with whips formed of serpents, they scourge,
   And fast from her wounds the blood flows.

"Oh! welcome!" she cried, and her voice spoke despair;
"Oh! welcome, Sir Osric, the torments to share,
   Of which thou hast made me the prey.
Twelve years have I languished thy coming to see;
Ulrilda, who perished dishonoured by thee
   Now calls thee to anguish away!

The Conference of the Dead

"Thy passion once sated, thy love became hate;
Thy hand gave the draught which consigned me to fate,
   Nor thought I death lurked in the bowl:
Unfit for the grave, stained with lust, swelled with pride,
Unblessed, unabsolved, unrepenting, I died,
   And demons straight seized on my soul.

"Thou com'st, and with transport I feel my breast swell:
Full long have I suffered the torments of hell,
   And now shall its pleasures be mine!
See, see, how the fiends are athirst for thy blood!
Twelve years has *my* panting heart furnished their food.
   Come, wretch, let them feast upon thine!"

She said, and the demons their prey flocked around;
They dashed him, with horrible yell, on the ground,
   And blood down his limbs trickled fast;
His eyes from their sockets with fury they tore;
They fed on his entrails, all reeking with gore,
   And his *heart* was Ulrilda's repast.

But now the grey cock told the coming of day!
The fiends with their victim straight vanished away,
   And Carloman's heart throbbed again;
With terror recalling the deeds of the night,
He rose, and from Falkenstein speeding his flight,
   Soon reached his paternal domain.

Since then, all with horror the ruins behold;
No shepherd, though strayed be a lamb from his fold,
   No mother, though lost be her child,
The fugitive dares in these chambers to seek,
Where fiends nightly revel, and guilty ghosts shriek
   In accents most fearful and wild!

Oh! shun them, ye pilgrims! though late be the hour,
Though loud howl the tempest, and fast fall the shower;
   From Falkenstein Castle begone!
There still their sad banquet hell's denizens share;
There Osric the Lion still raves in despair:
   Breathe a prayer for his soul, and pass on!

The Conference of the Dead

A legend of later date than most of the Rhineland tales,
but still of sufficient interest to merit inclusion among

these, is that which attaches to the palace of Biberich. Biberich lies on the right bank of the river, not very far from Mainz, and its palace was built at the beginning of the eighteenth century by George Augustus, Duke of Nassau.

The legend states that not long after the erection of the palace a Duchess of Nassau died there, and lay in state as befitted her rank in a room hung with black velvet and lighted with the glimmer of many tapers.

Outside in the great hall a captain and forty-nine men of the Duke's bodyguard kept watch over the chamber of death.

It was midnight. The captain of the guard, weary with his vigil, had gone to the door of the palace for a breath of air. Just as the last stroke of the hour died away he beheld the approach of a chariot, drawn by six magnificent coal-black horses, which, to his amazement, drew up before the palace. A lady, veiled and clad in white, alighted and made as though she would enter the building. But the captain barred the way and challenged the bold intruder.

"Who are you," he said sternly, "who seek to enter the palace at this hour? My orders are to let none pass."

"I was first lady of the bedchamber to our late Duchess," replied the lady in cold, imperious tones; "therefore I demand the right of entrance."

As she spoke she flung aside her veil, and the captain, instantly recognizing her, permitted her to enter the palace without further hindrance.

"What can she want here at this time of night?" he said to his lieutenant, when the lady had passed into the death-chamber.

The Conference of the Dead

"Who can say?" replied the lieutenant. "Unless, perchance," he mused, "we were to look."

The captain took the hint, crept softly to the keyhole, and applied his eye thereto. "Ha!" he said, shrinking back in amazement and terror, and beckoning to his lieutenant. "In Satan's name what have we here?"

The lieutenant hastened to the chamber door, full of alarm and curiosity. Putting his eye to the keyhole, he also ejaculated, turned pale, and trembled. One by one the soldiers of the guard followed their officers' example, like them to retreat with exclamations of horror. And little wonder; for they perceived the dead Duchess sitting up in bed, moving her pale lips as though in conversation, while by her side stood the lady of the bedchamber, pale as she, and clad in grave-clothes. For a time the ghastly conversation continued, no words being audible to the terror-stricken guard; but from time to time a hollow sound reached them, like the murmur of distant thunder. At length the visitor emerged from the chamber, and returned to her waiting coach. Duty, rather than inclination, obliged the gallant captain to hand her into her carriage, and this task he performed with praiseworthy politeness, though his heart sank within him at the touch of her icy fingers, and his tongue refused to return the adieu her pale lips uttered. With a flourish of whips the chariot set off. Sparks flew from the hoofs of the horses, smoke and flame burst from their nostrils, and such was their speed that in a moment they were lost to sight. The captain, sorely puzzled by the events of the night, returned to his men, who were huddled together at the end of the hall furthest from the death-chamber.

On the morrow, ere the guard had had time to inform the Duke of these strange happenings, news reached the palace that the first lady of the bedchamber had died on the previous night at twelve o'clock. It was supposed that sorrow for her mistress had caused her death.

Eppstein

Of the castle of Eppstein, whose ruins still remain in a valley of the Taunus Mountains, north of Biberich, the following curious story is told.

Sir Eppo, a brave and chivalrous knight—and a wealthy one to boot, as were his successors of Eppstein for many generations—was one day hunting in the forest, when he became separated from his attendants and lost his way. In the heat of the chase his sense of direction had failed him, and though he sounded his bugle loud and long there was no reply.

Tired out at length with wandering hither and thither, he rested himself in a pleasant glade, and was surprised and charmed to hear a woman's voice singing a mournful melody in soft, clear tones. It was a sheer delight to Sir Eppo to listen to a voice of such exquisite purity, yet admiration was not the only feeling it roused in his breast. There was a note of sadness and appeal in the song, and what were knighthood worth if it heeded not the voice of fair lady in distress? Sir Eppo sprang to his feet, forgetting his own plight in the ardour of chivalry, and set off in the direction from which the voice seemed to come. The way was difficult, and he had to cut a passage with his sword through the dense thicket that separated him from the singer. At length, guided by the melancholy notes, he arrived before a grotto, in which he beheld a maiden of surpassing beauty, but of sorrowful mien. When she saw the handsome knight gazing at her with mingled surprise and admiration she ceased her song and implored his aid. A cruel giant, she said, had seized her and brought her thither. At the moment he was asleep, but he had tied her to a rock so that she might not escape.

Her beauty and grace, her childlike innocence, her piteous plight, moved Sir Eppo strangely. First pity, then a stronger emotion dawned in his breast. He severed her bonds with a stroke of his keen falchion.

"What can I do to aid thee, gentle maiden?" he said. "You have but to command me; henceforth I am thy knight, to do battle for thee."

The damsel blushed at the courteous words, but she lifted her eyes bravely to the champion who had so unexpectedly appeared to protect her.

"Return to my castle," she said, "and there thou wilt find a consecrated net. Bring it hither. If I lay it upon the giant he will become as weak as a babe and will be easily overcome."

Eagerly the young knight obeyed the command, and having found the net according to the damsel's directions, he made all haste to return. At the grotto he paused and hid himself, for the strident voice of the giant could be heard within. Presently the monster emerged, and departed in search of reeds wherewith to make a pipe. No sooner had he disappeared than the maiden issued from the grotto, and Sir Eppo came out of his concealment and gave her the consecrated net. She spoke a few words of heartfelt gratitude, and then hurried with her treasure to the top of the mountain, where she knew the giant had intended to go.

Arrived at her destination, she laid down the net and covered it with moss, leaves, and sweet-smelling herbs. While engaged in her task the giant came up, and the damsel smilingly told him that she was preparing a couch whereon he might take some rest. Gratified at her solicitude, he stretched himself unsuspectingly on the fragrant pile. In a moment the damsel, uttering the name of the Trinity, threw a portion of the net over him, so that he was completely enveloped. Immediately there arose such loud oaths and lamentations that the damsel ran in terror to the knight, who had now come upon the scene.

" Let us fly," she said, " lest he should escape and pursue us."

But Sir Eppo strode to the place where the howling monster lay entangled in the net, and with a mighty effort rolled him over a steep precipice, where he was instantly killed.

The story ends happily, for Sir Eppo and the maiden he had rescued were married soon after; and on the spot where they had first met was raised the castle of Eppstein. It is said that the bones of the giant may still be seen there.

Flörsheim : The Shepherd Knight

In the now ruined castle of Wilenstein, overlooking the wooded heights of the Westrich, dwelt Sir Bodo of Flörsheim and his fair daughter Adeline. The maiden's beauty, no less than her father's wealth, attracted suitors in plenty from the neighbouring strongholds, but the spirit of love had not yet awakened in her bosom and each and all were repulsed with disconcerting coldness and indifference, and they left the schloss vowing that the lovely Adeline was utterly heartless.

One day there came to Sir Bodo a youth of pleasing manners and appearance, picturesquely clad in rustic garb, who begged that he might enter the knight's service in the capacity of shepherd. Though he hinted that he was of noble birth, prevented by circumstances from revealing his identity, yet he based his request solely on his merits as a tender of flocks and herds, and as Sir Bodo found that he knew his work well and that his intelligence was beyond question, he gave him the desired post. As time went on Sir Bodo saw no reason to regret his action, for his flocks and herds prospered as they had never done before, and none but good reports reached him concerning his servant.

Meantime Adeline heard constant references to Otto (as the shepherd was called) both from her father and her waiting-women. The former praised his industry and abilities, while the latter spoke of his handsome looks and melancholy air, his distinction and good breeding, and the mystery which surrounded his identity. All this excited the maiden's curiosity, and her pity was aroused as well, for it seemed that the stranger had a secret grief, which sometimes found vent in tears when he thought himself unobserved.

Adeline saw him for the first time one afternoon while she was walking in the castle grounds. At sight of her he paused as though spell-bound, and the maiden blushed under his earnest scrutiny. A moment later, however, he recovered himself, and courteously asked her pardon for his seeming rudeness.

" Forgive me, fair lady," said he; " it seemed that I saw a ghost in your sweet face."

Adeline, who had recognized him from the descriptions she had received, now made herself known to him, and graciously granted him permission to walk with her to the castle. His offence was readily pardoned when he declared that the cause of it was a fancied resemblance between Adeline and a dear sister whom death had lately robbed him of. Ere they parted the young people were already deeply in love with one another, and had promised to meet again on the following day. The spot where they had first encountered each other became a trysting-place which was daily hallowed by fresh vows and declarations. On one such occasion Otto told his beloved the story of his early life and revealed to her his identity. It was indeed a harrowing tale, and one which drew a full meed of sympathy from the maiden.

Otto and his sister—she whose likeness in Adeline's face had first arrested his attention—had been brought up by a cruel stepfather, who had treated them so brutally that Otto was at length forced to flee to the castle of an uncle, who received him kindly and gave him an education befitting his knightly station. A few years later he had returned home, to find his sister dead—slain by the ill-treatment of her stepfather, who, it was even said, had hastened her death with poison. Otto, overcome with grief, confronted her murderer, heaped abuse on his head, and demanded his share of the property. The only answer was a sneer, and the youth, maddened with grief and indignation, drew his sword and plunged it in his tormentor's heart. A moment later he saw the probable consequences of his hasty action, concealed himself in the woods, and thenceforth became a fugitive, renounced even by his own uncle, and obliged to remain in hiding in order to escape certain death at the hands of the murdered man's kindred. In a fortunate moment he had chanced to reach Flörsheim, where, in his shepherd's guise, he judged himself secure.

Adeline, deeply moved by the tale, sought to put her sympathy in the practical form of advice.

Flörsheim : The Shepherd Knight

"Dear Otto," she said, "let us go to my father and tell him all. We must dispatch an embassy to your uncle in Thuringen, to see whether he may not consent to a division of the property. Take courage, and your rightful position may yet be assured."

So it was arranged that on the following day the lovers should seek Sir Bodo and ask his advice in the matter. But alas! ere their plans could be carried out Bodo himself sent for his daughter and informed her that he had chosen a husband for her, Sir Siegebert, a wealthy and noble knight, just returned from Palestine.

In vain Adeline wept and implored. Her father remained adamant, and at last lost his temper and confined her within strict bounds till she should consent to the marriage. Sir Siegebert was but ill pleased with her pale cheeks and haggard eyes and her obvious distaste for his society; and seeing this, Bodo was more than ever wroth, and swore to send her to a nunnery if she did not greet her lover with a better face.

Day after day Otto waited at the trysting-place, yet his mistress did not appear, nor did she send him any message. He was filled with anguish at the thought that her ardent vows were forgotten, and wandered through the woods like one distraught, seeking solace and finding none. At length news reached him that on the morrow his beloved was to wed with the knight Siegebert, and his last shred of hope vanished. He made his way to a bridge where he had often watched for Adeline's coming, and with a prayer flung himself into the turbid stream beneath.

Meanwhile the unceasing cruelty to which Adeline had been subjected had reduced her to a state of terrified submission, so that, scarce knowing what she did, she consented to wed Siegebert. At length all was in readiness

247

for the ceremony; the bells were ringing gaily, the feast was spread, and the bride arrayed in her wedding dress. Unseen she slipped out by a little postern gate and made her way quickly to the hut of her shepherd. Alas! it stood empty. In despair she ran hither and thither, calling his name in anguished accents. Suddenly she espied some shepherds endeavouring to draw something out of the water. A strange instinct told her the truth, and she crept closer to the little group. One glance sufficed to show her that it was her lover's corpse which was being taken ashore. No need to ask how he had perished, or why! With a wild cry she flung herself into the stream where Otto had met his death, and was speedily overwhelmed.

The bridal party sought high and low for the bride, but she was nowhere to be seen. Bodo loudly vented his indignation at his daughter's rebelliousness, but his anger was changed to mourning when the body of the drowned maiden was washed ashore a few days later. Too late he repented him of his rash folly. All his lamentations could not restore poor Adeline to life. He caused the lovers to be buried together, and spent the remainder of his days in prayer and penitence.

Frankfort

Frankfort, the castle of the Franks, was, it is said, founded by Charlemagne at the time of the overthrow of the pagan Saxons, which has already been recorded in the *Song of the Saxons*. Here Charlemagne was led across the Rhine by deer, escaping with his army from certain slaughter at the hands of the savage horde who sought to ambush him. Other picturesque stories cluster round the city, the best of which are the following.

The Poacher of Frankfort

The Poacher of Frankfort

In the city of Frankfort-on-the-Main stands a five-pointed tower, and in the midst of one of these points is a vane containing nine round holes, forming the figure 9. The origin of this figure is as follows:

A notorious poacher lay in the tower condemned to death for numerous offences against the stringent game-laws of the country. He awaited his end in silence, and sat moodily unobservant of the bright rays of the sun which poured into his cell through the grated window. Others, he pondered, were basking in the joyous light outside yonder in the verdant summer fields, whilst he, who even now felt the noose tighten round his neck, was plunged in semi-darkness. Well, as darkness was to be his element, he might as well make present use of it for its special purpose—to aid sleep; especially as sleep would remove him for the time being from gloomy contemplation upon his approaching end.

As he slept a pleasant smile took the place of the sombre expression natural to his waking moments. But on a sudden he started in his slumber, grating his teeth, his face transformed with violent rage.

"Ha, villain, that was a trap," he muttered, but almost immediately his countenance resumed the sad expression which had lately become habitual to it. In the course of a few moments, however, this gave way to a look of resolution and conscious strength, and even in sleep he appeared to have made up his mind unalterably upon some matter of importance.

At this juncture the turnkey entered the cell, accompanied by two officials, one of whom read to him a missive from those in authority which stated that a petition for mercy which he had made could not be entertained, and that he must suffer the extreme penalty of the law.

"I protest against such a sentence," cried the poacher, "for, after all, I have only killed those animals which were given us by God for our common use. Would you forfeit the life of a man because he has slain the beasts of chase?"

"That is not the only charge against you," retorted one of the officials harshly. "Your comrades, as well as the honourable Company of Foresters, accuse you of being in league with the enemy of mankind, and of procuring from him charmed bullets."

The poacher laughed. "It is false," he cried. "They are jealous because I am such a good shot. Provide me with a gun and with powder and shot blessed by a priest, and I will undertake to place through the vane of this tower nine shots which shall form the figure 9."

"Such an opportunity shall be afforded you," said one of the officials, who had not as yet spoken. "It would be an injustice not to give you such a chance, especially as, if you are successful, you will remove the most odious portion of the charge against you."

The news of the poacher's challenge spread quickly through Frankfort, and even the foresters who had given evidence against him were so impressed that they forced their way into the council and insisted that, should he be successful, a free pardon should be granted to him. To this the council agreed, and an intimation of the decision was conveyed to the poacher. But he was assured that if one bullet missed its mark he would certainly die. To this he agreed, and the succeeding day was fixed for the trial of skill. At an early hour the square in which the tower was situated was thronged by an immense

The Knave of Bergen

crowd. The walls of the city, of which the tower was a part, were thronged by members of the Foresters' Guild. Soon the prisoner was led forth, and was publicly admonished by a monk not to tempt God if his skill had its origin in diabolic agencies. But to all such exhortations the poacher replied: "Fear not, I will write my answer upon yonder tower."

The master of the Foresters' Guild loaded the gun and handed it to him. Amidst a deep silence he aimed at the vane and fired. The shot found its mark. Once more he fired. Again the vane swung round, and another hole appeared therein. The crowd vented its feelings by loud huzzahs. Nine times did he fire, and nine times did the bullet hit its mark. And as the last bullet sang through the weather-cock the figure 9 showed clearly therein, and the poacher, sinking to his knees, bared his head and gave thanks for his life to God. All there, also, bared their heads and accompanied him in his thanksgiving.

That night, loaded with gifts, he quitted Frankfort, nevermore to return. But the vane on the tower remains there to this day as a witness of his prowess with the long rifle.

The Knave of Bergen

The city of Frankfort was once the scene of a great coronation festival, during the course of which a *bal masqué* was given by the King and Queen to a brilliant assembly of high-born ladies and nobles. The knights and princes in their fancy costumes were hardly less resplendent than the ladies in their jewels and brocaded silks, and the masks they all wore added to the excitement and gaiety of the scene. In all the gathering there was but one sombre note—a knight in coal-black armour,

visored, of great stature and stately in motion. His grace-
ful mien won the admiration of the ladies and the envy of
the gallants, and the question of his identity excited much
speculation.

With courtly air the Black Knight approached the Queen,
knelt before her, and begged that she would deign to be
his partner in the dance. The charm of his voice and
the modest yet dignified manner in which he proffered his
request so touched the Queen that she stepped down from
the dais and joined in the waltz. Never had she known
a dancer with a lighter step or a more delightful gift of
conversation. When that dance was over she granted
him another and yet another, till the company became
very curious to know who the gallant knight might be on
whom the Queen bestowed her favours with such a lavish
hand. At last the time came for the guests to unmask,
and the dancers made themselves known to each other—
with one exception, that is, for the Black Knight refused
to lift his visor. The King and Queen, however, shared
to the full the curiosity of their guests as to the identity
of their strange guest, and they commanded him to uncover
his face, whereupon the knight raised his visor, though with
some reluctance. Neither the royal hosts nor any of the
noble guests recognized him, but a moment later two
officials of the Court advanced and to the astonishment
and indignation of the company declared that the stranger
was no other than the executioner of Bergen! The King's
wrath knew no bounds. He commanded that the knave
should be seized and put to death immediately. To think
that he had allowed the Queen to dance with a common
executioner! The bare idea was intolerable!

The knave fell humbly on his knees before his irate
sovereign.

Darmstadt : The Proxy

"I acknowledge my crime, sire," he said, "but your Majesty must be aware that even my death would not be sufficient to wipe out my disgrace, and the disgrace of her Majesty, who has danced with an executioner. There is one other way to efface my guilt and to wipe out the humiliation of your Majesty's gracious consort. You must make a knight of me, sire, and I will challenge to mortal combat any who dares to speak ill of my King!"

The King was astounded by this bold proposition, but the very audacity of it caught his fancy. He struck the executioner gently with his sword.

"Rise, Sir Knight," he said, adding, as the Black Knight rose to his feet: "You have acted like a knave this night. Henceforth you shall be called the Knave of Bergen."

Darmstadt: The Proxy

In the days of chivalry there dwelt in Birbach a knight named Walther, no less renowned for his piety than for his skill in arms, and the Virgin, according to the following legend, was not unmindful of her humble worshipper.

A great tournament—so runs the tale—was to take place in Darmstadt, and Sir Walther, who was about to enter the lists for the first time, was not feeling confident as to the issue. He knew that there were to be present many knights whose strength and skill far exceeded his own, and, brave though he was, he could not but recognize that his chances of victory were small. Yet he felt that he dared not suffer defeat; he must not be disgraced before the spectators. In particular, there was a certain fair lady whose colours he wore; he must not be shamed before *her*. His mind, as he rode on his way to Darmstadt, was filled with conflicting emotions, love, hope, fear, shame, in turn dominating his thoughts. Suddenly he came to a wayside altar, upon which was set an image of the Virgin, and he decided to carry his troubles to her as he was wont to do. So he descended from his horse, which he secured to a tree, and made his way to the altar.

So deep were his emotions and so ardent his prayer that he passed into a sort of trance and fell at the foot of the altar like one dead. While he lay thus unconscious the Virgin descended from the altar, unlaced his armour, and donned it herself. Then taking sword and shield and lance, she mounted his steed and rode into Darmstadt. She was absent for some time, but when she returned the knight still lay in the death-like state in which she had left him. She tied his horse once more to the tree, replaced his armour, and then took her accustomed place on the altar.

Shortly after Walther recovered consciousness and rose hastily, then, after another prayer to the Virgin, he rode as quickly as he might into the town. Here, to his intense surprise, he was greeted with joyful shouts and congratulations. His friends hailed him as a mighty champion, and she who had won his affections bestowed upon him the reward of knightly valour—her promise of marriage. The bewildered Walther scarce knew whether he was awake or asleep, but at length it was borne in upon him that someone had won great triumphs in his name. Who could have so successfully personated him as to deceive even his dearest friends? Who, indeed, save she to whom he had turned in his distress, the Holy Virgin herself?

Soon he was wedded to the lady of his choice; and to show his gratitude for the intervention of Mary he built her a magnificent chapel on the spot where the miracle had taken place. Nor did he grow any less diligent in her service, but continued to live a noble and pious life, in which he was ever encouraged and assisted by his wife.

The Cooper of Auerbach

It is said that from the ruined castle of Auerbach a fragrant perfume of wine sometimes steals upon the air, and then the country folk whisper, "The cooper is tasting his wine." And if asked for the reason of this saying they tell the following story.

Once when the sun shone golden on the vine-clad hills, deepening the heavy clusters of grapes to a darker purple, a peasant, passing by the ruins, thought longingly upon the wine that, in the past, had been stored in those dark, cool cellars, wondering if perhaps some might not yet be found there, or if all had been wasted and lost. And while he yet pondered a rubicund little man, with leathern apron dark with wine-stains girded about his portly waist, stood at his side looking up at him with twinkling eyes.

"So, my friend, you think upon the wine, eh? Come and spend an hour with me and you shall taste it." As he spoke a warm, sweet wine-scent rose like incense about him, making the peasant's brain reel with delight. He could not but follow the little man, tripping under the vines, thrusting his way through thorn-hedges and over crumbling walls, till he came to a flight of ancient steps, streaked grey and green with moss, leading down to a weather-stained cellar-door. The door opened into dusky vaults and from a niche in the wall the little cooper took a candle and a huge bowl. Then on he went over the

moist floor until there rose before them in the candle-light, darker than the gloom about it, a gigantic tun. In·
a crooning murmur the cooper began to tell of his posses-sions. He called the vaults his realm, the tuns his dearly
loved subjects—for, as the peasant gazed, he saw a long
procession of tuns stretching away into the darkness. He
shouted with mad delight at the sight, he clapped his
hands and smacked his lips in anticipation, he declared
the tuns glittered like pure gold. At this the cooper
laughed and pointed out that the wine had fashioned its
own casks, gleaming crusts, from which the ancient wood
had fallen away long ago.

And next he filled the huge bowl with deep glowing wine
and drank to the peasant, whose hands ached to hold the
bowl and lift it to his lips. At last, with a courtly bow,
the cooper put it into his hands, and then the rustic
emptied the bowl in one draught and drew a deep sigh of
satisfaction.

In rapture he sang the praises of the wine, but the cooper
assured him that there was better to come. Again he
tasted, and again the little man led on from cask to cask.
Then, mad with delight, the peasant sang aloud, but the
song broke into wild howling; he danced about the tuns,
then fell to embracing them, stroking and kissing them,
babbling love-words to the dusky fragrant wine. And
still the cooper led on to the next cask, still he filled
the bowl, and still the peasant drank, till at last in
very joy tears ran down his face, and before his eyes
the tuns danced round him in a giddy whirl; then
slumber fell upon him and he sank down to sleep in
the gloom.

When he awoke next morning his body lay stretched in a
muddy ditch, his lips pressed to clammy moss. Stumbling

The Cooper of Auerbach

to his feet, he looked around for the door of the wine vault, for the flight of steps leading down to that realm of delight, but though he searched long and carefully, yet never again could he find it, nor did his eyes see the little cooper with his wine-stained leathern apron and his rubicund face.

CHAPTER VI : WORMS AND THE NIBELUNGENLIED

WORMS is celebrated as the locality of the *Nibelungenlied* and the epic of *Walthar of Aquitaine.* But it has other claims to fame. Before entering on the consideration of Germany's greatest epic we will recount several of the lesser legends of the locality.

The Rose Garden: A Tale of Dietrich of Bern

Dietrich of Bern is the King Arthur of German story. Like his prototype of Britain, he has become the central figure of innumerable medieval tales and epics, a model of chivalry and martial prowess, distinguished everywhere by high deeds and mighty feats of arms, and in not a few cases displacing the rightful hero of still older myths, which thus became grafted on to the Dietrich legends. Originally he was a *bona-fide* historical personage, Theodoric the Ostrogoth, and as such gained a widespread popularity among his people. His historical character, however, was soon lost in the maze of legendary lore which surrounded his name, and which, as time went on, ascribed to him feats ever more wildly heroic. Among the various traditions there is one relating to the Rhenish town of Worms which calls for inclusion here as much on account of its intrinsic merit as because of its undoubted popularity. The legend of the Rose Garden of Worms is a quaint and fanciful tale, and even the circumstance that it ends with the death of several good knights and true does not rob it of a certain humorous quality it possesses.

By the time Dietrich had reached the prime of his adventurous life—so runs the story—he had gathered

The Rose Garden

a considerable company of doughty paladins at his court
—he formed, in fact, a kind of Round Table—and the
knights who composed it were as eager as their lord to
seek fresh fields wherein to display their prowess, and
were second only to him in skill and valour. Among
them were numbered such illustrious warriors as Herbrand, his son Hildebrand, Eckehart, Wolfhart, and
Amelung.

On one occasion, as Dietrich was seated at table with his
followers, he vowed that no court in Christendom could
boast of such warriors as he could muster. The assembled
knights greeted the assertion with hearty acclamations—
all, that is, save the old warrior Herbrand, and he was
silent. Dietrich looked at him in surprise.

"Hast thou nothing to say, Herbrand?" he asked.
"Thinkest thou to find better knights than these?"—
indicating his followers with a wave of his hand.

Herbrand seemed somewhat reluctant to uphold his tacit
objection to Dietrich's claim. "Ay," he said at length,
"there are such warriors to be found."

"And where may we seek such paragons?" inquired the
king, none too well pleased.

"In the town of Worms," replied the old knight, "there
lies a wondrous rose garden, of great extent, where the
queen and her ladies take their pleasure. None save
these may enter its precincts unless the queen give him
leave, and that the sacred boundaries may not be overstepped twelve warriors are set to guard the garth.
Such is their strength and courage that none has ever
succeeded in passing them, whatever his skill and
renown."

"But wherefore should one seek to pass the guard?"
asked a young knight. "Is there a prize to be won, then?"

"Truly," sighed old Herbrand, "I would not give a hair of my head for the prize. 'Tis but a crown of roses and a kiss from one of the queen's ladies; though it is said, indeed, that they are as lovely as women may be."

"Are there no fair maids in Bern?" cried the warriors indignantly. "Must we go to the Rhine for them?"

"For myself," said Dietrich, "I care little for the reward; yet methinks that for the honour and glory I would e'en meet these doughty warriors, and peradventure overcome them. Who will follow me to Burgundy?"

As with one voice his knights responded to his appeal, and he chose eight from among them to accompany him on his quest. As there were still but nine, including Dietrich himself, to meet the twelve guardians of the Rose Garden, the king decided to send for three knights who were absent from the court. At the suggestion of Hildebrand he selected Rüdiger of Bechlarn, Dietleib of Styria, and Ilsan, who was brother to Hildebrand and at that time a monk in the monastery of Munchenzell. Rüdiger was margrave to King Etzel, and had to obtain his lord's permission to venture forth on the romantic undertaking; Dietleib's father strongly recommended that the quest be abandoned, though the youth himself was as eager as any to accompany Dietrich; while as for Ilsan, he found it especially difficult to obtain leave of absence, for, naturally, his abbot deemed the enterprise a strange one for a monk who had fled all earthly delights. However, all difficulties were eventually overcome, and when the party was ready for departure Rüdiger was sent on an embassy to King Gibich at Worms, to prepare him for their coming. Gibich gave his ready consent to the proposed trial of strength, whereupon the warriors set out

The Market and Cathedral, Worms

Louis Weirter, R.B.A.

(See page 258)

Odin and Brunhilde

Ferd. Lecke

(See page 270)

for the Rhine to see whether they might not win a kiss and
a garland from some fair lady,

An imposing array did the knights of the Rose Garden
make as they awaited the approach of the strangers, but
no less imposing were Dietrich and his warriors. Each
chose an opponent and immediately engaged in a fierce
hand-to-hand struggle, which was to end disastrously for
more than one brave knight. The first to dispatch his
antagonist was Wolfhart, who submitted to being crowned
with a rose-wreath, but disdained to accept the rest of the
reward. The monk, who was the next victor, took the
roses and kissed the maiden heartily. But alas! a bristly
beard covered his chin, and the maid was left ruefully
rubbing her pouting lips. One by one Dietrich's knights
overcame their adversaries, some of whom were slain and
some wounded. Toward nightfall a truce was called, and
Dietrich and his company set out to return to Bern, well
satisfied with having disproved the assertion of Herbrand
that there were better warriors in the world than Dietrich
and his noble company.

The Devil's Vineyard

There is a curious legend told to account for the excellent
quality of the wine of Worms. An old nobleman who at
one time lived in that neighbourhood was in the habit of
drinking more of the Rhenish wine than was good for him.
In every other respect he was a most worthy man, kind,
generous, and pious.

His piety, in an age when such qualities were rare, roused
the ire of the Devil, who determined to bring about his
fall, and as the old man's love of wine was his only serious
weakness, it was through this that the Fiend set himself
to compass the nobleman's destruction.

The Devil therefore disguised himself as a strolling musician and made the acquaintance of the old man. The latter set before him some of the wine of the country, extolling meanwhile its rare qualities. The guest seemed not at all impressed by the recital, but spoke of a wine which he had tasted in the South and which far surpassed any other vintage. The nobleman was all curiosity. The stranger talked of the wonderful wine with feigned reluctance, and at length his host promised to give him anything he should ask if only he would fetch him some of the wine. Satan promised to plant a vineyard in Worms, asking in exchange the soul of his host, to be forfeited at the end of a fixed period.

To this the old man consented, and the strolling musician planted a vineyard which sprang up as though by magic. When the first vintage was produced it was found to be delicious beyond the dreams of the old nobleman, who was indeed a connoisseur in wines. In his delight he christened the wine *Liebfrauenmilch,* signifying 'Milk of our Blessed Lady.' The Devil was furious at this reference to the Holy Virgin, but he consoled himself with the thought that in due course the man's soul would be his. But the Virgin herself was pleased with the christening of the vineyard, and rather sorry for the foolish old nobleman who had bartered his soul for the Devil's wine. When, therefore, the time arrived for the Evil One to claim his fee, she sent her angels to drive him away, and thus he was robbed of his prey.

The old man, having learned the danger of treating with the Devil, now built a chapel to the Virgin in his vineyard. He lived for a long time to enjoy the luscious wine, under the protection of the saints, and never again did he make a compact with Satan.

The Maiden's Caprice

Now, if anyone requires a proof of this marvellous story, is there not the *Liebfrauenmilch*, most delicious of wines to convince him of its truth?

The Maiden's Caprice

In the town of Worms there stands an old manor, built in the style of the Renaissance and known as the Wampolder Hof. At one time it belonged to the lord of Wampold, a wealthy noble of Mainz, who had appointed as castellan a kinsman of his, himself a nobleman, though landless and poor and no longer able to uphold his former dignities. In his youth the keeper had lived a gay and careless life, but now he was old and infirm and cared no longer for worldly vanities. His sole pride was his young daughter, a bewitching maiden who had more lovers than one could readily count, and who smiled upon them all impartially. With so many lovelorn youths at her beck and call it is hardly surprising that she should grow exacting and capricious, but this, as usually happens, only made them love her the more.

There was one among her suitors, however, for whom she cherished a real affection. Handsome, cultured, and, like herself, of noble birth, he was, notwithstanding his poverty, by far the most eligible of the youths who sought her in marriage, and the castellan readily granted his consent to their betrothal. So for a time everything seemed to indicate happiness in store for the young couple.

Yet the maiden remained as capricious as ever. On Walpurgis-night, when a party of lads and lasses were gathered in the Wampolder Hof, and tales of witches and witchcraft were being told in hushed tones, she conceived a wild scheme to test her lover's affection: she bade him go to the cross-roads at midnight, watch the procession of witches, and return to tell her what he saw. The awed company protested vigorously against the proposed test, but the girl persisted, and at last her lover, seeing that she was already piqued at his refusal, laughingly set out for the bewitched spot, convinced that no harm would befall him.

Meantime the company in the manor anxiously awaited his return. One o'clock came, then two—three; still there was no sign of him. Glances of horror and pity were cast at the castellan's daughter, who now wrung her hands in futile grief. At length a few braver spirits volunteered to go in search of their comrade, but no trace of him could they find. His widowed mother, of whom he had been the only son, cursed the maid who was the cause of his ghastly fate, and not long afterward the castellan's daughter lost her reason and died. On Walpurgis-nights she may still be heard in Worms calling for her lost lover, whom she is destined never to find.

The fate of the youth remains uncertain. The most popular account is that he was torn limb from limb by the infuriated witches and his remains scattered to the winds. But some, less superstitious than their neighbours, declared that he had been murdered by his rivals, the disappointed suitors, and that his body had been cast into the Rhine—for not long afterward a corpse, which might have been that of the missing youth, was drawn from the river by fishermen.

The Nibelungenlied

The greatest Rhine story of all is that wondrous German Iliad, the *Nibelungenlied*, for it is on the banks of the Rhine in the ancient city of Worms that its action for the most part takes place. The earliest actual form of the

The Nibelungenlied

epic is referred to the first part of the thirteenth century, but it is probable that a Latin original founded on ballads or folk-songs was in use about the middle or latter end of the tenth century. The work, despite many medieval interpolations and the manifest liberties of generations of bards and minnesingers, bears the unmistakable stamp of a great antiquity. A whole literature has grown up around this mighty epic of old Germanic life, and men of vast scholarship and literary acumen have made it a veritable battle-ground of conflicting theories, one contending for its mythical genesis, another proving to his satisfaction that it is founded upon historic fact, whilst others dispute hotly as to its Germanic or Scandinavian origin.

So numerous are the conflicting opinions concerning the origin of the *Nibelungenlied* that it is extremely difficult to present to the reader a reasoned examination of the whole without entering rather deeply into philological and mythical considerations of considerable complexity. We shall therefore confine ourselves to the main points of these controversies and refrain from entering upon the more puzzling bypaths which are only to be trodden by the 'Senior Wranglers' of the study, as they have been called.

Its Original Form

In the beginning of the nineteenth century Karl Lachmann, a philologist of some repute, put forward the theory that the poem was made up of a number of distinct ballads or lays, and he eliminated from it all parts which appeared to him to be interpolations. This reduced the whole to twenty lays, which he considered the work of twenty separate minstrels; but if certain ballads relating to episodes in the *Nibelungenlied* once existed in Germany it is the spirit of these more than the matter which is incorporated into the great epic. In medieval times, when the *Nibelungenlied* story was popular, minnesingers and harpers, in an attempt to please their audiences, would cast about for fresh incidents to introduce into the story. Popular as was the tale, even a medieval audience could tire of the oft-repeated exploits of its *dramatis personae*, and the minstrel, dependent upon their goodwill for bed and board, would be quick to note when the tale fell flat. Accordingly he would attempt to infuse into it some new incident or series of incidents, culled from other stories more often than not self-created. Such an interpolation is probably to be noted in the presence of Dietrich of Bern, otherwise Theodoric the Ostrogoth, at the court of Etzel or Attila. To say nothing of the probability of anachronism, geographical conditions are not a little outraged in the adoption of this incident, but the question arose who was to worst the mighty Hagen, whose sombre figure dominates in its gloomy grandeur the latter part of the saga. It would not do for any Hunnish champion to vie successfully with the Burgundian hero, but it would be no disgrace for him to be beaten by Dietrich, the greatest champion of antiquity, who, in fact, is more than once dragged into the pages of romance for the purpose of administering an honourable defeat to a hitherto unconquered champion. We can thus see how novel and subsidiary passages might attach themselves to the epic.

But a day came when the minnesingers of Germany felt that it behoved them to fix once and for all time the shape of the Lay of the Nibelungs. Indeed, not one, but several poets laboured at this task. That they worked with materials immediately to their hand is seen from the circumstance that we have proof of a Low German account, and a Rhenish version which was evidently moulded into its present shape by an Austrian or Tyrolese craftsman— a singer well versed in court poetry and courtly etiquette. The date when the *Nibelungenlied* received its latest form was probably about the end of the twelfth century, and this last version was the immediate source of our present manuscripts. The date of the earliest known manuscript of the *Nibelungenlied* is comparatively late. We possess in all twenty-eight more or less complete manuscripts preserved in thirty-one fragments, fifteen of which date from the thirteenth and fourteenth centuries.

Its Fragmentary Nature

Even a surface examination is sufficient to testify to the fragmentary nature of the *Nibelungenlied*. We can discern through the apparent unity of texture of the work as we now possess it the patchwork where scribe or minstrel has interpolated this incident or joined together these passages to secure the necessary unity of narrative. Moreover, in none of the several versions of the Siegfried epic do we get the ' whole story.' One supplements another. And while we shall follow the *Nibelungenlied* itself as closely as possible we shall in part supplement it from other kindred sources, taking care to indicate these where we find it necessary to introduce them.

Kriemhild's Dream

In the stately town of Worms, in Burgundy, dwelt the noble and beauteous maiden Kriemhild, under the care of her mother Ute, and her brothers Gunther, Gernot, and Giselher. Great was the splendour and state which they maintained, and many and brave were the warriors who

drank wine at their board. Given to martial exercises were
those men of might, and day by day the courts of the palace
rang to the clangor of sword-play and manly sport. The
wealth of the chiefs was boundless, and no such magnificence as theirs was known in any German land, or in any
land beyond the German frontiers.

But with all this stateliness and splendour Kriemhild, the
beautiful, was unhappy. One night she had had an ominous
dream. She dreamed that she had tamed a falcon strong
and fierce, a beauteous bird of great might, but that
while she gazed on it with pride and affection two great
eagles swooped from the sky and tore it to pieces before
her very eyes. Affected by this to an extent that seemed
inexplicable, she related her dream to her mother, Ute,
a dame of great wisdom, who interpreted it as fore-
telling for her a noble husband, " whom God protect, lest
thou lose him too early." Kriemhild, in dread of the
omen, desired to avert it by remaining unwed, a course
from which her mother attempted to dissuade her, telling
her that if ever she were destined to know heartfelt joy it
would be from a husband's love.

Siegfried

Siegfried, of the Netherlands, son of Siegmund and
Sieglind, a warrior bold as he was young and comely,
having heard of the great beauty of Kriemhild, desired to
visit Worms that he might see the far-famed princess for
himself. Until this time he had been wandering through
the world doing great deeds : he had won the sword and
treasure of the Nibelungs, had overcome their monarchs,
had conquered a dwarf Alberich, gaining possession of his
cloak of darkness. Hagen, a mighty Burgundian paladin
(in a passage which is obviously adapted from another

version for the purpose of recounting Siegfried's previous adventures), tells how "he had slain a dragon and made himself invulnerable by bathing in its blood. We must receive him graciously, and avoid making him our enemy." Siegfried sojourned at Worms for over a year, distinguishing himself in all the martial exercises of the Burgundians and rendering them splendid service in their wars against the Saxons and Danes. A year passed without his having been allowed to meet Kriemhild, who in secret cherished the utmost admiration for him. Chagrined at the treatment meted out to him, he finally made up his mind to depart. But his hosts did not desire to lose such a valuable ally, and brought about a meeting between him and the lady of his dreams. The passage describing their first sight of one another is full of the essence of romance.

We are told that Kriemhild appeared before his eyes as does the rosy flush of dawn breaking from sombre clouds. As he beheld her his heart was soothed and all his trouble vanished, for there stood she who had cost him many a love-pang, her eyes sparkling with pleasure, brighter than the rich jewels which covered her raiment, her cheeks suffused with the blushes of maidenhood. No one had, he thought, ever seen so much beauty before. As the silver moon obscures the light of the stars by its superior splendour, so did Kriemhild obscure the beauty of the ladies who surrounded her. When he beheld her each hero drew himself up more proudly than ever and appeared as if ready to do battle for such a paragon of beauty. She was preceded by chamberlains in rich attire, but no ushers might keep back the knights from sight of her, and they crowded about her to catch a glimpse of her face. Pleased and sad was Siegfried, for, thought he, "How may I ever hope to win so peerless a creature? The hope is a rash one. Better were I to forget her—but then, alas, my heart would have ceased to beat, and I should be dead!" Pale and red he grew. He recked not of his own great worth. For all there agreed that so handsome a warrior had never come to the Rhineland, so fair of body, so debonair was he.

The Wooing of Brunhild

Siegfried now resolved to win Kriemhild, and on Gunther's asking him to accompany him on an adventure the purpose of which is to gain the hand of Queen Brunhild of Isenstein, he accepted on condition that on their return he should be rewarded by the hand of his sister. To this Gunther gave assent, and they set out, accompanied by Hagen and his brother Dankwart. But the *Nibelungenlied* proper is silent regarding Siegfried's previous relations with Brunhild. In Scandinavian versions—such as the *Volsunga Saga*, where this legend, originally a German one, is preserved in its pagan form—Brunhild was a Valkyr, or warmaiden of Odin, who sent her to sleep with a prick of a magic thorn and imprisoned her within a circle of flame, through which Siegfried (in this version almost certainly the god of nature, springtide, and the sun) broke, delivered the captive, and took her as his bride, soon, however, departing from her. In the *Nibelungenlied* this ancient myth is either presupposed or intentionally omitted as unfitting for consumption by a Christianized folk, but it is hinted that Brunhild had a previous claim upon Siegfried's affections.

Brunhild had made it a condition that the hero whom she would wed must be able to overcome her in three trials of prowess, losing his head as a penalty of failure. Siegfried,

The Wooing of Brunhild

donning the magic cloak of invisibility he had won from Alberich, king of the dwarfs, took Gunther's place and won the three trials for him, Gunther going through a pantomime of the appropriate actions while Siegfried performed the feats. The passage which tells of the encounter is curious. A great spear, heavy and keen, was brought forth for Brunhild's use. It was more a weapon for a hero of might than for a maiden, but, unwieldy as it was, she was able to brandish it as easily as if it had been a willow wand. Three and a half weights of iron went to the making of this mighty spear, which scarce three of her men could carry. Sore afraid was Gunther. Well did he wish him safe in the Burgundian land. "Once back in Rhineland," thought he, "and I would not stir a foot's distance to win any such war-maid."

But up spake Dankwart, Hagen's valiant brother: "Now is the day come on which we must bid farewell to our lives. An ill journey has this been, I trow, for in this land we shall perish at the hands of women. Oh, that my brother Hagen and I had but our good swords here! Then would these carles of Brunhild's check their laughter. Without arms a man can do nothing, but had I a blade in hand even Brunhild herself should die ere harm came to our dear lord."

This speech heard the warrior-maid. "Now put these heroes' swords into their hands," she commanded, "and accoutre them in their mail."

Right glad was Dankwart to feel iron in his hand once more and know its weight upon his limbs. "Now I am ready for such play as they list," he cried. "Since we have arms, our lord is not yet conquered."

Into the ring of contest mighty men bore a great stone. Twelve of them it took to carry it, so ponderous it was.

271

Woe were they of Burgundy for their lord at sight of the same.

Brunhild advanced on Gunther, brandishing her spear. Siegfried was by his side and touched him lightly to give him confidence, but Gunther knew not it was he and marvelled, for no one saw him there.

"Who hath touched me?" said he.

"'Tis I, Siegfried," replied his friend. "Be of good cheer and fear not the maiden. Give me thy shield and mark well what I say. Make thou motions as if to guard and strike, and I will do the deeds. Above all hearken to my whispered advice."

Great was Gunther's joy when he knew that Siegfried was by him. But he had not long to marvel, for Brunhild was on him, her great spear in hand, the light from its broad blade flashing in his eyes. She hurled the spear at his shield. It passed through the iron as if it had been silk and struck on the rings of Gunther's armour. Both Gunther and Siegfried staggered at the blow. But the latter, although bleeding from the mouth with the shock of the thrown weapon, seized it, reversing the point, and cast it at Brunhild with such dreadful might that when it rang on her armour she was overthrown.

Right angry was Brunhild. But she weened that the blow was Gunther's, and respected him for his strength. Her anger, however, overcame her esteem, and seizing the great stone which had been placed in the ring of combat, she cast it from her twelve fathoms. Leaping after it, she sprang farther than she had thrown it. Then went Gunther to the stone and poised it while Siegfried threw it. He cast the stone farther than Brunhild had done, and so great was his strength that he raised King Gunther from the earth and leapt with him a greater distance than Brunhild had leapt herself. Men saw Gunther throw and leap alone.

Red with anger grew Brunhild when she saw herself defeated. Loudly she addressed her men.

"Ho, ye liegemen of mine," she cried, "now are ye subject to Gunther the King, for, behold, he has beaten me in the sports."

The knights then acclaimed Gunther as the victor. By his own strength of arm had he won the games, said they, and he in turn greeted them lovingly. Brunhild came forward, took him by the hand, and granted to him full power throughout her dominions. They proceeded to her palace and Gunther's warriors were now regaled with better cheer than before. But Siegfried carefully concealed his magic cloak.

Coming to where Gunther and Brunhild sat, he said: "My lord, why do you tarry? Why are the games of which Queen Brunhild doth speak not yet begun? I long to see how they may be played." He acted his part so well that Brunhild really believed that he was not aware the games were over and that she was the loser.

"Now, Sir Siegfried," said she, "how comes it that you were not present when the games, which Gunther has won, were being played?"

Hagen, fearing that Siegfried might blunder in his reply, took the answer out of his mouth and said: "O Queen, the good knight Siegfried was hard by the ship when Gunther won the games from you. Naught indeed knew he of them."

Siegfried now expressed great surprise that any man living had been able to master the mighty war-maid. "Is it possible," he exclaimed, "is it possible, O Queen, that you have been vanquished at the sports in which you excel so greatly? But I for one am glad, since now you needs must follow us home to the Rhineland."

"You are speedy of speech, Sir Siegfried," replied Brunhild. "But there is much to do ere yet I quit my lands. First must I inform my kindred and vassals of this thing. Messengers must be sent to many of my kinsmen ere I depart from Isenstein."

With that she bade couriers ride to all quarters, bidding her kinsmen, her friends, and her warriors come without delay to Isenstein. For several days they arrived in troops: early and late they came, singly and in companies. Then with a large escort Brunhild sailed across the sea and up the Rhine to Worms.

Siegfried and Brunhild

It now became increasingly clear that Siegfried and Brunhild had had affectionate relations in the past. [Indeed, in the *Volsunga Saga*, which is an early version of the *Nibelungenlied*, we find Grimhild, the mother of Gudrun (Kriemhild), administering to Sigurd (Siegfried) a magic potion in order that he should forget about Brunhild.] On seeing Siegfried and Kriemhild greet each other with a kiss, sadness and jealousy wrung the heart of the war-maiden, and she evinced anything but a wifely spirit toward her husband Gunther, whom, on the first night of their wedded life, she wrestled with, defeated, and bound with her girdle, afterward hanging him up by it on a peg in the wall! Next day he appealed to Siegfried for assistance, and that night the hero donned his magic cloak of invisibility, contended with Brunhild in the darkness, and overcame her, she believing him to be Gunther, who was present during the strife. But

The Plot against Siegfried

Siegfried was foolish enough to carry away her ring and girdle, "for very haughtiness." These he gave to Kriemhild, and sore both of them rued it in after-time. Brunhild's strength vanished with her maidenhood and thenceforth she was as any other woman.

Siegfried and Kriemhild now departed to the capital of Santen, on the Lower Rhine, and peace prevailed for ten years, until Brunhild persuaded Gunther to invite them to a festival at Worms. She could not understand how, if Siegfried was Gunther's vassal, as Gunther had informed her, he neither paid tribute nor rendered homage. The invitation was accepted cordially enough. But Kriemhild and Brunhild quarrelled bitterly regarding a matter of precedence as to who should first enter church, and at the door of the minster of Worms there was an unseemly squabble. Then Kriemhild taunted Brunhild with the fact that Siegfried had won and deserted her, and displayed the girdle and ring as proof of what she asserted.

Siegfried, confronted with Brunhild, denied that he had ever approached her in any unseemly way, and he and Gunther attempted to make peace between their wives. But all to no avail. A deadly feud had sprung up between them, which was to end in woe for all. Hagen swore a great oath that Siegfried should pay for the insult his wife had put upon Brunhild.

The Plot against Siegfried

Now, but four days after, news came to Gunther's court that war was declared against him. But this was merely a plot to draw Siegfried from the court and compass his death. The heroes armed for war, among them Siegfried. When Hagen bade farewell to Kriemhild she recommended Siegfried to his care. Now, when Siegfried slew the dragon which guarded the treasure of the Nibelungs, he bathed in its blood and became, like Achilles, invulnerable, save at a spot where a linden leaf had fallen between his shoulders as he bathed, and so prevented contact with the potent stream. Hagen inquired of Kriemhild the whereabouts of this vulnerable spot, pretending that he would guard Siegfried against treachery in battle; and she, fully believing in his good faith, sewed a silken cross upon Siegfried's mantle to mark the place.

On the following morning Siegfried, with a thousand knights, took horse and rode away, thinking to avenge his comrades. Hagen rode beside him and carefully scanned his vesture. He did not fail to observe the mark, and having done so, he dispatched two of his men with another message. It was to the effect that the King might know that now his land would remain at peace. This Siegfried was loath to hear, for he would have done battle for his friends, and it was with difficulty that Gunther's vassals could hold him back. Then he rode to Gunther, who thanked him warmly for having so quickly granted his prayer. Gunther assured him that if need be he would at any time come to his aid, and that he held him the most trusty of all his friends. He pretended to be so glad that the threat of war was past that he suggested that they should ride hunting to the Odenwald after the bear and the boar, as they had so often done before. This was the counsel of the false Hagen.

It was arranged that they should start early for the greenwood, and Gunther promised to lend Siegfried several dogs that knew the forest ways well. Siegfried then hurried home to his wife, and when he had departed

Siegfried's Farewell to Kriemhild

Hagen and the King took counsel together. After they had agreed upon the manner in which they would compass the destruction of Siegfried, they communicated their plans to their comrades. Giselher and Gernot would not take part in the hunt, but nevertheless they abstained from warning Siegfried of his danger. For this, however, they paid dearly in the end.

The morning dawned bright and clear, and away the warriors cantered with a clatter of hoofs and a boasting of bugles.

Siegfried's Farewell to Kriemhild

Before departing Siegfried had said farewell to Kriemhild, who, she knew not why, was filled with dark forebodings.

" God grant I may see thee safe and well again," said Siegfried. " Keep thou a merry heart among thy kin until I return."

Then Kriemhild thought on the secret she had betrayed to Hagen, but she could not tell Siegfried of it. Sorely she wept, wishing that she had never been born, and keen and deep was her grief.

" Husband," she said, " go not to the hunt. A baleful dream I had last night. You stood upon the heath and two wild boars approached. You fled, but they pursued you and wounded you, and the blossoms under your feet were red with blood. You behold my tears. Siegfried, I dread treachery. Wot you not of some who cherish for us a deadly hate ? I counsel you, I beg you, dear lord, go not to the greenwood."

Siegfried tried to laugh her fears away, " It is but for a few days that I leave thee, beloved," he said. " Who can bear me hate if I cherish none against them ? Thy brothers wish me well, nor have I offended them in any wise."

But Kriemhild would not be comforted. "Greatly do I dread this parting," she wailed, "for I dreamed another dream. You passed by two mountains, and they rocked on their bases, fell, and buried you, so that I saw you no more. Go not, for bitterly will I grieve if you depart."

But with a laugh and a kiss Siegfried was gone. Leaping on his steed, he rode off at a gallop. Nevermore was she to see him in life.

Into the gloomy forest, the abode of the bear, the wolf, and the wild boar, plunged the knights in their lust of royal sport. Brilliant, brave, and goodly of cheer was the company, and rich was their entertainment. Many pack-horses laden with meats and wines accompanied them, and the panniers on the backs of these bulged with flesh, fish, and game, fitting for the table of a great king.

On a broad meadow fringing the greenwood they camped, near to the place where they were to begin the hunt, and watchers were sent round the camp, so that no one with a message of warning on his lips might win to the ears of Siegfried.

Siegfried waxed restless, for he had come not to feast but to hunt, and he desired to be home again with Kriemhild. "Ha, comrades," he cried; "who will into the forest with me and rouse the game?"

"Then," said the crafty Hagen, "let us find who is the best sportsman. Let us divide the huntsmen and the hounds so that each may ride alone where he chooses; and great praise shall be to him who hunts the best and bears off the palm."

To this Siegfried agreed, and asked only for one hound that had been well broken to the chase to accompany him.

Siegfried's Farewell to Kriemhild

This was granted. Then there came an old huntsman with a limehound and led the sportsmen to where there was an abundance of game. Many beasts were started and hunted to the death, as is ever the way with good huntsmen.

Nothing that the limehound started could escape Siegfried. Swift was his steed as the tempest, and whether it was bear or boar he soon came up with it and slew it. Once he encountered a stark and mighty lion. Aiming an arrow at the monster, he shot it through the heart. The forest rang with acclaim at the deed.

Then there fell by his hand a buffalo, an elk, four grim aurochs, and a bear, nor could deer or hind escape him, so swift and wight was he. Anon he brought a wild boar to bay. The grisly beast charged him, but, drawing his sword, Siegfried transfixed it with the shining blade.

"I pray thee, lord," said the huntsman, "leave to us something living, for in truth thy strong arm doth empty both mountain and forest."

Merrily rang the noise of the chase in the greenwood that day. The hills and the leafy aisles of the forest resounded with the shouts of the hunters and the baying of dogs. In that hunting many a beast met its death-day and great was the rivalry. But when the hunting was over and the heroes met at the tryst-fire, they saw that Siegfried had proved himself the greatest huntsmen of them all.

One by one they returned from the forest to the trysting-place, carrying with them the shaggy fell of the bear, the bristly boar-skin, and the grey pelt of the wolf. Meat abounded in that place, and the blast of a horn announced to the hungry knights that the King was about to feast. Said Siegfried's huntsman to him: "I hear the blast of a horn bidding us return to the trysting-place," and raising his bugle to his lips, he answered it.

Siegfried was about to leave the forest, ambling quietly on horseback through the green ways, when he roused a mighty bear. The limehound was slipped and the bear lumbered off, pursued by Siegfried and his men. They dashed into a ravine, and here Siegfried thought to run the beast down, but the sides were too steep and the knight could not approach it on horseback. Lightly he sprang from his steed, and the bear, seeing his approach, once more took flight. So swift, however, was Siegfried's pursuit that ere the heavy beast could elude him he had caught it by its shaggy coat and had bound it in such a manner that it was harmless; then, tying it across his horse's back, he brought it to the tryst-fire for pastime.

Proudly emerged Siegfried from the forest, and Gunther's men, seeing him coming, ran to hold his horse. When he had dismounted he dragged the bear from his horse's back and set it loose. Immediately the dogs pursued it, and in its efforts to escape into the forest it dashed madly through a band of scullions who were cooking by the great fire. There was a clatter of iron pots, and burning brands were strewed about. Many goodly dishes were spoiled. The King gave order to slip the hounds that were on leash. Taking their bows and spears, the warriors set off in chase of the bear—but they feared to shoot at it through fear of wounding any among the great pack of dogs that hung upon its flanks. The one man who could keep pace with the bear was Siegfried, who, coming up with it, pierced it with his sword and laid it dead on the ground. Then, lifting the carcass on his shoulders, he carried it back to the fire, to the marvel of all present.

The Slaying of Siegfried

Then began the feasting. Rich meats were handed around, and all was festive and gay. No suspicion had Siegfried that he was doomed, for his heart was pure of all deceit. But the wine had not yet been brought from the kitchen, whereat Sir Siegfried wondered.

Addressing Gunther, he said: "Why do not your men bring us wine? If this is the manner in which you treat good hunters, certes, I will hunt no more. Surely I have deserved better at your hands."

And the false Gunther answered: "Blame me not, Siegfried, for the fault is Hagen's. Truly he would have us perish of thirst."

"Dear master," said Hagen of Trony, "the fault is mine—if fault it be—for methought we were to hunt to-day at Spessart and thither did I send the wine. If we go thirsty to-day, credit me I will have better care another time."

But Siegfried was athirst and said: "If wine lacks, then must we have water. We should have camped nearer to the Rhine."

The Slaying of Siegfried

And Hagen, perceiving his chance, replied: "I know of a cool spring close at hand. If you will follow me I will lead you thither."

Sore athirst was Siegfried, and starting up from his seat, he followed Hagen. But the crafty schemer, desiring to draw him away from the company so that none else would follow them, said to him as they were setting out for the spring: " Men say, Siegfried, that none can keep pace with you when you run. Let us see now."

"That may easily be proved," said Siegfried. "Let us run to the brook for a wager, and see who wins there first. If I lose I will lay me before you in the grass. Nay, I

281

will more, for I will carry with me spear, shield, and hunting gear."

Then did he gird on his weapons, even to his quiver, while the others stripped, and off they set. But Siegfried easily passed them and arrived at the lime-tree where was the well. But he would not drink first for courtesy, even although he was sore athirst.

Gunther came up, bent down to the water, and drank of the pure, cool well. Siegfried then bent him to drink also. But the false Hagen, carrying his bow and sword out of reach, sprang back and gripped the hero's mighty spear. Then looked he for the secret mark on his vesture that Kriemhild had worked.

As Siegfried drank from the stream Hagen poised the great spear and plunged it between the hero's shoulders. Deeply did the blade pierce through the spot where lay the secret mark, so that the blood spurted out on the traitor's garments. Hagen left the spear deep in Siegfried's heart and flew in grim haste from the place.

Though wounded to the death, Siegfried rose from the stream like a maddened lion and cast about him for a weapon. But nothing came to his hand but his shield. This he picked up from the water's edge and ran at Hagen, who might not escape him, for, sore wounded as he was, so mightily did he smite that the shield well-nigh burst and the jewels which adorned it flew in flinders. The blow rang across the meadow as Hagen fell beneath the stroke.

It was Siegfried's last blow. His countenance was already that of a dead man. He could not stand upright. Down he crashed among the flowers; fast flowed his blood; in his agony he began to upbraid those who had contrived his death.

The Funeral of Siegfried

Hermann Hendrich

(See page 283)

Sigurd is instructed by the Birds

Ferd. Lecke

(See page 300)

The Slaying of Siegfried

"Cowards and caitiffs," he cried, "is this the price you pay me for my fealty to you? Ill have you done by your friends, for sons of yours as yet unborn will feel the weight of this deed. You have vented your spite on my body; but for this dastard crime all good knights shall shun you."

Now all surrounded him, and those that were true among them mourned for him. Gunther also wept. But the dying man, turning to him, said: "Does he weep for the evil from whom the evil cometh? Better for him that it had remained undone, for mighty is his blame."

Then said false Hagen: "What rue ye? Surely our care is past. Who will now withstand us? Right glad am I that Siegfried is no more."

Loud was Siegfried's dole for Kriemhild. "Never was so foul a murder done as thou hast done on me, O king," he said to Gunther. "I saved thy life and honour. But if thou canst show truth to any on earth, show it to my dear wife, I beg of thee, for never had woman such woe for one she loved."

Painfully he writhed as they watched him, and as he became weaker he spake prophetically.

"Greatly shall ye rue this deed in the days to come," he groaned, "for know, all of ye, that in slaying me ye have slain yourselves."

Wet were the flowers with his blood. He struggled grimly with death, but too deep had been the blow, and at last he spake no more.

They laid his body on a shield of ruddy gold and took counsel with one another how they should hide that the deed had been done by Hagen.

"Sure have we fallen on evil days," said many; "but let us all hide this thing, and hold to one tale: that is, that as Siegfried rode alone in the forest he was slain by robbers."

"But," said Hagen of Trony, "I will myself bear him back to Burgundy. It is little concern of mine if Kriemhild weep."

Kriemhild's Grief

Great was the grief of Kriemhild when she learned of the murder of her husband, whose body had been placed at her very door by the remorseless Hagen. He and the rest of the Burgundians pretended that Siegfried had been slain by bandits, but on their approach the wounds of Siegfried commenced to bleed afresh in mute witness of treachery. Kriemhild secretly vowed a terrible revenge and would not quit the land where her beloved spouse was buried. For four years she spake never a word to Gunther or Hagen, but sat silent and sad in a chamber near the minster where Siegfried was buried. Gunther sent for the Nibelungen treasure for the purpose of propitiating her, but she distributed it so freely among Gunther's dependents that Hagen conceived the suspicion that her intention was to suborn them to her cause and foment rebellion within the Burgundian dominions; therefore he seized it and sank it in the Rhine, forcing Kriemhild's brethren never to divulge its whereabouts.

It is a circumstance of some importance that when this treasure enters the land of the Burgundians they take the name of Nibelungs, as Siegfried was called Lord of the Nibelungs on first possessing the hoard, and for this reason that part of the poem which commences with the Burgundian acquirement of the treasure was formerly known as the *Nibelungen Not.*

The confiscation of the treasure was another sharp wound

Kriemhild Marries Attila

to Kriemhild, who appears to have bitterly cherished every hostile act committed against her by her uncle Hagen and her brothers, and to have secretly nursed her grievances throughout the remainder of her saddened existence.

Kriemhild Marries Attila

Thirteen years after the death of Siegfried, Helche, wife of Attila, or Etzel, King of the Huns, having died, that monarch was desirous of marrying again, and dispatched his faithful councillor, Rüdiger, Margrave of Bechlarn, to the Burgundian court to ask for the hand of Kriemhild. Her brethren, only too anxious to be rid of her accusing presence, gladly consented to the match, but Hagen had forebodings that if she gained power she would wreak a dreadful vengeance on them all. But he was overruled, and Rüdiger was permitted to interview Kriemhild. At first she would not hear of the marriage, but when Rüdiger expressed his surprise at the manner in which she was treated in her own country, and hinted that if she were to wed with Etzel she would be guarded against such insulting conduct, she consented. But first she made Rüdiger swear to avenge her wrongs, and this he did lightly, thinking it merely a woman's whim which would pass away after marriage. She accompanied Rüdiger to the court of Etzel, stopping at his castle of Bechlarn, where dwelt his wife Gotelind and his daughter Dietlinde. The journey to Vienna is described in detail. At length they met Etzel at Tulna with twenty-four kings and princes in his train and a mighty retinue, the greatest guest present being Dietrich of Bern, King of the Goths, who with his band of Wolfings was sojourning at the court of Etzel. The nuptials took place at Vienna amid great magnificence, but through all Kriemhild sorrowed only for

Hero Tales & Legends of the Rhine

Siegfried and brooded long and darkly on her schemes of vengeance.

Seven years passed, during which Kriemhild won the love of all Etzel's court. She bore the King a son, Ortlieb, and gained the confidence and respect of his advisers. Another six years passed, and Kriemhild believed that the time for vengeance had now arrived. To this end she induced Etzel to invite her brethren and Hagen to his court at Vienna. At first the Burgundians liked the hospitable message well, but suspicion of it was sown in their minds by Hagen, who guessed that treachery lurked beneath its honeyed words. In the end they accepted the invitation and journeyed to the land of the Huns, a thousand and sixty knights and nine thousand soldiers. On the way they encountered many ill omens.

The Journey

Through Eastern Frankland rode Gunther's men toward the river Main, led by Hagen, for well he knew the way. All men wondered when they saw the host, for never had any seen such lordly knights or such a rich and noble retinue. Well might one see that these were princes. On the twelfth day they came to the banks of the Danube, Hagen riding in the van. He dismounted on the river's sandy shore and tied his steed to a tree. The river was swollen with rains and no boats were in sight. Now the Nibelungs could not perceive how they were to win over the stream, for it was broad and strong.

And Hagen rebuked the King, saying: "Ill be with you, lord. See ye not that the river is swollen and its flood is mighty? Many a bold knight shall we lose here to-day."

"Not greatly do thy words help, Hagen," spake the King.

286

The Journey

"Meeter were it for thee to search for a ford, instead of wasting thy breath."

But Hagen sneered back: "I am not yet weary of life, O king, and I wish not to drown in these broad waves. Better that men should die by my sword in Etzel's land. Stay thou then by the water's edge, whilst I seek a ferryman along the stream."

To and fro he sought a ferryman. Soon he heard a splash of water and hearkened. In a spring not far off some women were bathing. Hagen spied them and crept stealthily toward them. But they saw his approach and went swiftly away. Hagen, approaching, seized their clothes.

Now these women were swan-maidens, or mermaids, and one of them, Hadburg, spake to him. "Sir Hagen," she said, "well wot I that ye wish to find a ferry. Now give to us our garments and we will show you where one is."

They breasted the waves like swans. Once more spake Hadburg: "Safely will ye go to Etzel's land and great honours will ye gain there; aye, greater than hero ever rode to find."

Right joyous was Hagen at this speech. Back he handed to the maidens their weeds.

Then spake another mermaid, Sieglind: "Take warning from me, Hagen. Believe not the word of mine aunt, for she has sore deceived thee. Go not to Etzel's land, for there you shall die. So turn again. Whoso rideth onward hath taken death by the hand."

"I heed not thy words," said Hagen, "for how should it be that all of us die there through the hate of anyone?"

"So must it be," said Sieglind, "for none of you shall live, save the King's chaplain, who alone will come again safe and sound to Gunther's land."

"Ye are wise wives," laughed Hagen bitterly. "Well would Gunther and his lords believe me should I tell him this rede. I pray thee, show us over the stream."

"So be it," replied Sieglind; "since ye will not turn you from your journey. See you yonder inn by the water's side? There is the only ferry over the river."

At once Hagen made off. But Sieglind called after him: "Stay, Sir Knight; credit me, you are too much in haste. For the lord of these lands, who is called Else, and his brother, Knight Gelfrat, will make it go hard with you an ye cross their dominions. Guard you carefully and deal wisely with the ferryman, for he is liegeman unto Gelfrat, and if he will not cross the river to you, call for him, and say thou art named Amelrich, a hero of this land who left it some time agone."

No more spake Hagen to the swan-maidens, but searching up the river banks, he found an inn upon the farther shore. Loudly he called across the flood. "Come for me, ferryman," he said, "and I will bestow upon thee an armlet of ruddy gold."

Now the ferryman was a noble and did not care for service, and those who helped him were as proud as he. They heard Hagen calling, but recked not of it. Loudly did he call across the water, which resounded to his cries. Then, his patience exhausted, he shouted:

"Come hither, for I am Amelrich, liegeman to Else, who left these lands because of a great feud." As he spake he raised his spear, on which was an armlet of bright gold, cunningly fashioned.

The haughty ferryman took an oar and rowed across, but when he arrived at the farther bank he spied not him who had cried for passage.

At last he saw Hagen, and in great anger said: "You may

The Journey

be called Amelrich, but you are not like him whom I thought to be here, for he was my brother. You have lied to me and there you may stay."

Hagen attempted to impress the ferryman by kindness, but he refused to listen to his words, telling the warrior that his lords had enemies, wherefore he never conveyed strangers across the river. Hagen then offered him gold, and so angry did the ferryman become that he struck at the Nibelung with his rudder oar, which broke over Hagen's head. But the warrior smote him so fiercely with his sword that he struck his head off and cast it on the ground. The skiff began to drift down the stream, and Hagen, wading into the water, had much ado to secure it and bring it back. With might and main he pulled, and in turning it the oar snapped in his hand. He then floated down stream, where he found his lords standing by the shore. They came down to meet him with many questionings, but Gunther, espying the blood in the skiff, knew well what fate the ferryman had met with.

Hagen then called to the footmen to lead the horses into the river that they might swim across. All the trappings and baggage were placed in the skiff, and Hagen, playing the steersman, ferried full many mighty warriors into the unknown land. First went the knights, then the men-at-arms, then followed nine thousand footmen. By no means was Hagen idle on that day.

On a sudden he espied the king's chaplain close by the chapel baggage, leaning with his hands upon the relics, and recalling that the wise women had told him that only this priest would return and none other of the Nibelungs, he seized him by the middle and cast him from the skiff into the Danube.

"Hold, Sir Hagen, hold!" cried his comrades. Giselher grew wroth; but Hagen only smiled.

Then said Sir Gernot of Burgundy: "Hagen, what availeth you the chaplain's death? Wherefore have ye slain the priest?"

But the clerk struck out boldly, for he wished to save his life. But this Hagen would not have and thrust him to the bottom. Once more he came to the surface, and this time he was carried by the force of the waves to the sandy shore. Then Hagen knew well that naught might avail against the tidings which the mermaids had told him, that not a Nibelung should return to Burgundy.

When the skiff had been unloaded of baggage and all the company had been ferried across, Hagen broke it in pieces and cast it into the flood. When asked wherefore he had done so, and how they were to return from the land of the Huns back to the Rhine, Hagen said:

"Should we have a coward on this journey who would turn his back on the Huns, when he cometh to this stream he will die a shameful death."

In passing through Bavaria the Burgundians came into collision with Gelfrat and his brother Else, and Gelfrat was slain. They were received at Bechlarn by Rüdiger, who treated them most hospitably and showered many gifts upon them, bestowing upon Gernot his favourite sword, on Gunther a noble suit of armour, and on Hagen a famous shield. He accompanied the strangers to the court of Etzel, where they were met first of all by Dietrich of Bern, who warned them that Kriemhild prayed daily for vengeance upon them for the murder of Siegfried. When Kriemhild beheld Hagen, her arch-enemy, she wept. Hagen saw, and "bound his helmet tighter."

Kriemhild's Welcome

"We have not made a good journey to this feast," he muttered.

Kriemhild's Welcome

"Ye are welcome, nobles and knights," said Kriemhild. "I greet you not for your kinship. What bring ye me from Worms beyond the Rhine that ye should be so welcome to me here? Where have ye put the Nibelung treasure? It is mine as ye know full well, and ye should have brought it me to Etzel's court."

Hagen replied that he had been ordered by his liege lords to sink it in the Rhine, and there must it lie till doomsday.

At this Kriemhild grew wroth. Hagen went on to say that he had enough to do to carry his shield and breast-plate. The Queen, alarmed, desired that all weapons should be placed in her charge, but to this Hagen demurred, and said that it was too much honour for such a bounteous princess to bear his shield and other arms to his lodging.

Kriemhild lamented, saying that they appeared to think that she planned treachery against them; but to this Dietrich answered in great anger that he had forewarned Gunther and his brothers of her treacherous intentions. Kriemhild was greatly abashed at this, and without speaking a word she left the company; but ere she went she darted furious glances upon them, from which they well saw with what a dangerous foe they had to deal.

King Etzel then asked who Hagen might be, and was told his name and lineage and that he was a fierce and grim warrior. Etzel then recognized him as a warrior who had been a hostage with him along with Walthar of Spain and who had done him yeoman service.

Events March

This last passage connects the *Nibelungenlied* with the Latin poem of *Walthar of Aquitaine*. Indeed, the great German epic contains repeated allusions to this work of the ninth or tenth century, which is dealt with later in this book. Events now march quickly. Kriemhild offered gold untold to him who would slay Hagen, but although her enemy was within her grasp, so doughty was the warrior and so terrible his appearance that none dared do battle with him. A Hun was killed by accident in a tournament, but Etzel protected his Burgundian guests. At length Blodelin was bribed by Kriemhild to attack Dankwart with a thousand followers. Dankwart's men were all slain, but he himself made good his escape by fighting his way through the closely packed Hunnish ranks. Dankwart rushed to the hall where the Burgundians were feasting with the Huns, and in great wrath acquainted Hagen with the treacherous attempt which had been made upon his life.

" Haste ye, brother Hagen," he cried, " for as ye sit there our knights and squires lie slain in their chambers."

" Who hath done this deed ? " asked Hagen.

" Sir Blodelin with his carles. But he breathes no longer, for myself I parted his head from his body."

" If he died as a warrior, then it is well for him," replied the grim Hagen ; " but, brother Dankwart, ye are red with blood."

" 'Tis but my weeds which ye see thus wet," said Dankwart carelessly. " The blood is that of other men, so many in sooth that I could not give ye tale of the number."

" Guard the door, brother," said Hagen fiercely ; " guard

it yet so that not a single Hun may escape. I will hold parley with these brave warriors who have so foully slain defenceless men."

" Well will I guard the doorway," laughed Dankwart; " I shall play ye the part of chamberlain, brother, in this great business."

The Beginning of the Slaughter

Hagen, mortally incensed at the slaughter of the Burgundians by the Huns, and wrongly suspecting Etzel of conspiracy in the affair, drew his sword, and with one blow of the weapon smote off the head of young Ortlieb, the son of Etzel and Kriemhild. Then began a slaughter grim and great. The Huns fought at first in self-defence, but as they saw their friends fall they laid on in good earnest and the combat became general. At length Dietrich of Bern, as a neutral, intervened, and succeeded in bringing about a half-truce, whereby Etzel, Kriemhild, and Rüdiger were permitted to leave the hall, the remainder of Etzel's attendants being slaughtered like sheep. In great wrath Etzel and Kriemhild offered heavy bribes to any who would slay Hagen. Several attempts were made, but without avail; and the terrible conflict continued till nightfall, when a truce was called. From his place of vantage in the hall Giselher reproached his sister with her treachery, and Kriemhild offered to spare her brothers if they would consent to give up Hagen. But this offer they contemptuously refused, holding death preferable to such dishonour. Kriemhild, in her bitter hate, set the hall on fire, and most of the Burgundians perished in the conflagration. Kriemhild and the Huns were astounded, however, when in the morning they discovered six hundred of the Burgundians

293

were still alive. The queen appealed to Rüdiger to complete the slaughter, but he, aghast at the idea of attacking friends whom he had sworn to protect, was about to refuse, when Kriemhild reminded him of his oath to her. With sorrow he proceeded to fulfil his promise, and Giselher, seeing his approach, imagined he came as an ally. But Rüdiger promptly disillusioned him. The Burgundians were as loath to attack Rüdiger as he them, and Hagen and he exchanged shields. The combat recommenced, and great was the slaughter of the Burgundians, until Gernot and Rüdiger came together and slew one another. At this, Wolfhart, Dietrich of Bern's lieutenant, led his men against the Burgundians to avenge Rüdiger's death, and Giselher and Wolfhart slew one another. Volker and Dankwart were also slain. At length all were dead save Gunther and Hagen, whom Dietrich accosted and whom he offered to save. But this offer Hagen refused. Then the Lord of Bern grew wroth.

Dietrich Intervenes

Dietrich then donned his armour and was assisted to accoutre himself by Hildebrand. He felt a heroic mood inspire him, a good sword was in his hand, and a stout shield was on his arm, and with the faithful Hildebrand he went boldly thence.

Hagen espied him coming and said: "Yonder I see Sir Dietrich. He desires to join battle with us after his great sorrow. To-day shall we see to whom must go the palm. I fear him not. Let him come on."

This speech was not unheard of Dietrich and Hildebrand, for Hagen came to where he found the hero leaning against the wall of the house. Dietrich set his shield on the ground

Dietrich Intervenes

and in woeful tones said: "O king, wherefore have ye treated me so? All my men are gone, I am bereft of all good, Knight Rüdiger the brave and true is slain. Why have ye done these things? Never should I have worked you such sorrow. Think on yourselves and on your wrongs. Do ye not grieve for the death of your good kinsmen? Ah, how I mourn the fall of Rüdiger! Whatsoever joy I have known in life that have ye slain. It is not for me to sorrow if my kin be slain."

"How so, Dietrich?" asked Hagen. "Did not your men come to this hall armed from head to heel with intent to slay us?"

Then spake Dietrich of Bern. "This is fate's work and not the doing of man," said the hero. "Gunther, thou hast fought well. Yield thee now as hostage, no shame shall it be to thee. Thou shalt find me true and faithful with thee."

"Nay, God forbid," cried Hagen; "I am still unfettered and we are only two. Would ye have me yield me after such a strife?"

"Yet would I save thy life, brave and noble Hagen," said Dietrich earnestly. "Yield thee, I beg, and I will convoy thee safe home to Rhineland."

"Nay, cease to crave this thing," replied Hagen angrily. "Such a tale shall never be told of me. I see but two of ye, ye and Hildebrand."

Hildebrand, addressing Hagen, then said that the hour would come when he would gladly accept the truce his lord offered, but Hagen in reply twitted Hildebrand with the manner in which he had fled from the hall. Dietrich interrupted them, saying that it ill beseemed heroes to scold like ancient beldams, and forbade Hildebrand to say more. Then, seeing that Hagen was grim of mood,

Dietrich snatched up his shield. A moment later Hagen's sword rang on his helm, but the Lord of Bern guarded him well against the dreadful blows. Warily did he guard him against Hagen's mighty falchion Balmung. At last he dealt Hagen a wound deep and wide. But he did not wish to slay him, desiring rather to have such a hero as hostage. Casting away his shield, in his arms he gripped Hagen of Trony, who, faint from loss of blood, was overthrown. At that Gunther began to wail greatly. Dietrich then bound Hagen and led him to where stood Kriemhild and gave him into her hand. Right merry was she at the sight and blessed Dietrich, bowing low before him, telling him that he had requited her of all her woes, and that she would serve him until death.

But Dietrich begged Hagen's life of the Queen, telling her that he would requite her of all that he had done against her. "Let him not suffer," said he, "because you see him stand there bound." But she ordered that Hagen be led away to durance.

Dietrich then went to where Gunther stood in the hall and engaged him in strife. Loudly rang the swords as the two heroes circled in fight, dealing mighty blows on each other's helm, and men there had great wonder how Sir Dietrich did not fall, so sorely angry was Gunther for the loss of Hagen. But the King's blood was seen to ooze through his armourings, and as he grew fainter Dietrich overcame him as he had done Hagen and bound him. Then was he too taken before Kriemhild, and once again the noble Dietrich begged a life from the Queen. This she gladly promised, but treachery was in her heart. Then went she to Hagen and said to him that if he would return the Nibelungs' treasure to her he might still go home safe and sound to Burgundy. The grim champion

The Death of Hagen & Kriemhild

answered that she wasted her words, and that he had sworn an oath not to show the hoard while any of his lords still lived. At that answer a terrible thought entered the mind of Kriemhild, and without the least compunction she ordered that her brother Gunther's life be taken. They struck off his head like that of a common malefactor, and by the hair she carried it to the Knight of Trony. Full sorrowfully he gazed upon it, then turning his eyes away from the haggard and distorted features, he said to Kriemhild:

"Dead is the noble King of Burgundy, and Giselher, and Gernot also. Now none knoweth of the treasure save me, and it shall ever be hid from thee, thou fiend."

The Death of Hagen and Kriemhild

Greatly wroth was Kriemhild when she heard that her stratagem had come to naught. "Full ill have ye requited me, Sir Hagen," she cried fiercely, and drawing the sword of Siegfried from its sheath, she raised it with both hands and struck off the Burgundian's head.

Amazed and sorrowful was King Etzel when he saw this. "Alas," cried he, "that such a hero should die bound and by the hands of a woman. Here lieth the best of knights that ever came to battle or bore a shield. Sorely doth this deed grieve me, however much I was his foe."

Then spake old Hildebrand, full of horror that such a thing had come to pass. "Little shall it profit her that she hath slain him so foully," he cried; "whatever hap to me, yet will I avenge bold Hagen."

With these words he rushed at Kriemhild. Loudly did she cry out, but little did that avail her, for with one great stroke Hildebrand clove her in twain. The victims of fate lay still. Sorely wept Dietrich and Etzel. So ended the high feast in death and woe. More is not to be said. Let the dead rest. Thus fell the Nibelungs, thus was accomplished the fate of their house!

The place of origin of the *Nibelungenlied* is much disputed, a number of scholars arguing for its Scandinavian genesis, but it may be said that the consensus of opinion among modern students of the epic is that it took its rise in Germany, along the banks of the Rhine, among the Frankish division of the Teutonic folk. Place-names lend colour to this assumption. Thus in the Odenwald we have a Siegfried Spring; a Brunhild Bed is situated near Frankfort; there is a Hagen Well at Lorch, and the Drachenfels, or Dragon's Rock, is on the banks of the Rhine. Singularly enough, however, if we desire a full survey of the *Nibelungenlied* story, we have to supplement it from earlier versions in use among the peoples of Scandinavia and Iceland. These are distinctly of a more simple and early form than the German versions, and it is to be assumed that they represent the original *Nibelungenlied* story, which was preserved faithfully in the North, whereas the familiarity of its theme among the Southern Teutons caused it to be altered again and again for the sake of variety, until to some extent it lost its original outline. Moreover, such poems as the Norse *Volsunga Saga* and *Thidreks Saga*, not to speak of other and lesser epics, afford many details relating to the *Nibelungenlied* which it does not contain in its present form. It may be interesting to give a summary of the *Volsunga Saga*, which is a prose paraphrase of the Edda Songs.

The Volsunga Saga

The epic deals with the history of the treasure of the Nibelungs, and tells how a certain Hreithmar had it given

The Volsunga Saga

him by the god Loki as a weregild for the slaying of the former's son, Otur or Otter, who occasionally took the shape of that animal. Loki in his turn obtained the ransom from the dwarf Andwari, who had stolen it from the river-gods of the Rhine. The dwarf, incensed at losing the treasure, pronounced a most dreadful curse upon it and its possessors, saying that it would be the death of those who should get hold of it. Thus Hreithmar, its first owner, was slain in his sleep by his son Fafnir, who carried the treasure away to the Gnita Heath, where, having taken the form of a dragon, he guarded it.

The treasure—and the curse—next passed into the keeping of Sigurd (the Norse form of Siegfried), a descendant of the race of the Volsungs, a house tracing its genealogy back to the god Woden. The full story of Sigurd's ancestry it is unnecessary to deal with here, as it has little influence on the connexion of the story of the Volsungs with the *Nibelungenlied*. Sigurd came under the tutelage of Regin, the son of Hreithmar and brother of Fafnir, received the magic steed Grani from the king, and then was requested by Regin to assist him in obtaining the treasure guarded by Fafnir. After forging a sword for himself out of the fragments of a blade left by his father Siegmund, he avenged his father's death and then set out to attack Fafnir. Meeting Woden, he was advised by the god to dig a ditch in the dragon's path. Encountering Fafnir, he slew him and the dragon's blood ran into the ditch, without which he would have been drowned by the flood of gore from the monster. As the dragon died he warned Sigurd against the treasure and its curse and against Regin, who, he said, was planning Sigurd's death.

When Regin saw that the dragon was quite dead, he crept from his hiding-place and quaffed its blood. Then, cutting out the heart, he begged Sigurd to roast it for him. In this operation Sigurd burnt his fingers and instinctively thrust them in his mouth, thus tasting of the dragon's blood, whereupon he was surprised to find that he comprehended the language of the birds. Hearkening intently to the strange, new sounds, he learned that if he himself should eat the heart, then he would be wiser than anyone in the world. The birds further betrayed Regin's evil intentions, and advised Sigurd to kill him. Seeing his danger, Sigurd went to where Regin was and cut off his head and ate Fafnir's heart. Following once again the advice of the birds, he brought the treasure from the cave and then journeyed to the mountain Hindarfjall, where he rescued the sleeping Valkyr, Brynhild or Brunhild, who had been pierced by the sleep-thorn of Woden and lay in slumber clad in full armour within a castle, surrounded by a hedge of flame. Mounting his horse Grani, Sigurd rode through the fiery obstacle to the gate of the castle. He entered it, and, finding the maiden asleep, cut the armour from her with his sword—for during her long slumber it had become very tight upon her. Brunhild hailed him with joy, for she had vowed never to marry a man who knew fear. She taught Sigurd much wisdom, and finally they pledged their troth. He then departed, after promising to remain faithful to her.

On his travels he arrived at the court of Giuki or Gibicho, a king whose domains were situated on the Lower Rhine. Three sons had he, Gunnar, Hogni, and Gutthorm, and a daughter Gudrun, a maiden of exquisite beauty. His queen bore the name of Grimhild, and was deeply versed in magical science, but was evil of nature.

The Volsunga Saga

They received Sigurd with much honour. Grimhild knew of his relations with Brunhild, and gave him a potion which produced forgetfulness of the war-maiden, so that he accepted the hand of Gudrun which Giuki offered him. The marriage was celebrated with great splendour, and Sigurd remained at Giuki's court, much acclaimed for his deeds of skill and valour.

Grimhild meanwhile urged upon her son Gunnar to sue for the hand of Brunhild. He resolved to accept her advice and set out to visit her, taking with him Sigurd and a few other friends. He first visited Brunhild's father Budli, and afterward her brother-in-law Heimir, from whom he heard that Brunhild was free to choose the man she desired, but that she would espouse no one who had not ridden through the hedge of flame. They proceeded to Brunhild's castle. Gunnar attempted to pierce the flames, but was unable to do so even when seated on Sigurd's horse, for Grani would not stir, knowing well that it was not his master who urged him on. At last they made use of a potion that had been given them by Grimhild, and Sigurd, in the shape of Gunnar, rode through the wall of fire. He explained to the war-maiden that he was the son of Giuki and had come to claim her hand. The destiny laid upon her by Woden compelled her to consent, but she did so with much reluctance. Sigurd then passed three nights at her side, placing his sword Gram between them as a bar of separation; but at parting he drew from her finger the ring with which he had originally plighted his troth to her, and replaced it with another taken from Fafnir's hoard. Shortly afterward the wedding of Gunnar and Brunhild was celebrated with lavish splendour, and they all returned to Giuki's court.

The Quarrel of Brunhild and Gudrun

Matters progressed happily for some time, until one day Brunhild and Gudrun went to bathe in the river. Brunhild refused to bathe farther down the stream than Gudrun—that is, in the water which flowed from Gudrun to her—asserting that her husband was the son of a king, while Sigurd had become a menial. Gudrun retorted to her sister-in-law that not Gunnar, but Sigurd had penetrated the hedge of fire and had taken from her the ring, which she then showed to Brunhild in proof of her words. A second and even more disturbing conversation followed, which served only to increase the hatred between the women, and Brunhild planned a dreadful vengeance. She feigned illness, retired to her bed, and when Gunnar inquired what ailed her, asked him if he recalled the circumstances of their wooing, and how Sigurd, and not he, rode through the flames to win her. So furious was she at the dreadful insult which had been placed upon her by Gudrun that she attempted to take Gunnar's life. She still loved Sigurd, and could never forgive Gunnar and his sister for robbing her of him. So terrible was her grief that she sank into a deep slumber in which she remained for seven days, no one daring to waken her. Finally Sigurd succeeded in doing so, and she lamented to him how cruelly she had been deceived; she declared that he and she had been destined for one another, and that now she had received for a husband a man who could not match with him. Sigurd begged her not to harbour a grudge against Gunnar, and told her of his mighty deeds —how that he had slain the king of the Danes, and also the brother of Budli, a great warrior—but Brunhild did not cease to lament, and planned Sigurd's death, threatening Gunnar with the loss of his dominions and his life if he would not kill Sigurd. Gunnar hesitated for a long time, but at length consented, and calling Hogni, ordered him to slay Sigurd that they might thus obtain the treasure of the Rhinegold. Hogni was aghast at this, and reminded him that they had pledged their oaths to Sigurd. Then Gunnar remembered that his brother Gutthorm had sworn no oath of loyalty to Sigurd, and so might perform the deed. They plied him with wolf and snake meat to eat, so that he might become savage by nature, and they tried to excite his greed with tales of the Rhinegold treasure. Twice did Gutthorm make the attempt as Sigurd lay in bed, but twice he was deterred from slaying him by the hero's penetrating glance. The third time, however, he found him asleep and pierced him with his sword. Sigurd awoke and hurled his own sword after Gutthorm, cutting him in two. He then died, stating that he knew Brunhild to be the instigator of the murder. Gudrun's grief was frantic, and at this Brunhild laughed aloud as if with joy; but later she became more grief-stricken than Sigurd's wife herself, and determined to be done with life. Donning her richest array, she pierced herself with a sword. As she expired she requested to be burned on Sigurd's funeral pyre, and also prophesied that Gudrun would marry Atli, and that the death of many heroes would be caused thereby.

Gudrun's Adventure

Gudrun in her great sorrow fled to the court of King Half of Denmark, at which she tarried for seven years. Her mother Grimhild learned of her place of concealment and attempted to bring about a reconciliation between her and Gunnar. She was offered much treasure if she would marry Atli, King of the Huns, and finally she consented. Atli became covetous of Gunnar's wealth—for the latter had taken possession of the Rhinegold—and invited him to his court. But Gudrun sent a message of warning to her brother. The runes which composed this, however, were so manipulated by Vingi, one of the messengers, that they read as a harmless invitation instead of a warning, and this Gunnar and Hogni determined to accept. They reached Atli's court in due season, and as they arrived Vingi disclosed his true character, stating that he had lured them into a snare. Hogni slew him, and as they rode to Atli's dwelling the Hunnish king and his sons armed themselves for battle and demanded Sigurd's treasure, which they declared belonged by right to Gudrun. Gunnar refused to part with it, and a great combat began. Gudrun armed herself and fought on the side of her brothers. A fierce battle raged with great loss on both sides, until nearly all the Nibelungs were slain, and Gunnar and Hogni, forced to yield to the power of numbers, were captured and bound.

Gunnar was now asked if he would purchase his life with the treasure, and he replied eventually that he would do so if he were given Hogni's heart. To humour his request the Huns cut out the heart of a slave and brought it to him; but Gunnar saw through the stratagem and recognized the heart as that of a coward. They then cut out Hogni's heart, and Gunnar, seeing that this was indeed the heart of a prince, was glad, for now he alone knew where the treasure of the Rhinegold was hid, and he vowed that Atli should never know of its whereabouts. In great wrath the Hunnish monarch ordered Gunnar to be thrown into a pit of snakes. His hands were bound, yet the hero from the Rhine played so exquisitely with his toes on a harp which Gudrun had sent to him that he lulled to sleep all the reptiles—with the exception of an adder, which stung him to the heart so that he died.

Atli, spurning the bodies of the fallen, turned to Gudrun, saying that she alone was to blame for what had happened. That evening she killed her two sons, Erp and Eitil, and served their flesh at the banquet which the King was giving for his warriors. When Atli asked for the boys to be brought to him, he was told that he had drunk their blood in his wine and had eaten their hearts.

That night, while he slept, Gudrun took Hogni's son Hnifling, who desired to avenge his slaughtered father, and entering Atli's chamber, the young man thrust a sword through the breast of the Hunnish king. He awoke through the pain of his wound, and was informed by Gudrun that she was his murderess. He bitterly reproached her, only to be told that she cared for no one but Sigurd. Atli's last request was that his obsequies should be such as were fitting for a king, and to ensure that he had proper funeral rites Gudrun set fire to his castle and burnt his body together with those of his dead retainers.

The further adventures of Gudrun are related in certain songs in the *Edda*, but the *Volsunga Saga* proper ends with the death of Atli.

Comparisons between the Epics

We see from this account that the *Volsunga Saga* presents in many respects an older form of the *Nibelungenlied* story. Sigurd is the same as Siegfried; Gunnar, Hogni, and Gudrun are parallels with Gunther, Hagen, and Kriemhild—although, strangely enough, that name is also borne by Gudrun's mother in the *Volsunga Saga*. We will recall that the events detailed in the first part of the lay of the Volsungs are vaguely alluded to in the *Nibelungenlied*, which assures us that the connexion we have thus drawn is a correct one.

Myth or History ?

We come now to the vexed question as to whether the *Nibelungenlied* is mythical or historical in origin. This question has been approached by certain scholars who, because of their lack of mythological knowledge, have rendered themselves ridiculous in attempting elucidations on a purely historical basis. An entirely mythological origin is not here pleaded for the *Nibelungenlied*, but it should surely be recognized, even by the historian who is without mythological training, that no story of any antiquity exists which does not contain a substantial substratum of mythical circumstance. So speedy is the crystallization of myth around the nucleus of historical fact, and so tenacious is its hold, that to disentangle it from the factors of reality is a task of the most extreme difficulty, requiring careful handling by scholars who possess a wide and accurate knowledge of mythological processes. Even to-day, when students of history have recovered from the first shock of the intrusion into their domain of the mythologist and the folklorist, so much remains to be effected in the disentanglement of what is believed to be absolute historical fact from the mythical growths which surround it that, were they conscious of the labour which yet remains in this respect, even the most advanced of our present-day historians would stand aghast at the task which awaits their successors.

In the *Nibelungenlied* we have a case in point. What the exact mythological elements contained in it represent it would indeed be difficult to say. Students of the Müllerian school have seen in Siegfried a sun-god, who awakens Brunhild, a nature goddess. This aspect is not without its likelihood, for in one passage Brunhild tells how Odin thrust into her side a thorn—evidently the sharp sting of icy winter—and how the spell rendered her unconscious until awakened by Siegfried. There are many other mythological factors in the story, and either a diurnal or seasonal myth may be indicated by it. But it would require a separate volume to set forth the arguments in favour of a partial mythological origin of the *Nibelungenlied*. One point is to be especially observed— a point which we have not so far seen noted in a controversy where it would have seemed that every special circumstance had been laboured to the full—and that is that, besides mythological matter entering into the original scheme of the *Nibelungenlied*, a very considerable mass of mythical matter has crystallized around it *since it was cast into its first form*. This will be obvious to any folklorist of experience who will take the trouble to compare the Scandinavian and German versions.

The Historical Theory

Abeling and Boer, the most recent protagonists of the historical theory, profess to see in the *Nibelungenlied* the misty and confused traditions of real events and people. Abeling admits that it contains mythical elements, but identifies Siegfried with Segeric, son of the Burgundian king Sigismund, Brunhild with the historical Brunichildis, and Hagan with a certain Hagnerius. The basis of the story, according to him, is thus a medley of Burgundian historical traditions round which certain mythological details have crystallized. The historical nucleus is the

307

overthrow of the Burgundian kingdom of Gundahar by the Huns in A.D. 436. Other events, historical in themselves, were torn from their proper epochs and grouped around this nucleus. Thus the murder of Segeric, which happened eighty-nine years later, and the murder of Attila by his Burgundian wife Ildico, are torn from their proper historical surroundings and fitted into the story. Boer, on the other hand, will not have it that there is any mythology at all in the *Nibelungenlied*, and, according to him, the nucleus of the legend is an old story of the murder of relatives. This became grafted on the Siegfried legend according to some authorities, but Boer will not admit this, and presents a number of arguments to disprove the mythical character of the Siegfried story. The reasoning is ingenious, but by no means valuable. We know that the mythologies of the ancient Germans and the Scandinavians were in many respects, though not in all, one and the same system, and we find many of the characters of the *Nibelungenlied* among the divine beings alluded to in the *Edda*. It is unlikely that the *dramatis personae* of a German murder story would find its way into even the most decadent form of Scandinavian belief. There is every reason to conclude that a great many historical elements are to be discovered in the *Nibelungenlied*, but to discount entirely those which are mythical is absurd and even more futile than it would be to deny that many of the incidents related in the great epic reflect in some measure historical events.

The Klage

The *Klage*, a sequel to the *Nibelungenlied*, recounts somewhat tamely the events which follow upon the dire catastrophe pictured in the great German epic. It is on

The Klage

the whole more modern than the *Lied*, and most critics
ascribe it to a period so late as the fourteenth century. It
is highly artificial and inartistic, and Grimm points out
that it is obvious that in penning it the author did not
have the *Nibelungenlied*, as we know it, before him. As
it is practically unknown to English-speaking readers, a
résumé of it may not be out of place here. It describes
the search among the dead bodies in the house of slaughter,
the burying of them, the journey of Etzel's "fiddler,"
Swemmelin, to the Rhine by way of Bechlarn and Passau
to give the tidings of the massacre to Queen Brunhild, his
return, and the final parting from Etzel of Dietrich and his
wife Herrat, who also take Bechlarn on their way. Level
and poor as the narrative is, it reaches pathos in the
description of the arrival of the messengers at Bechlarn.
To spare his niece (Gotelint) Dietrich tells them not to
mention the terrible events which have happened, but to
say that he and Rüdiger will soon come to see her, or at
all events himself. They are received with great rejoicing
—Gotelint and her daughter think "both to receive love
without sorrow, as often before, from beloved glances."
The young margravine has a foreboding of evil at seeing
the messengers so few—only seven. Then her mother
tells her of an evil dream which she has had, and she in
turn has to tell of another which has come to herself.
Meanwhile the messengers are at hand, and are observed
to be sad. They give to Rüdiger's wife the false tidings
of peace which they have been instructed to relate, and
the younger lady wonders that her father should have sent
no message to herself specially. The ladies continue to
question the messengers about Kriemhild: how has she
received her brother? what did she say to Hagen? what
to Gunther? How is it, asks the younger one, that

Giselher has sent her never a message? Each lying answer costs the speaker more and more sorrow, and at last his tears begin to flow. The young margravine exclaims that there must be ill news, that evil has befallen them, and that the guests and her father must be dead. As she speaks one of the messengers can contain himself no longer, and a cry breaks with blood from his mouth. All his companions burst into tears at the same time. The margravine conjures them by their troth to tell how they parted from her husband, saying that the lie must have an end. "Then spake the fiddler, Swemmelin the messenger: 'Lady, we wished to deny to you that which we yet must say, since no man could conceal it; after this hour, ye see Margrave Rüdiger no more alive.'" The margravine, we are afterward told, dies of grief at the news, as does old Queen Ute at her abbey of Lors. Brunhild survives, and is prevailed upon by her vassals to have her son crowned. Etzel, after parting with Dietrich, loses his mind; according to another version, his fate remains altogether uncertain. Dietelint, the young margravine, is taken under Dietrich's protection, who promises to find her a husband. Bishop Pilgrin has the story written out in Latin letters, "that men should deem it true." A writer, Master Konrad, then began to set it down in writing; since then it has been often set to verse in Teuton tongues; old and young know well the tale. "Of their joy and of their sorrow I now say to you no more; this lay is called *Ein Klage.*"

Walthar of Aquitaine

One of the grandest and most heroic epics of the great age of romance is that of *Walthar of Aquitaine.* It is indissolubly connected with the Rhine and with the city

Walthar of Aquitaine

of Worms because in the vicinity the hero whose feats of arms it celebrates fought his greatest battle. It was written in monkish Latin at any time between the eighth and ninth centuries, and is connected with later versions of the *Nibelungenlied,* which contains numerous allusions to it. Founded upon traditional materials collected and edited by some gifted occupant of the cloister, it opens in the grand manner by telling how the empire of the Huns had already lasted for more than a thousand years, when Attila invaded the territory of the Franks, ruled over by Gibicho. Gibicho, trembling for his throne, by the advice of his counsellors determined to pay tribute and give hostages to the terrible Hun; but as his son Gunther was too young to be sent as a hostage, he put in his place a noble youth named Hagen, and paying the invaders a great indemnity in treasure, thus secured the safety of his kingdom. The Huns then turned their attention to the Burgundians, whose king Herric had an only daughter, the beautiful Hildegund. Herric shut himself up in the town of Châlons, and calling together his ministers imparted to them his deliberations.

"Since the Franks, who are so much stronger than we, have yielded," he said, "how can we of Burgundy hope to triumph against such a host? I will give my daughter Hildegund as a hostage to the Huns. Better that one should suffer than that the realm should be laid waste." The Huns accepted Hildegund as a hostage, and with much treasure turned their faces westward to the kingdom of Aquitaine, whose king, Alphere, had an only son, Walthar, who was already affianced to Hildegund. He, too, had to give up his son as hostage and pay tribute. Although ruthless as an invader and cruel as a conqueror, Attila displayed the utmost kindness to the children. He treated them in every way as befitted their rank, and handing the girl over to the queen, had the boys trained in martial exercises and intellectual arts, till in a few years' time they easily surpassed all of the Huns in every accomplishment that becomes a knight. So greatly did Attila's queen trust the maiden, Hildegund, that she placed in her charge all the treasures Attila had won in war. Life was pleasant for the youthful hostages, but one day news came to the ear of Attila that Gibicho was dead and that Gunther was his successor. Learning this, Hagen succeeded in making his escape by night, and fearing that Walthar would follow his example, Attila's queen suggested to her husband that he should marry the youthful warrior, who had greatly distinguished himself at the head of the Huns, to a Hunnish maiden. But Walthar had no mind for such a match and declared himself unworthy of marriage, urging that if wedded he might neglect his military duties, and declaring that nothing was so sweet to him as for ever to be busy in the faithful service of his lord. Attila, never doubting him, and lulled from all suspicion by further victories won by him over a rebellious people, dismissed the matter from his mind; but on returning from his successful campaign Walthar had speech with Hildegund on the subject of their betrothal, hitherto untouched between them.

At first she thought that he merely mocked her, but he protested that he was weary of exile, was anxious to escape, and would have fled ere this but that it grieved him to leave her alone at the Hunnish court. Her reply is one characteristic of women in medieval days.

"Let my lord command," she said; " I am ready for his love to bear evil hap or good."

She then provided him, out of the treasure-chests of

312

Attila, with helm, hauberk, and breast-plate. They filled
two chests with Hunnish money in the shape of golden
rings, placed four pairs of sandals on the top and several
fish-hooks, and Walthar told Hildegund that all must be
ready in a week's time.

The Escape

On the seventh day after this Walthar gave a great feast
to Attila, his nobles, and his household. He pressed food
and wine on the Huns, and when their platters were clear
and the tables removed, he handed to the king a splendid
carven goblet, full to the brim of the richest and oldest
wine. This Attila emptied at a draught, and ordered all
his men to follow his example. Soon the wine overcame
the Huns, who, pressed by Walthar, caroused so deeply
that all were at last rendered unconscious.

Walthar gave the sign to Hildegund, and they slipped
from the hall and from the stable took his noble war-
horse Lion, so named for his courage. They hung the
treasure-chests like panniers on each flank of the charger,
and taking with them some food for the journey, set off.
Hildegund took the reins, Walthar in full armour sitting
behind her. All night they did not draw rein, and during
the day they hid in the gloomy woods. At every breath,
at the snapping of a twig, or the chirping of a bird, Hildegund trembled. They avoided the habitations of men and
skirted the mountains, where but few faces were to be seen,
and so they made good their flight.

But the Huns, roused from their drunken sleep, gazed
around stupidly and cried loudly for Walthar, their boon
companion as they thought, but nowhere was he to be
found. The queen, too, missed Hildegund and, realizing
that the pair had escaped, made loud wail through the

palace. Angry and bewildered, Attila could touch neither food nor drink. Enraged at the manner in which he had been deceived, he offered great gifts to him who would bring back Walthar in chains; but none of the Hunnish champions considered themselves fit for such a task, and at length the hue and cry ceased, and Walthar and Hildegund were left to make their way back to Aquitaine as best they could.

Full of the thought that they were being pursued, Walthar and the maiden fled onward. He killed the birds of the wood and caught fish to supply them with food. His attitude to Hildegund was one of the deepest chivalry, and he was ever mindful for her comfort. Fourteen days had passed when at last, issuing from the darkness of the forest, they beheld the silver Rhine gleaming in the sunlight and spied the towers of Worms. At length he found a ferry, but, fearing to make gossip in the vicinity, he paid the ferryman with fishes, which he had previously caught. The ferryman, as it chanced, sold the fish to the king's cook, who dressed them and placed them before his royal master. The monarch declared that there were no such fishes in France, and asked who had brought them to Worms. The ferryman was summoned, and related how he had ferried over an armed warrior, a fair maiden, and a great war-horse with two chests. Hagen, who sat at the king's table, exclaimed full joyfully:

" Now will I avow that this is none other than my comrade Walthar returning from the Hunnish land."

" Say ye so? " retorted King Gunther. " It is clear that by him the Almighty sends me back the treasure of my father Gibicho."

So ordered he a horse to be brought, and taking with him twelve of his bravest chiefs besides Hagen, who sought in vain to dissuade him, he went in search of Walthar.

The Cave

Journeying from the banks of the Rhine, Walthar and the maiden had by this time reached the forest of the Vosges. They halted at a spot where between two hills standing close together is situated a pleasant and shady cave, not hollowed out in the earth, but formed by the beetling of the rocks, a fit haunt for bandits, carpeted with green moss. But little sleep had Walthar known since his escape from the Hunland, so, spying this cool retreat, he crept inside it to rest. Putting off his heavy armour, he placed his head on Hildegund's lap, bidding her keep watch and wake him by a touch if she saw aught of danger. But the covetous Gunther had seen his tracks in the dust, and ever urging on his companions soon came near the cave where Walthar reposed. Hagen warned him of Walthar's powers as a champion, and told him that he was too great a warrior to permit himself to be despoiled easily.

Hildegund, noticing their approach, gently aroused Walthar, who put on his armour. At first she thought the approaching band were Huns pursuing them, and implored him to slay her ; but Walthar smilingly bade her be of good cheer, as he had recognized Hagen's helm. He was evidently aware, however, of the purpose for which he had been followed, and going to the mouth of the cave, he addressed the assembled warriors, telling them that no Frank should ever return to say that he had taken aught of his treasure unpunished.

Hagen advised a parley in case Walthar should be ready to give up the treasure without bloodshed, and Camillo, the prefect of Metz, was sent to him for this purpose. Camillo told him that if he would give up his charger, the two chests, and the maiden, Gunther would grant him life ; but Walthar laughed in his face.

"Go tell King Gunther," he said, "that if he will not oppose my passage I will present him with one hundred armlets of red metal."

Hagen strongly advised the king to accept the offer, for on the night before he had had an evil dream of a bear which tore off one of the king's legs in conflict, and put out one of his own eyes when he came to Gunther's aid. Gunther replied with a sneer, and Hagen, greatly humiliated, declared that he would share neither the fight nor the spoil.

"There is your foe," he said. "I will stay here and see how you fare at his hands."

Now only one warrior could attack Walthar at a time. It is needless to go into details of his several conflicts, which are varied with very considerable skill and fancy, but all of which end in his triumph. The sixth champion he had to meet was Patavrid, sister's son to Hagen, who vainly endeavoured to restrain him, but who also was worsted, and after the fall of the next warrior the Franks themselves urged Gunther to end the combat; but he, furious at his want of success, only drove them to it the more vehemently.

At last four of them made a combined attack on Walthar, but because of the narrowness of the path they could not come at him with any better success than could one single warrior, and they too were put out of the fight.

Then Gunther was left alone and, fleeing to Hagen, besought him to come to his aid. Long did Hagen resist his entreaties, but at last he was moved by

The Cave

Gunther's description of the manner in which his kinsfolk had been slain by Walthar. Hagen's advice was to lure Walthar into the open, when both should attack him, so Hagen and the king departed and selected a spot for an ambush, letting their horses go loose.

Uncertain of what had passed between Hagen and the king, Walthar decided upon remaining in the cave till the morning, so after placing bushes around the mouth of the cave to guard against a surprise, he gave thanks to heaven for his victory.

Rising from his knees, he bound together the six horses which remained, then, loosing his armour, comforted Hildegund as best he might and refreshed himself with food, after which he lay down upon his shield and requested the maiden to watch during his sleep. Although she was tired herself, Hildegund kept awake by singing in a low tone. After his first sleep Walthar rose refreshed, and bidding Hildegund rest herself, he stood leaning upon his spear, keeping guard at the cave-mouth. When morning had come he loaded four of the horses with spoils taken from the dead warriors, and placing Hildegund on the fifth, mounted the sixth himself. Then with great caution he sent forward first of all the four laden horses, then the maiden, and closed the rear with the horse bearing the two treasure-chests.

For about a mile they proceeded thus, when, looking backward, Hildegund espied two men riding down the hill toward them and called to Walthar to flee. But that he would not do, saying: " If honour falls, shame shall attend my last hour." He bade her take the reins of Lion, his good charger, which carried the gold, and seek refuge in the neighbouring wood, while he ascended the hill to await his enemies.

Gunther advanced, hurling insulting epithets at the champion, who ignored him, but turned to Hagen, appealing to their old friendship and to the recollections of the many hours of childhood they had spent together. He had thought that Hagen would have been the first to welcome him, would have compelled him to accept his hospitality, and would have escorted him peacefully to his father's kingdom. If he would break his fealty to Gunther, said Walthar, he should depart rich, his shield full of red gold. Irritated at such an offer, Hagen replied that he would not be deluded, and that for Walthar's slaying of his kinsmen he must have vengeance. So saying, he hurled his spear at Walthar, which the latter avoided. Gunther then cast a shaft which was equally harmless. Then, drawing their swords and covering themselves with their shields, the Franks sought to close with the Aquitainian, who kept them at bay with his spear. As their shorter swords could not reach past Walthar's mighty shaft, Gunther attempted to recover the spear which he had cast and which lay before the hero's feet, and told Hagen to go in front; but as he was about to pick it up from the ground Walthar perceived his device and, placing his foot upon it, flung Gunther on his knees, and would have slain him had not Hagen, rushing to his aid, managed to cover him with his shield.

The struggle continued. The hot sunshine came down, and the champions were bathed in sweat. Walthar, tired of the strife, took the offensive, and springing at Hagen, with a great stroke of his spear carried away a part of his armour. Then with a marvellous blow of his sword he smote off the king's leg as far as the thigh. He would have dispatched him with a second blow, but Hagen threw himself over Gunther's body and received

The Cave

the sword-stroke on his own head. So well tempered was his helm that the blade flew in flinders, shivered to the handle.

Instantly Walthar looked about him for another weapon, but quick as thought Hagen seized the opportunity and cut off his right hand, "fearful to peoples and princes." But, undismayed, the hero inserted the wounded stump into the shield, and drawing with his left hand a Hunnish half-sword girt to his right side, he struck at Hagen so fiercely that he bereft him of his right eye, cutting deep into the temple and lips and striking out six of his teeth. But neither might fight more: Gunther's leg, Walthar's hand, and Hagen's eye lay on the ground. They sat down on the heath and stanched with flowers the flowing stream of their blood. They called to them Hildegund, who bound up their wounds and brought them wine.

Wounded as they were, they cracked many a joke over their cups, as heroes should.

" Friend," said Hagen, "when thou huntest the stag, of whose leather mayest thou have gloves without end, I warn thee to fill thy right-hand glove with soft wool, that thou mayest deceive the game with the semblance of a hand. But what sayest thou to break the custom of thy people in carrying thy sword at thy right side and embracing thy wife with thy left arm?"

" Ha," retorted Walthar, laughing grimly, "thou wilt have to greet the troops of heroes with a side glance. When thou gettest thee home, make thee a larded broth of milk and flour, which will both nourish and cure thee." Then they placed on horseback the king, who was in sore pain. Hagen bore him back to Worms, whilst Walthar and Hildegund pursued their way to Aquitaine, and, on arrival, magnificently celebrated their wedding.

319

For thirty years did Walthar rule his people after his father's death. "What wars after this, what triumphs he ever had, behold, my blunted pen refuses to mark. Thou whosoever readest this, forgive a chirping cricket. Weigh not a yet rough voice but the age, since as yet she hath not left the nest for the air. This is the poem of Walthar. Save us, Jesus Christ."

CHAPTER VII : HEIDELBERG TO SÄCKINGEN

HEIDELBERG is known all over the world as one of Germany's great university towns, as the site of an unrivalled if ruined schloss, and of a view at the junction of the Rhine with the Neckar which is one of the most famous in the world. It lies between lofty hills covered with vineyards and forests, flanked by handsome villas and gardens, and is crowned by its castle, which has suffered equally from siege and the elements, being partially blown up by the French in 1609, and struck by lightning in 1704.

The Wolf's Spring

The name of Jette, a beautiful prophetess of the ancient goddess Herthe, is linked with the neighbourhood of Heidelberg by the following tragic tale.

When the old heathen gods and goddesses were still worshipped in the Rhine country, a certain priestess of Herthe took up her abode in an ancient grove, where she practised her occult arts so successfully that the fame of her divinations spread far and wide, and men came from all parts of Europe to learn from her what the future had in store for them. Frequently a warrior left her abode with a consuming fire kindled in his breast which would rob him of sleep for many a long night, yet none dared to declare his love to her, for, lovely though she was, there was an air of austerity, an atmosphere of mysticism about her which commanded awe and reverence, and forbade even the smallest familiarity.

One evening there came to the grove of Herthe a youth from a far distant land, seeking to know his destiny. All day he had journeyed thitherward, and the dusk had already fallen ere he reached the sacred spot. Jette sat on the glimmering altar-steps, clad in a flowing white robe, while on the altar itself burned a faint and fitful flame. The tall, slender trees, showing fantastic and ghostly in the fading light, made a fitting background for the gleaming shrine; and the elusive, unearthly beauty of the priestess was quite in keeping with the magic scene. Her mantle of austerity had fallen from her; she had forgotten that she was a prophetess; for the moment she was but a woman, full of grace and charm. The youth paused as though held by a spell.

"Fair prophetess," he said in a low voice, fearing to break in rudely upon her meditations, "wilt thou read me my fate?"

Jette, roused from her reverie, fixed her startled gaze on the handsome stranger, whose dark, burning eyes met hers in deepest admiration. Something stirred in her heart at the ardent glance, the thrilling tones, and her wonted composure deserted her.

"Youth," she faltered at length, "thou comest at a time when my prophetic skill hath failed me. Ere I tell thee thy fate I must offer sacrifice to Herthe. If thou wilt come to-morrow at this hour I will tell thee what the stars say concerning thy destiny."

It was true that her skill had deserted her under the admiring scrutiny of the young warrior, yet she delayed also because she wished to hear his voice again, to meet the ardent yet courteous glance of his dark eyes.

"I will return, O prophetess," said he, and with that he was gone.

Jette's peace of mind had gone too, it seemed, for she could think of naught but the handsome stranger.

The Wolf's Spring

On the following evening he returned, and again she delayed to give him the information he sought. He was no less rejoiced than was Jette at the prospect of another meeting.

On the third day the priestess greeted him with downcast eyes.

"I cannot read thy destiny, youth," she said; "the stars do not speak plainly. Yet methinks thy star and mine are very close together." She faltered and paused.

"Dost thou love me, Jette?" cried the young man joyfully. "Wilt thou be my bride?"

The maiden's blushing cheeks and downcast glance were sufficient answer.

"And wilt thou come with me to my tower?" pursued the youth eagerly.

Jette started back in affright.

"Nay, that I cannot," she cried. "A priestess of Herthe is doomed an she marry. If I wed thee we must meet in secret and at night."

"But I will take thee to Walhalla, and Freya shall appease Herthe with her offerings."

Jette shook her head.

"Nay," said she; "it is impossible. The vengeance of Herthe is swift—and awful. I will show thee a spring where we may meet."

She led him to a place where the stream branched off in five separate rivulets, and bade him meet her there on the following night at a certain hour. The lovers then parted, each full of impatience for the return of the hour of meeting.

Next evening, when the dusk had fallen on the sacred grove of Herthe, Jette made her way to the rendezvous. The appointed time had not yet arrived, but scarcely had she reached the spot ere she fancied she heard a step among the undergrowth, and turned with a glad smile, prepared to greet her lover. Imagine her dismay when instead of the youth a grisly wolf confronted her! Her shriek of terror was uttered in vain. A moment later the monster had sprung at her throat.

Her lover, hastening with eager steps toward the place of meeting, heard the agonized shriek and, recognizing the voice of Jette, broke into a run. He was too late! The monster wolf stood over the lifeless body of his beloved, and though in his despairing fury the youth slew the huge brute, the retribution of Herthe was complete.

Henceforth the scene of the tragedy was called the 'Wolf's Spring,' and the legend is enshrined there to this day.

The Jester of Heidelberg

Considering the wide fame of Rhenish vintages, it is perhaps not surprising that wine should enter as largely into the Rhine legends as the 'barley bree' is supposed to enter into Scottish anecdote. In truth there runs through these traditions a stream of Rhenish which plays almost as important a part in them as the Rhine itself. We are told that the Emperor Wenzel sold his crown for a quantity of wine; in the tale connected with Thann, in Alsace, mortar is mixed with wine instead of water, because of the scarcity of the latter commodity during the building of a steeple; while in the legends of " The Devil's Vineyard," and "The Cooper of Auerbach" the vintage of Rhineland provides the main interest of the plot. The following quaint little story, attaching to the castle of Heidelberg, is a 'Rhenish' tale in every sense of the word.

The Jester of Heidelberg
Hiram Ellis

(See page 324)

Strassburg Cathedral, from the old Pig Market

Louis Weirter, R.B.A.

(See page 341)

The Jester of Heidelberg

In the days when the Schloss Heidelberg was in its most flourishing state the lord of the castle numbered among his retainers a jester, small of stature and ugly of feature, whose quips and drolleries provided endless amusement for himself and his guests. Prominent among the jester's characteristics was a weakness for getting tipsy. He was possessed of an unquenchable thirst, which he never lost an opportunity of satisfying.

Knowing his peculiarity, some youthful pages in the train of the nobleman were minded to have some amusement at his expense, and they therefore led him to a cellar in which stood a large vat filled with fragrant wine. And there for a time they left him.

The jester was delighted at the propinquity of his favourite beverage and decided that he would always remain in the cellar, regaling himself with the vintage. His thirst increased at the prospect, so he produced a gimlet, bored a hole in the vat, and drank and drank till at length he could drink no more; then the fumes of the wine overcame him and he sank down in a drunken stupor. Meanwhile the merry little stream flowed from the vat, covered the floor of the cellar, and rose ever higher.

The pages waited at the top of the stairs, listening for the bursts of merriment which were the usual accompaniments of the jester's drinking bouts; but all was silent as the grave. At last they grew uneasy and crept below in a huddled group. The fool lay quite still, submerged beneath the flood.

He had been drowned in the wine.

The joke now seemed a sorry one, but the pages consoled themselves with the thought that, after all, death had come to the jester in a welcome guise.

The Passing Bells

There is a legend connected with the town of Speyer in which poetic justice is meted out to the principal characters, although not until after they have died.

The tale concerns itself with the fate of the unfortunate monarch Henry IV. History relates that Henry was entirely unfit to wear the ermine, but weak as he was, and ignominious as was his reign, it was a bitter blow that his own son was foremost among his enemies. At first the younger Henry conspired against his father in secret; outwardly he was a model of filial affection, so that he readily prevailed upon the weak monarch to appoint him as his successor. After that, however, he openly joined himself to his father's foes; and when the Pope excommunicated the monarch, gradually the Emperor's following went over to the side of his son, who then caused himself to be invested with imperial honours. The deposed sovereign, deprived of power and supporters, was compelled to go into exile; even his personal freedom was secured only as the price of his renunciation of the crown. Broken and humiliated, feeling intensely the disgrace of his position, he determined to undertake a pilgrimage to Liége, accompanied only by his servant Kurt, who alone of all his train had remained faithful to him. The pilgrimage was successfully accomplished, but ere he could enter upon the return journey the wretched Emperor died, in want and misery, utterly neglected by his kindred. Even after death the Pope's ban was effective, so that his corpse was not allowed interment for several years. During that period the faithful Kurt kept guard unceasingly over his master's coffin and would not suffer himself to be drawn therefrom.

The Passing Bells

At length, however, Henry V, under pressure from his princes and nobles, gave orders that his father's remains be conveyed to Speyer and there interred in the royal vault with such honours as befitted the obsequies of a monarch. The messengers found old Kurt still holding his vigil beside the Emperor's body, and in recognition of his faithfulness he was permitted to follow the funeral *cortège* to Speyer. There were in the town certain good and pious folk who were touched by the servant's devotion, and by these he was kindly treated. But all their kindness and attention could not repair the havoc which his weary vigil and long privations had wrought on his health, and a few months later he followed his master to the grave.

Strange to relate, as he expired all the bells of Speyer tolled out a funeral peal such as was accorded to an emperor, and that without being touched by human hands. Meanwhile Henry V also lay dying. All the luxury of his palace could not soothe his last moments ; though he was surrounded by courtiers who assumed sorrow and walked softly, and though all his kindred were around him, he saw ever before him the image of his dead father, pointing at him with a grim, accusing finger. Stricken with terror and remorse, and tortured by disease, he longed for death to end his torments, and at last it came.

Again the passing bell was tolled by invisible hands, but not this time the peal which announced the passing of an emperor. The citizens heard the awful sound which told that a criminal had paid the law's last penalty, and asked one another what poor wretch had been executed. Awe and astonishment seized upon everyone when it was known that the Emperor had died, for they knew then that it was no earthly hand that had rung his death-knell.

Legends of Windeck

Concerning the neighbourhood of Windeck, some eight miles from Baden, several interesting tales are current. The castle itself has long enjoyed the reputation of being haunted by the ghost of a beautiful girl, though when or wherefore this originated tradition does not relate. We are told that a young huntsman, whom the chase had driven thitherward, saw the spectre and was so stricken with her charms that day after day he visited the castle, hoping to see her once more. But being disappointed, he at length took up his solitary abode in the deserted fortress, renouncing his former pursuits and ceasing from all communication with his friends.

One day he was found dead in his bed with so peaceful an expression of countenance that those who saw him could not doubt that his end had been a pleasant one. On his finger was a ring of quaint design which he had not been known to wear, and it was whispered among the peasantry that the ghost-maid of Windeck had claimed her lover.

The Hennegraben

Hard by the Schloss Windeck lay a deep trench, known as the Hennegraben, of which traces may still be found. It is rendered immortal by reason of the following romantic legend, which tells of its magical origin.

A certain young knight, lord of the castle of Windeck, for some unknown reason had seized and imprisoned the worthy Dean of Strassburg. It is true that the Churchman was treated with every consideration, more like a guest than a captive, but he nevertheless resented strongly the loss of his liberty, as did also the good folk of Strassburg when they learned what had happened.

328

The Hennegraben

Two of the Dean's young kinsfolk resolved to journey to Windeck and beg that their uncle might be set free. On their way thither they had to pass through a forest, where they met an old woman.

"Whither away, my pretty boys?" said she. "Will you not tell an old gossip your destination?"

The elder of the two replied courteously that they were on their way to Windeck, where their uncle was imprisoned. "Perchance," he added timidly, "the lord may accept us as hostages till the ransom be paid."

"Perchance," mimicked the old woman, "aye, perchance! Think you the knight of Windeck will take such lads as you are for hostages?"

And in truth they were not an imposing couple—the elder a slim, fragile youth, whose eyes were already tearful at the prospect of confronting his uncle's captor; while the younger was a mere boy, sanguine and adventuresome as children often are.

"I will challenge this knight," said the boy seriously. "I will draw sword for my uncle, for I also am a knight."

"Hush, Cuno," said his brother, smiling in spite of himself at the boy's ardour. "We must not talk of fighting. We must entreat the knight to let our uncle go free."

"What would you have, Imma? Entreat? Nay, that we shall not."

He stopped awkwardly, and his sister's rising colour showed plainly her embarrassment at having her sex thus suddenly revealed.

The old woman looked at her kindly.

"I knew from the first that thou wert a maid disguised," she said. "Go, and God speed you! Tell the knight of Windeck that the people of Strassburg mean to attack his castle on the morrow, and that his only means of resisting them is to dig a deep trench across the one possible approach. But stay—there is no time for that; I will give you something wherewith to dig the trench."

She whistled shrilly and in answer to her call a grey hen fluttered toward her; this she gave to the young people. "When the moon rises," she said, "take the hen and place it where you wish the trench to be."

Then with a few words to the hen in a strange tongue, she bade the brother and sister farewell and went on her way.

The two continued their journey and upon arriving at Windeck they were agreeably surprised in the lord of the castle, for he was young and handsome and very courteous, not at all the ogre they had imagined. In faltering tones Imma told him their mission, conveyed to him the old witch's warning, and presented the grey hen.

When he heard that they proposed to gain their uncle's freedom by themselves taking his place, the knight regarded his visitors with mingled feelings of pity and astonishment. The gentle, appealing glance of the elder, no less than the naïve candour of the younger, appealed to his sympathies. In a very short time Cuno, who had quite forgotten to challenge his host, was on the best of terms with him.

Meanwhile the Dean, very impatient and incensed, paced his small chamber like a caged lion, or bemoaned his lost liberty and meditated on the chances of escape. He was roused from a reverie by the sound of familiar voices outside his cell, and a moment later the door was flung open and Cuno entered unceremoniously.

"You are free, uncle, you are free! Imma and I have come to save you!"

The Klingelkapelle

Once more Imma flushed crimson at the revelation of her sex. The astonished knight glanced with a new interest at her beautiful face, with its rosy colour and downcast eyes. Turning to the Dean, he greeted him cordially.

"You are free," he said. "Your nephews have promised to remain with me as hostages till you have provided a ransom." Then, turning humorously to Imma, he added: "Wilt thou be a soldier in my employ, youth? Or wouldst have a place in my household?"

Imma vouchsafed no other reply than a deepening of her colour. She must, however, have found words to utter when, later, the gallant knight begged her seriously to remain at Windeck as his wife—for ere nightfall the old Dean, grumbling and somewhat reluctant, was called upon to consent to his niece's betrothal. This he did at length, when Imma had joined her entreaties to those of her lover.

That night the grey hen was placed as the witch had advised, and it was as she had said. With the dawn the Strassburgers arrived before the castle, to find a newly made trench filled with the castle troopers. When they learned that the Dean was free they called for a truce, and it was not blood, but wine, which flowed that day, for all were invited to share the wedding-feast of Imma and the knight of Windeck.

The Klingelkapelle

On the road between Gernsbach and Eberstein there once stood an ancient, moss-grown cell. It had been occupied by a beautiful pagan priestess, a devotee of Herthe, but when the preaching of the white monks had begun to spread Christianity among the people she left the neigh-

331

bourhood. In passing by that way a Christian monk noticed the deserted retreat and took possession of it, issuing at intervals to preach to the inhabitants of the surrounding country.

One stormy night as he sat within his cell he fancied he heard a pleading voice mingling with the roar of wind and waters. Going to the door, he beheld a young girl who seemed to be half dead with cold and fatigue. The good monk, who was never indifferent to human suffering, drew her quickly inside, bade her seat herself by the fire, and set food and wine before her. When she had recovered a little from the effects of the storm the hermit questioned her with regard to her presence in such a lonely spot and at such an unseasonable hour. The maid replied that she had once dwelt in just such a pleasant and peaceful cell as that in which she now reposed, but that cruel persecution had driven her from her retreat.

"Then you, too, are a hermit?" said the young monk inquiringly, looking down at his fair guest. The wine had brought some colour to her pale cheeks and he could see that she was beautiful, with a beauty beyond that of any maiden he had ever seen.

"Yes," she replied, "I am a priestess of Herthe. This cell in which I beg for shelter was once my own. It was those of your religion who drove me from it."

"You are not a Christian?" asked the monk, startled in spite of himself by the passionate tones in which she spoke.

The maiden laughed.

"Am I not as beautiful as your Christian maids?" said she. "Am I not human even as they are?" She moved about the cell as she spoke, and picked up a piece of embroidery. "See, this is my handiwork; is it less beautiful because it is not the work of a Christian? Why should we suffer persecution at your hands?"

The young monk endeavoured to show that she was unjust in her estimate of his religion. Gravely he told her the story of Christianity, but his thoughts were of her weird beauty and he spake less earnestly than was usual. And the maid, with an appearance of child-like innocence, waited until he had finished his recital. She saw that she had him completely in her power and pressed her advantage to the uttermost. She drew closer to him, raised his hand, and pressed it to her lips. The monk surrendered himself to her caresses, and when at length she begged him to break the symbol of his religion he was too much fascinated to refuse. He raised the cross and would have dashed it to the ground, but at that very moment he heard high above the storm the sound of a bell. Contrite and ashamed, he fell on his knees and prayed for pardon. When he looked up again the girl had disappeared.

The hermit found the warning bell suspended on a bough outside his cell; how it came there he never knew, but he was sure that it had been sent to rescue him from the wiles of Satan and he treasured it as a sacred relic. Many came from far and near to see the wonder, and on the site of the cell the monk founded a chapel which became known as the *Klingelkapelle*, or 'Tinkling-chapel.'

The Water-Nymph of Staufenberg

A charming story is linked with the castle of Staufenberg. One day while its owner was out hunting he lost his way in the forest. The day was hot, and the hunter was well-nigh overcome with thirst and fatigue when he entered a pleasant glade in which a spring of limpid water bubbled and sparkled. Having quenched his thirst, he seated himself on a mossy bank to rest before proceeding homeward. Suddenly he saw at a little distance a damsel of unique and marvellous beauty, braiding her wet hair by the side of the spring. He watched her for a time in silence, then, conscious that the damsel had observed his scrutiny, he hastened to her side and courteously begged her permission to remain a little longer in the glade.

"You are the lord of these domains," she replied graciously. "It is I who am grateful to you for suffering me to dwell here."

The young knight protested eagerly that she honoured the forest with her presence, and, indeed, he had already begun to wish that she might dwell not only in the forest but in the schloss itself as his wife and its mistress—for he had fallen in love with her at first sight. Indeed, so ardent was his passion that he could not conceal his infatuation; he told her of his love and begged that she would give him a little hope. The maid's hesitation only drove him to urge his suit with increasing ardour.

"I will say neither 'yes' nor 'no,'" she replied, smiling. "Meet me to-morrow at this hour and you shall have your answer."

The knight parted reluctantly from the fair lady and promised to return on the following day. When the appointed time arrived he was already at the tryst, eagerly awaiting the approach of his beloved. When at length she came he renewed his pleadings with even greater ardour, and to his unbounded delight the answer was favourable.

"I am a water-nymph," said the lady, "the spirit of the stream from which you drank yesterday. You saw me then for the first time, but I have often seen you in the forest—and I have long loved you."

334

The Water-Nymph of Staufenberg

The knight was more than ever enchanted by this naïve confession, and begged that their wedding should not be long delayed.

"There is one condition," said the nymph. "If you marry me you must remain for ever faithful. Otherwise you must suffer death, and I eternal unhappiness."

The knight laughed at the bare idea of his proving unfaithful to his beloved, and his vows were sincere.

Shortly afterward they were married, and none supposed the beautiful being to be aught but a very attractive woman; in time there was born to them a little son. The knight adored both wife and child, and for some years lived a life of ideal domestic happiness. But there came a time when another interest entered into his life. Rumours of fighting reached him from France; he saw the knights of neighbouring fortresses leading their troops to the war, and a martial spirit stirred within him. His wife was not slow to observe that his world was no longer bounded by the castle-walls of Staufenberg, and she wisely resolved not to stand in the way of her lord's ambitions, but rather, if possible, to help them to an honourable realization. So with much labour and skill she made him a strangely wrought belt, which she gave him at once as a love-token and a charm to secure success in battle. She concealed her grief at his departure and bade him farewell bravely.

At the head of his troop the knight rode boldly into France and offered his services to a distinguished French leader, to whom he soon became indispensable—so much so, in fact, that the nobleman cast about for a means of retaining permanently in his train a knight of such skill and courage. But he could think of nothing with which to tempt the young man, who was already possessed of gold and lands, till the artless glances of his youngest daughter

gave him his cue. For he saw that she had lately begun
to look with some favour on the simple knight of Staufenberg, and it occurred to him that the hand of a lady of
rank and beauty would be a very desirable bait.

Nor was he mistaken, for the gaieties of the Frankish
court had dazzled the knight, and the offer of the lady's
hand completely turned his head; not that he felt a great
affection for her, but because of the honour done to him.
So he accepted the offer and drowned, as best as he could,
the remembrance of his wife and child at Staufenberg.
Nevertheless he sometimes felt that he was not acting
honourably, and at length the struggle between his love for
his wife and his pride and ambition became so severe that
he determined to consult a priest.

The good man crossed himself when he heard the story.
"She whom you married is an evil spirit," said he.
"Beneficent spirits do not wed human beings. It is your
duty to renounce her at once and do penance for your sin."
Though he hardly found it possible to believe the priest's
assertion, the knight strove to persuade himself that it was
true, and that he was really acting virtuously in renouncing
the water-nymph and marrying again. So he performed
the penances prescribed by the priest, and allowed the
wedding preparations to proceed.

When the day of his wedding arrived, however, he was
strangely perturbed and pale. The rejoicings of the
people, the gay processions, even the beautiful bride,
seemed to have no interest for him. When the hand of
the lady was placed in his he could not repress an
exclamation; it was cold to the touch like the hand of a
corpse.

On returning the wedding procession was obliged to cross
a bridge, and as they approached it a great storm arose

so that the waters of the stream washed over the feet of the bridegroom's horse, making it prance and rear. The knight was stricken with deadly terror, for he knew that the doom of which the water-nymph had spoken was about to overtake him. Without a word he plunged into the torrent and was nevermore seen.

At the very hour of this tragedy a great storm raged round the castle of Staufenberg, and when it abated the mother and child had disappeared for ever. Yet even now on a stormy night she can still be heard among the tree-tops weeping passionately, and the sound is accompanied by the whimpering of a child.

Trifels and Richard Cœur-de-Lion

As a troop of horsemen rode through Annweiler toward the castle of Trifels, in which Richard Cœur-de-Lion was imprisoned by the Archduke of Austria, his deadly enemy, the plaintive notes of a familiar lay fell on their ears. The singer was a young shepherd, and one of the knights, a troubadour, asked him to repeat his ditty. The youth complied, and the knight accompanied him as he sang, their voices blending tunefully together.

Giving him generous largess, the knight asked the minstrel who had taught him that song. The shepherd replied that he had heard it sung in the castle of Trifels. At this intelligence the stranger appeared highly gratified, and, turning to his companions, ejaculated: "The King is found!"

It was evident to the shepherd that the new-comers were friends of Richard, and he warned them earnestly that danger lay before them. Only by guile could they hope to succour their King. The warning was heeded, and the tuneful knight rode forward alone, disguised in a minstrel's tunic, in which he was welcomed at the castle. His courtly bearing soon won him the favour of the castellan's pretty niece, who persuaded her uncle to listen to his songs. During one of their stolen interviews the girl betrayed the place where the King of England was imprisoned, and that night, from beneath a window, the minstrel heard his King's well-remembered voice breathing a prayer for freedom. His hopes being thus confirmed, he took his harp and played the melody which he himself had composed for Richard. The King immediately joined in the familiar lay. When its strains had ended, "Blondel!" cried the captive excitedly. The minstrel cautiously replied by singing another song, telling how he was pledged to liberate his master.

But suspicion was aroused, and Blondel was requested to depart on the following day. Deeming it prudent to make no demur, he mounted his horse, after having arranged with the castellan's niece to return secretly at nightfall. He rode no further than an inn near Annweiler, which commanded a view of the castle. There his host informed him that the Emperor was presently to be crowned at Frankfort, and that on the evening of that day the garrison would celebrate the event by drinking his health.

The minstrel said that he would certainly join the company, ordered wine for the occasion, and promised to pay the reckoning. He then withdrew to seek his comrades. At dusk he returned stealthily to the castle, and at his signal the maid appeared at a little postern and admitted him.

On the day of the Emperor's coronation stealthy forms crept among the trees near by the castle, and concealed themselves in the thick foliage of the underbrush. The garrison, gaily dressed, quitted the keep, the drawbridge was lowered, and the men were soon quaffing the choice wine which the stranger had ordered.

Meanwhile Blondel had appeared before the postern and had given his accustomed signal; for a time there was no response, and the minstrel was becoming impatient, when the gate was suddenly opened and the maiden appeared.

The minstrel now told the girl his reason for coming hither: how he hoped to liberate the captive monarch. As a reward for her connivance he promised to take her with him to England. Then he beckoned to his friends, there was a sudden rush, and armed forms thronged the postern. The frightened maid, dreading lest violence should overtake her uncle, shrieked loudly; but her cries were unheeded, and the English knights pressed into the courtyard.

The assailants met with little resistance, seized the keys, threw open the prison door, and liberated their King. The castellan protested loudly, and threatened Richard with mighty words, but all to no purpose. When the garrison returned they were powerless to render aid, for the castellan was threatened with death should his followers attack the castle. In the end a truce was made, and the English were allowed to retire unmolested with their King. Although urged by him, the maid refused to accompany Blondel, so, giving her a gold ring as a memento, he parted from her.

Returning again many years afterward, the minstrel once more heard the same song which the King had sung to his harp in the castle of Trifels. Entering the inn, he recognized in the landlord the one-time shepherd-boy. From him he learnt that the castellan had perished by an unknown hand, and that his pretty niece, having, as she thought, plumbed the depths of masculine deceit, had entered the nunnery of Eberstein at Baden.

Thann in Alsace

Thann is known to legend by two things: a steeple and a field. The steeple was built in a season of great drought. Water had failed everywhere; there was only the thinnest trickle from the springs and fountains with which the people might allay their thirst. Yet, strangely, the vine-yards had yielded a wonderful harvest of luscious grapes, and the wine was so abundant that the supply of casks and vessels was insufficient for the demand. Therefore did it happen that the mortar used for building the steeple was mixed with wine, wherefore the lime was changed to must. And it is said that even to this day, when the vines are in blossom, a delicate fragrance steals from the old steeple and on the stones a purple dew is seen, while some declare that there is a deeper tone in the harmony of the bells.

The Lying-field

The field is a terrible place, barren and desolate, for it is avoided as a spot accursed. No living thing moves upon it; the earth is streaked with patches of dark moss and drifts of ghastly skulls, like a scattered harvest of death. Once, says the legend, a wayfarer, surprised by the swift-fallen night, lost himself on the plain. As he stumbled in the darkness he heard the clocks of the town near by strike the hour of midnight. At this the stillness about the wanderer was broken. Under his feet the earth seemed to tremble, there was a rattling of weapons, and there sounded the tramp of armed men and the tumult of battle.

340

Strassburg

Suddenly the shape of a man in armour appeared before him, terrific and menacing.

"What do you seek here, in a field that has been accursed through many centuries?" he asked. "Do you not know that this is a place of terror and death? Are you a stranger that you stand on the place where a king, Louis the Pious, betrayed by his own sons, was handed over to his enemies, his crown torn from his head by his own troops? And he who would have died gladly in battle suffered the shame and dishonour that were worse than death. He lifted up his hands to heaven and cried with bitterness: 'There is no such thing on earth as faith and loyalty. Accursed be sons and warriors, accursed be this field whereon such deeds have been done, accursed be they for ever!'"

The spectre paused and his words echoed across the field like the cry of a lost soul. Again he spoke to the trembling wanderer: "And that curse has endured through the centuries. Under this plain in mile-wide graves we faithless warriors lie, our bones knowing no repose; and never will that curse of our betrayed king be lifted from us or this place!"

The spectral warrior sank into the gloomy earth, the tumult of fighting died away. The wayfarer, seized with terror, stumbled blindly on in the night.

Strassburg

Strassburg, the capital of Alsace-Lorraine, is only two miles west of the Rhine. The city is of considerable antiquity, and boasts a cathedral of great beauty, in which the work of four centuries is displayed to wonderful advantage. By the light of the stained-glass windows the famous astronomical clock in the south transept can be descried,

341

still containing some fragments of the horologe constructed by the mathematician Conrad Dasypodius in 1574. This, however, does not tally with the well-known legend of the clock, which now follows.

The Clockmaker of Strassburg

There dwelt in the town of Strassburg an old clockmaker. So wrapped up was he in his art that he seemed to live in a world of his own, quite indifferent to the customs and practices of ordinary life; he forgot his meals, forgot his sleep, cared nothing for his clothes, and would have been in evil case indeed had not his daughter Guta tended him with filial affection. In his absent-minded fashion he was really very fond of Guta, fonder even than he was of his clocks, and that is saying not a little.

The neighbours, busy, energetic folk who performed their daily tasks and drank wine with their friends, scoffed at the dreamy, unpractical old fellow and derided his occupation as the idle pastime of a mind not too well balanced. But the clockmaker, finding in his workroom all that he needed of excitement, of joy and sorrow, of elation and despondency, did not miss the pleasures of social life, nor did he heed the idle gossip of which he was the subject.

It need hardly be said that such a man had but few acquaintances; yet a few he had, and among them one who is worthy of especial note—a wealthy citizen who aspired to a position of civic honour in Strassburg. In appearance he was lean, old, and ugly, with hatchet-shaped face and cunning, malevolent eyes; and when he pressed his hateful attentions on the fair Guta she turned from him in disgust.

One day this creature called on the clockmaker, announced

The Clockmaker of Strassburg

that he had been made a magistrate, and demanded the hand of Guta, hinting that it would go ill with the master should he refuse.

The clockmaker was taken completely by surprise, but he offered his congratulations and called the girl to speak for herself as to her hand. When Guta heard the proposal she cast indignant glances at the ancient magistrate, whereupon he, without giving her an opportunity to speak, said quickly:

"Do not answer me now, sweet maid; do not decide hastily, I beg of you, for such a course might bring lasting trouble on you and your father. I will return to-morrow for your answer."

When he was gone Guta flung herself into her father's arms and declared that she could never marry the aged swain.

"My dear," said the clockmaker soothingly, "you shall do as you please. Heed not his threats, for when I have finished my great work we shall be as rich and powerful as he."

On the following day the magistrate called again, looking very important and self-satisfied, and never doubting but that the answer would be favourable. But when Guta told him plainly that she would not marry him his rage was unbounded, and he left the house vowing vengeance on father and daughter.

Scarcely was he gone ere a handsome youth entered the room and looked with some surprise at the disturbed appearance of Guta and her father. When he heard the story he was most indignant; later, when the clockmaker had left the young people alone, Guta confessed that the attentions of the magistrate were loathsome to her, and burst into tears.

The young man had long loved the maiden in secret, and he could conceal his passion no longer. He begged that she would become his bride, and Guta willingly consented, but suggested that they should not mention the matter to her father till the latter had completed his great clock, which he fondly believed was soon to bring him fame and fortune. She also proposed that her lover should offer to become her father's partner—for he, too, was a clockmaker—so that in the event of the master's great work proving a failure his business should still be secure. The young man at once acted upon the suggestion, and the father gratefully received the proffered assistance.

At last the day came when the clockmaker joyfully announced that his masterpiece was finished, and he called upon Guta and his young partner to witness his handiwork. They beheld a wonderful clock, of exquisite workmanship, and so constructed that the striking of the hour automatically set in motion several small figures. The young people were not slow to express their admiration and their confidence that fame was assured.

When the clock was publicly exhibited the scepticism of the citizens was changed to respect; praise and flattery flowed from the lips that had formerly reviled its inventor. Nevertheless the civic authorities, urged thereto by Guta's discarded lover, refused to countenance any attempt to procure the wonderful clock for the town. But soon its fame spread abroad to other cities. Members of the clockmakers' guild of Basel travelled to see it, and raised their hands in surprise and admiration. Finally the municipal authorities of Basel made arrangements to purchase it.

But at this point the citizens of Strassburg stepped in and

The Clockmaker of Strassburg

insisted on preserving the clock in their own city, and it was therefore purchased for a round sum and erected in a chapel of the Strassburg Cathedral. The corporation of Basel, having set their hearts on the wonderful time-piece, commissioned the clockmaker to make another like it, and offered substantial remuneration. The old man gladly agreed, but his arch-enemy, hearing of the arrangement and scenting a fine opportunity for revenge, contrived to raise an outcry against the proposal. "Where was the advantage," asked the magistrates, "in possessing a wonderful clock if every city in Germany was to have one?" So to preserve the uniqueness of their treasure they haled the old clockmaker before a tribunal and ordered him to cease practising his art. This he indignantly refused to do, and the council, still instigated by his enemy, finally decided that his eyes be put out, so that his skill in clockmaking should come to a decided end. Not a few objections were raised to so cruel a decision, but these were at length overruled. The victim heard the dreadful sentence without a tremor, and when asked if he had any boon to crave ere it were carried out, he answered quietly that he would like to make a few final improvements in his clock, and wished to suffer his punishment in its presence.

Accordingly when the day came the old man was conducted to the place where his masterpiece stood. There, under pretence of making the promised improvements, he damaged the works, after which he submitted himself to his torturers. Hardly had they carried out their cruel task when, to the consternation of the onlookers, the clock began to emit discordant sounds and to whirr loudly. When it had continued thus for a while the gong struck thirteen and the mechanism came to a standstill.

"Behold my handiwork!" cried the blind clockmaker. "Behold my revenge!"

His assistant approached and led him gently away. Henceforward he lived happily with Guta and her husband, whose affectionate care compensated in part for the loss of his eyesight and his enforced inability to practise his beloved art.

When the story became known the base magistrate was deprived of his wealth and his office and forced to quit the town.

And as for the clock, it remained in its disordered state till 1843, when it was once more restored to its original condition.

The Trumpeter of Säckingen

A beautiful and romantic tale which has inspired more than one work of art is the legend of the Trumpeter of Säckingen; it shares with "The Lorelei" and a few other legends the distinction of being the most widely popular in Rhenish folklore.

One evening in early spring, so the legend runs, a gallant young soldier emerged from the Black Forest opposite Säckingen and reined in his steed on the banks of the Rhine. Night was at hand, and the snow lay thickly on the ground. For a few moments the wayfarer pondered whither he should turn for food and shelter, for his steed and the trumpet he carried under his cavalry cloak were all he possessed in the world; then with a reckless gesture he seized the trumpet and sounded some lively notes which echoed merrily over the snow.

The parish priest, toiling painfully up the hill, heard the martial sound, and soon encountered the soldier, who saluted him gravely. The priest paused to return the

The Trumpeter of Säckingen

greeting, and entering into conversation with the horseman, he learned that he was a soldier of fortune, whereupon he invited him with simple cordiality to become his guest. The proffer of hospitality was gratefully accepted, and the kindly old man led the stranger to his home.

The old priest, though not a little curious with regard to his guest's previous history, forbore out of courtesy to question him, but the warmth and cheer soon loosened the trumpeter's tongue, and he volunteered to tell the old man his story. Shorn of detail, it ran as follows:

The soldier's youth had been passed at the University of Heidelberg, where he had lived a gay and careless life, paying so little attention to his studies that at the end of his course his only asset was a knowledge of music, picked up from a drunken trumpeter in exchange for the wherewithal to satisfy his thirst. The legal profession, which his guardian had designed for him, was clearly impossible with such meagre acquirements, so he had joined a cavalry regiment and fought in the Thirty Years' War. At the end of the war his horse and his trumpet were his sole possessions, and from that time he had wandered through the world, gaining a scanty livelihood with the aid of his music. Such was his history.

That night Werner—for so the young man was called—slept soundly in the house of the old priest, and next morning he rose early to attend the festival of St. Fridolin, in celebration of which a procession was organized every year at Säckingen. There, at the head of a band of girls, he beheld a maid who outshone them all in beauty and grace, and to her he immediately lost his heart. From that moment the gaieties of the festival had no attraction for him, and he wandered disconsolately among the merrymakers, thinking only of the lovely face that had caught his fancy.

Toward nightfall he embarked in a little boat and floated idly down the Rhine. Suddenly, to his amazement, there arose from the water the handsome, youthful figure of the Rhine-god, who had recognized in his pale cheek and haggard eye the infallible signs of a lover. Indicating a castle at the edge of the river, the apparition informed Werner that his lady-love dwelt therein, and he bade him take heart and seek some mode of communicating with her. At this Werner plucked up courage to row ashore to his lady's abode. There in the garden, beneath a lighted window, he played an exquisite serenade, every perfect note of which told of his love and grief and the wild hopes he would never dare to express in words.

Now, the lord of the castle was at that very moment telling to his beautiful daughter the story of his own long-past wooing; he paused in his tale and bade his daughter listen to the melting strains. When the notes had died away an attendant was dispatched to learn who the musician might be, but ere he reached the garden Werner had re-embarked and was lost to sight on the river. However, on the following day the nobleman pursued his inquiries in the village and the musician was discovered in an inn.

In obedience to a summons the trumpeter hastened to the castle, where the old lord greeted him very kindly, giving him a place with his musicians, and appointing him music-master to the fair Margaretha. Henceforward his path lay in pleasant places, for the young people were thrown a great deal into each other's society, and in time it became evident that the lady returned the young soldier's tender passion. Yet Werner did not dare to declare his

The Trumpeter of Säckingen

love, for Margaretha was a maiden of high degree, and he but a poor musician who not so very long ago had been a homeless wanderer.

One day Werner heard strange, discordant sounds issuing from the music-room, and thinking that some mischievous page was taking liberties with his trumpet, he quietly made his way to the spot, to find that the inharmonious sounds resulted from the vain attempt of his fair pupil to play the instrument. When the girl observed that her endeavours had been overheard, she joined her merriment with that of her teacher, and Werner then and there taught her a bugle-call.

A few weeks later the nobleman, hearing of a rising of the peasants, hastened to Säckingen to restore order, leaving his daughter and Werner to guard the castle. That night an attempt was made upon the stronghold. Werner courageously kept the foe at bay, but was wounded in the *mêlée*, and Margaretha, seeing her lover fall and being unable to reach him, took the trumpet and sounded the bugle-call he had taught her, hoping that her father would hear it and hasten his return. And, sure enough, that was what happened; the nobleman returned with all speed to the assistance of the little garrison, and the remnant of the assailants were routed. Werner, who was happily not wounded seriously, now received every attention.

Her lover's peril had taught Margaretha beyond a doubt where her affections lay, and she showed such unfeigned delight at his recovery that he forgot the difference in their rank and told her of his love. There on the terrace they plighted their troth, and vowed to remain true to each other, whatever might befall. Werner now ventured to seek the nobleman that he might acquaint him of the circumstances and beg for his daughter's hand, but ere he could prefer his request the old man proceeded to tell him that he had but just received a letter from an old friend desiring that his son should marry Margaretha. As the young man was of noble birth, he added, and eligible in every respect he was disposed to agree to the arrangement, and he desired Werner to write to him and invite him to Säckingen. The unfortunate soldier now made his belated announcement; but the old man shook his head and declared that only a nobleman should wed with his daughter. It is true he was greatly attached to the young musician, but his ideas were those of his times, and so Werner was obliged to quit his service and fare once more into the wide world.

Years passed by, and Margaretha, who had resolutely discouraged the advances of her high-born lover, grew so pale and woebegone that her father in despair sent her to Italy. When in Rome she went one Sunday with her maid to St. Peter's Church, and there, leading the Papal choir, was her lover! Margaretha promptly fainted, and Werner, who had recognized his beloved, was only able with difficulty to perform the remainder of his choral duties. Meanwhile the Pope had observed that the young man was deeply affected, and believing this to be caused by the lady's indisposition, he desired that the couple should be brought before him at the conclusion of the service. With kindly questioning he elicited the whole story, and was so touched by the romance that he immediately created Werner Marquis of Santo Campo and arranged that the marriage of the young people should take place at once. Immediately after the ceremony, having received the Papal blessing, they returned to Säckingen, where the father of the bride greeted them cordially, for Margaretha was restored to health and happiness, and his own condition was satisfied, for had she not brought home a noble husband?

The Charcoal-Burner

In the woods of Zähringen there dwelt a young charcoal-burner. His parents before him had followed the same humble calling, and one might have supposed that the youth would be well satisfied to emulate their simple industry and contentment. But in truth it was not so. On one occasion, while on an errand to the town, he had witnessed a tournament, and the brilliant spectacle of beauty and chivalry had lingered in his memory and fired his boyish enthusiasm, so that thenceforth he was possessed by 'divine discontent.' The romance of the ancient forests wherein he dwelt fostered his strange longings, and in fancy he already saw himself a knight, fighting in the wars, jousting in the lists, receiving, perchance, the prize of the tourney from the fair hands of its queen. And, indeed, in all save birth and station he was well fitted for the profession of arms—handsome, brave, spirited, and withal gentle and courteous.

Time passed, and his ambitions seemed as far as ever from realization. Yet the ambitious mind lacks not fuel for its fires; the youth's imagination peopled the woody solitudes with braver company than courts could boast—vivid, unreal dream-people, whose shadowy presence increased his longing for the actuality. The very winds whispered mysteriously of coming triumphs, and as he listened his unrest grew greater. At length there came a time when dreams no longer satisfied him, and he pondered how he might attain his desires.

" I will go out into the world," he said to himself," and take service under some great knight. Then, peradventure——"

At this point his musings were interrupted by the approach of an old man, clad in the garb of a hermit.

"My son," he said, "what aileth thee? Nay"—as the youth looked up in astonishment—"nay, answer me not, for I know what thou wouldst have. Yet must thou not forsake thy lowly occupation; that which thou dost seek will only come to thee whilst thou art engaged thereon. Follow me, and I will show thee the spot where thy destiny will meet thee."

The young man, not yet recovered from his surprise, followed his aged guide to a distant part of the forest. Then the hermit bade him farewell and left him to ponder on the cryptic saying: "Here thy destiny will meet thee."

"Time will show the old man's meaning, I suppose," he said to himself; "in any case, I may as well burn charcoal here as elsewhere."

He set to work, hewed down some great trees, and built a kiln, which, before lighting, he covered with stony earth. What was his amazement when, on removing the cover of the kiln in due course, he discovered within some pieces of pure gold! A moment's reflection convinced him that the precious metal must have been melted out of the stones, so he again built a kiln, and experienced the same gratifying result. Delighted with his good fortune, he concealed his treasure in an appropriate hiding-place and proceeded to repeat the process till he had obtained and hidden a large fortune, of whose existence none but himself was aware.

One night, as he lay awake listening to the wind in the trees—for his great wealth had this drawback, that it robbed him of his sleep—he fancied he heard a knock at the door. At first he thought he must have been mistaken, but as he hesitated whether to rise or not the knock was repeated. Boldly he undid the door—a feat requiring no small courage in that remote part of the forest, where robbers and freebooters abounded—and there, without, stood a poor wayfarer, who humbly begged admittance. He was being pursued, he declared ; would the charcoal-burner shelter him for a few days? Touched by the suppliant's plight, and moved by feelings worthy of his chivalrous ideals, the youth readily extended the hospitality of his poor home, and for some time the stranger sojourned there in peace. He did not offer to reveal his identity, nor was he questioned on that point. But one morning he declared his intention of taking his departure. "My friend," he said warmly, "I know not how I may thank you for your brave loyalty. The time has come when you must know whom you have served so faithfully. Behold your unfortunate Emperor, overcome in battle, deprived of friends and followers and fortune!"

At these astounding words the young charcoal-burner sank on his knees before the Emperor.

"Sire," he said, "you have yet one humble subject who will never forsake you while life remains to him."

"I know," replied the Emperor gently, raising him to his feet, "and therefore I ask of you one last service. It is that you may lead me by some secret path to the place where the remnant of my followers await me. Alas, that I, once so powerful, should be unable to offer you any token of a sovereign's gratitude!"

"Sire," ventured the youth, "methinks I may be privileged to render yet one more service to your Majesty." Straightway he told the story of his hidden treasure and with simple dignity placed it at the disposal of his sovereign, asking for nothing in return but the right to spend his strength in the Emperor's service—a right which was readily accorded him.

The gold, now withdrawn from its place of concealment, proved to be a goodly store, and with it the Emperor had no difficulty in raising another army. Such was the courage and confidence of his new troops that the first battle they fought resulted in victory. But the most valiant stand was made by the erstwhile charcoal-burner, who found on that field the opportunity of which he had long dreamt. The Emperor showed his recognition of the gallant services by knighting the young man on the field of battle. On the eminence whither the old hermit had led him the knight built a castle which was occupied by himself and his successors for many generations.

And thus did the charcoal-burner become the knight of Zähringen, the friend of his Emperor, the first of a long line of illustrious knights, honoured and exalted beyond his wildest dreams.

Conclusion

With this legend we close on a brighter and more hopeful note than is usually associated with legends of the Rhine. The reader may have observed in perusing these romances how closely they mirror their several environments. For the most part those which are gay and buoyant in spirit have for the places of their birth slopes where is prisoned the sunshine which later sparkles in the wine-cup and inspires song and cheerfulness. Those, again, which are sombre and tragic have as background the gloomy forest, the dark and windy promontory which overhangs the darker river, or the secluded nunnery. In such surroundings is fostered the germ of tragedy, that feeling of the inevitable which is inherent in all great literature. It

Conclusion

is to a tragic imagination of a lofty type that we are
indebted for the greatest of these legends, and he who
cannot appreciate their background of gloomy grandeur
will never come at the true spirit of that mighty literature
of Germany, at once the joy and the despair of all who
know it.

Countless songs, warlike and tender, sad and passionate,
have been penned on the river whose deathless tales we
have been privileged to display to the reader.   But no
such strains of regret upon abandoning its shores have
been sung as those which passed the lips of the English
poet, Byron, and it is fitting that this book should end
with lines so appropriate :

> Adieu to thee, fair Rhine! How long delighted
> The stranger fain would linger on his way!
> Thine is a scene alike where souls united
> Or lonely Contemplation thus might stray ;
> And could the ceaseless vultures cease to prey
> On self-condemning bosoms, it were here,
> Where Nature, nor too sombre nor too gay,
> Wild but not rude, awful yet not austere,
> Is to the mellow Earth as Autumn to the year.

> Adieu to thee again ! a vain adieu !
> There can be no farewell to scene like thine ;
> The mind is colour'd by thy every hue ;
> And if reluctantly the eyes resign
> Their cherish'd gaze upon thee, lovely Rhine !
> 'Tis with the thankful heart of parting praise ;
> More mighty spots may rise, more glaring shine,
> But none unite in one attaching maze
> The brilliant, fair, and soft,—the glories of old days.

> The negligently grand, the fruitful bloom
> Of coming ripeness, the white city's sheen,
> The rolling stream, the precipice's gloom,
> The forest's growth, and Gothic walls between,
> The wild rocks shaped as they had turrets been,
> In mockery of man's art: and there withal
> A race of faces happy as the scene,
> Whose fertile bounties here extend to all,
> Still springing o'er thy banks, though Empires near them fall.

355

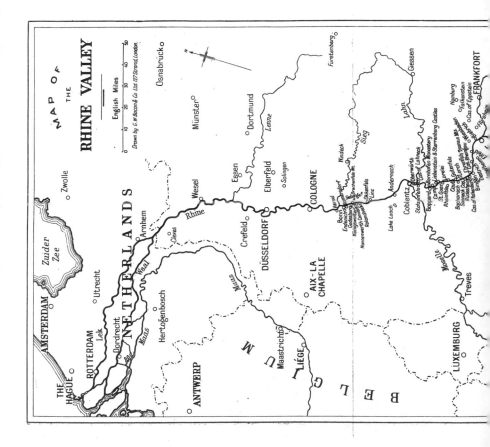

MAP OF
THE
RHINE VALLEY

English Miles
0 10 20 30 40 50

Drawn by G.W.Bacon & Co. Ltd 127 Strand, London.

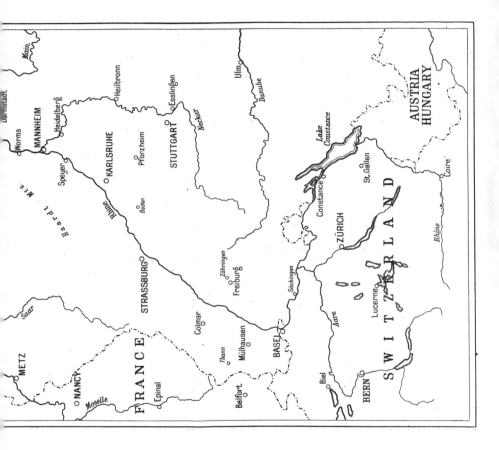

GLOSSARY & INDEX

A

AAR. Tributary of the Rhine, 6

ABELING, T. And the historical theory of the origin of the *Nibelungenlied*, 307

ABRAHAM. A Jew; in the legend of the Treasure-seeker, 137

ACRE. The city, in Syria, 171

ADALBERT. Lord of Ehrenfels; in a legend of Bishop Hatto, 209–211

ADELINE. Daughter of Sir Bodo of Flörsheim; in the legend of the Shepherd Knight, 244–248

ADOLF. Duke of Holland; a claimant to the German throne after the death of Conrad IV, 181

ADUCHT, SIR. A knight of Cologne; in the legend of the White Horses, 118–120

AEGIDIUS. A Roman general; elected King of the Franks, 25–26

AGATHE. A maiden; in a legend of Aix-la-Chapelle, 128–129

AGRIPPUS. A German prince; in the legend of St. Ursula, 75–77

AIX - LA - CHAPELLE. The city; Charlemagne's tomb at, 29, 40; Charlemagne's affection for, 40; legends of, 127–133; Charlemagne's capital, 127; the legend of the Cathedral of, 129–133; mentioned, 176

ALBERICH. In the *Nibelungenlied*, a dwarf; vanquished by Siegfried, 268, 271

ALBERTUS MAGNUS. A famous magician; in the legend of the Magic Banquet, 120–121

ALCHEMIST, THE. A legend of Stolzenfels, 164–168

ALCHEMY. A common pursuit in the Middle Ages, 164; in a legend of Stolzenfels, 164–168

ALEMANNI. Early inhabitants of the Rhine-country, 15, 23, 24; conflicts with the Romans, 23

ALFONSO X. King of Castile; a claimant to the German throne after the death of Conrad IV, 181

ALPHERE. In *Walthar of Aquitaine*, King of Aquitaine; yields to Attila, 311

ALSACE. The province; Germany cedes, under the Peace of Westphalia, 51

ALSACE-LORRAINE. The province; restored to Germany, 51–52

ALTA VILLA. Roman station which afterward became the town of Elfeld, 225

ALTAR OF BACCHUS. A stone in the Rhine near Bacharach; a superstition connected with, 89

ALTDÖRFER, ALBRECHT. Painter; the gruesome element in his work, 105

AMELRICH. A hero; in the *Nibelungenlied*, Hagen pretends to be, 288–289

AMELUNG. A knight at the court of Dietrich of Bern, 259

AMINA. Daughter of a robber-baron; in a legend of Fürstenberg, 189–192

ANDERNACH. The town; claimed as the home of the Merovingians, 25; Childeric before, 26; a legend of the castle of, 82–84; Sigebert has his court at, 174

ANDWARI. In the *Volsunga Saga*, a dwarf from whom Loki obtained the treasure of the Nibelungs, 299

ANNWEILER. The town, 337, 338

AQUITAINE. The province; in *Walthar of Aquitaine*, Attila invades, 311; Walthar reaches, and rules over, 319–320

AQUITAINE, WALTHAR OF. See *Walthar of Aquitaine*

ARCHBISHOP OF COLOGNE. At the trial of the maiden Lorelei, 62–63

ARCHBISHOP'S LION, THE. A legend of Cologne, 115–118

ARCHITECT OF COLOGNE CATHEDRAL, THE. The legend, 78, 104–108

ARGENFELS. The castle of; a legend of, 87–88

ARMINIUS. Teutonic chieftain; defeats the Romans under Q. Varus, 21–22

359

Hero Tales & Legends of the Rhine

Hero Tales & Legends of the Rhine

associated with Ingelheim, 218–
225; said to have founded the
city of Frankfort-on-the-Main,
248

CHARLEMAGNE THE ROBBER. A
legend of Ingelheim, 218–225

CHARLES THE BALD. Emperor of
the Romans, 41

CHARLES THE FAT. Emperor of
the Romans, 41

CHATTI. Germanic tribe; in the
Frankish confederacy, 23

CHAUCI. Germanic tribe; in the
Frankish confederacy, 23

CHERUSCI. Germanic tribe, 21;
in the Frankish confederacy, 23

CHEVALIER AU CYGNE, LE. A
French version of the Lohengrin
legend, 92

CHILDERIC I. King of the Franks,
son of Merovig, 25; his vision
of the fall of the Merovingians,
26–27

CHILPERIC I. King of the Franks,
24–25

CHRISTIANITY. A legend of, 331–
333

CLEVES. The castle of; in the
Lohengrin legend, Elsa of Brabant imprisoned in, 92–93

CLOCKMAKER OF STRASSBURG, THE.
The legend of, 342–346

CLODIO. Reputed father of Merovig,
25

CLOVIS I. King of the Franks,
28

COBLENTZ. The city; the junction
of the Rhine and Aar at, 6; the
island and nunnery of Oberwörth near, 158, 159; Charlemagne at, 176

COIRE. The town; the Nearer
and Farther Rhine unite near, 5

COLOGNE. 1. The city, 7, 20, 29; the
Heinzelmännchen associated with,
74–75; in the legend of St. Ursula,
76–77; the legend of the Architect of the cathedral of, 104–
108; legends explaining why
the building of the cathedral was
never completed, 108–112; the
legend of the Fire-bell of, 112–
114; becomes a free city, 115;
the legend of the Archbishop's
Lion, 115–118; the legend of
the White Horses, 118–120; the
legend of the Magic Banquet,

120–122; the legend of Truenfels, 122–125; a tourney at,
in the legend of Gutenfels, 179–
180, 182. 2. Bishop of; in the
legend of Truenfels, 122–123.
3. Archbishop of; in the legend
of Gutenfels, 179

COMAN, PRINCE. Husband of St.
Ursula, 76–77

COMPANY OF FORESTERS, THE. A
guild; in a legend of Frankfort,
250

CONFEDERATION OF THE RHINE.
A League of Rhenish cities;
German princes join and re-
pudiate their allegiance to the
Empire, 51

CONFERENCE OF THE DEAD, THE.
A legend of Biberich, 239–242

CONGRESS OF VIENNA. Conference
of Great Powers; Rhenish territory restored to Prussia as a result
of, 51

CONRAD. 1. A son of Kurt; in the
legend of Liebenstein and Sterrenberg, 172–174. 2. Brother of the
Emperor Ludwig; imprisoned in
the castle of Ehrenfels, 209

CONRAD I. King of Germany, 41

CONRAD III. King of Germany,
85

CONRAD IV. King of Germany;
dispute as to the succession to,
181

CONSTANCE. 1. Lake, 6, 163.
2. The town, 6

CONSTANTINE. Roman Emperor;
the vision of, occurred at Mainz,
227–228

CONSTANTINOPLE. The city, 173

COOPER OF AUERBACH, THE. The
legend of, 73, 255–257, 324

CORNWALL, EARL OF. See Richard

COUNT PALATINE. Ruler of the
Palatinate, 42–43

CRANACH, LUCAS. The painter; the
gruesome element in his work,
105

CRESCENTIUS. One of the first
apostles of Christianity on the
Rhine, and first Archbishop of
Mainz; martyred at Mainz, 227

CRUSADE, THIRD, 168

CRUSADER, THE. In Rhenish
legend, 79

CRUSADERS, 213, 215

CUNO. Nephew of the Dean of

362

Glossary & Index

FERDINAND III. Emperor of the Romans, 50

FERRYMAN, THE. In the *Nibelungenlied*, 288–289

FIDDLER, THE. A legend of Mainz Cathedral, 228–230

FIELD OF THE HOLY CROSS. The place in the vicinity of Mainz where Constantine's vision is supposed to have occurred, 228

FIRE-BELL OF COLOGNE CATHEDRAL, THE. The legend of, 112–114

FLÖRSHEIM. A village near Mainz; Kunigunda von—see Kunigunda; Sir Bodo of, in the legend of the Shepherd Knight, 244–248

FOLKLORE. The comparatively small element of, in the Rhine legends, 59, 78

FRANCE. In the Thirty Years' War, 50–51; extends her boundaries to the Rhine, 51; loses her Rhine provinces as a result of the war of 1870–71, 51–52

FRANCO - PRUSSIAN WAR. Of 1870–71; France forfeits her Rhenish territory as a consequence of, 51–52

FRANCONIA. The province, 28, 48

FRANKENSTEIN. The castle of, 40

FRANKFORT - ON- THE - MAIN. The city; said to have been founded by Charlemagne, 248; the legend of the Poacher of, 249–251; the legend of the Knave of Bergen, 251–253; the Brunhild Bed near, 298; mentioned, 338

FRANKLAND. The country of the Franks; in the *Nibelungenlied*, Gunther and Hagen journey through Eastern, 286; in *Walthar of Aquitaine*, Attila invades, 11

FRANKS. Early inhabitants of the Rhine country, 23, 24; the *Nibelungenlied* probably had its origin among, 298; in *Walthar of Aquitaine*, 311

FREDEGONDA. Queen of the Frankish king Chilperic, 25; her feud with her sister-in-law of Austrasia, 28

FREDERICK. Younger son of Count Louis III; in a story of Heidelberg Castle, 44–48

FREDERICK I. Emperor of the Romans; and Charlemagne's tomb, 40; and the Third Crusade, 168

FREDERICK II. Emperor of the Romans; and Charlemagne's tomb, 40

FRENCH REVOLUTION. Political effect upon the Rhine-country, 51

FREYA. Northern goddess of love; in the legend of the Wolf's Spring, 323

FRIEDEL. A hunchback of Aix-la-Chapelle; the legend of, 128–129

FÜRST, FRANZ VON. In a legend of Fürstenberg, 189–192

FÜRSTENBERG. The castle of; the legend of the Phantom Mother of, 189–192; the legend of the Blind Archer, 192–195

G

GALLIENUS. Roman Emperor; and the Germanic risings, 23

GAUTIER, THÉOPHILE. Mentioned, 56

GELFRAT. In the *Nibelungenlied*, knight, brother to Else, 288; slain by Gunther's men, 290

GENEVA. Canton, 5

GENOFEVA. Wife of Count Siegfried of Andernach; in a legend of Andernach, 83–84

GERBERT VON ISENBURG. A young squire; in a legend of Oberwörth, 158–161

GERDA. Daughter of the Lord of Rheinstein; the legend of Kuno and, 195–200

GERMANICUS. Roman Emperor; in the Rhine-country, 22

GERMANS, EARLY. *See* Teutons

GERMANY. In the Thirty Years' War, 50–51; regains Rhenish territory as a result of the war of 1870–71, 51–52

GERNOT. In the *Nibelungenlied*, brother of Kriemhild, 267; and the plot to slay Siegfried, 277; with Gunther and Hagen on the journey to Etzel's court at Vienna, 290; slain by Rüdiger, 294; mentioned, 297

GERNSBACH. The town, 331

365

Glossary & Index

Glossary & Index

Glossary & Index

OELBERG. One of the mountains of the Siebengebirge ; Truenfels near, 122

OESTRICH. The town ; the legend of the Nun of, 216–218

OKKENFELS. A ruined stronghold near Linz ; a legend of, 154–158

OPPENHEIM. The town ; a story of, connected with the Thirty Years' War, 52–55

ORTLIEB. In the *Nibelungenlied*, son of Kriemhild and Etzel, 286 ; slain by Hagen, 293

OSRIC THE LION. A legend of Falkenstein Castle, 236–239

OSWALD, SIR. Lord of Fürstenberg ; a legend of, 192–195

OTTO. 1. Count of Reuss-Marlinberg of Hammerstein ; in a legend of Rosebach, 142–144. 2. A knight who took service as a shepherd ; in a legend of Flörsheim, 244–248

OTTO I. Emperor of the Romans, 41, 42

OTTO III. Emperor of the Romans ; and Charlemagne's tomb at Aix-la-Chapelle, 40

OTUR, or OTTER. In the *Volsunga Saga*, son of Hreithmar ; slain by Loki, 299

OUDE RIJN. A branch of the Rhine, 7

P

PALATINATE, THE. A German state, 42–43

PALESTINE. Mentioned in the legend of Boppard, 169–171 ; in the legend of Liebenstein and Sterrenberg, 172 ; in the legend of Minna of Rüdesheim, 213 ; in the legend of Gisela, 215 ; in the legend of the Shepherd Knight, 247

PALSGRAVE. = Count Palatine ; mentioned, 201

PANNONIA. The province, 14, 16

PANTULUS. A saint; in the legend of St. Ursula, 76

PARSIFAL. One of the knights of the Grail ; in the Lohengrin legend, sends Lohengrin to help Elsa, 93–94

PARZIVAL. Wolfram von Eschenbach's romance, 92

PASSAU. The city ; mentioned in the *Klage*, 309

PASSING BELLS, THE. A legend of Speyer, 326–327

PATAVRID. In *Walthar of Aquitaine*, nephew of Hagen ; fights with Walthar, 316

PATER, WALTER. His story *Duke Karl of Rosenwald*, 43

PEACE OF WESTPHALIA. Treaty which ended the Thirty Years' War ; effect upon the Rhine-country, 51

PEPIN. King of Italy, son of Charlemagne ; quarrels with his brother Karloman, and is reconciled at the shrine of St. Goar, 177–178

PEPIN OF HERISTAL. A ruler of the Franks ; overthrows the Merovingian dynasty, 28

PEPIN THE SHORT. King of the Franks, father of Charlemagne, 8

PERRON, JACQUES. A blacksmith; in a legend of Liége, 97–101

PFALZ. An island, near Bacharach ; the legend of, 185–189

PFALZGRAFENSTEIN. A castle on the island of Pfalz ; in the legend of Pfalz, 185–188

PHANTOM MOTHER OF FÜRSTENBERG, THE. The legend of, 189–192

PHILIP OF FALKENSTEIN, SIR. See Falkenstein

PICARD. A robber leader ; a story of, 57

PILGRIN, BISHOP. Of Passanform ; has the *Nibelungenlied* story recorded, 310

PLAGUE. Of 1440, in Germany, 118

POACHER OF FRANKFORT, THE. The legend of, 249–251

POPE, THE. Under the German Emperors of the Holy Roman Empire, 41

PRIESTS' GATE. Gate of a monastery in Cologne, associated with the legend of the Archbishop's Lion, 118

PROBUS. Roman Emperor ; subdues the Rhenish peoples and builds a wall, 23–24

PROXY, THE. A legend of Darmstadt, 253–255

PRUSSIA. Cedes to France her territory on the left bank of the Rhine, 51

Glossary & Index

ROMANS, THE. In the Rhine-country, 20–24

ROME. St. Ursula's pilgrimage to, 76; in the legend of the Trumpeter of Säckingen, Werner and Margaretha reunited at, 350

RONCEVAUX. A gorge in the Pyrenees; Roland's last great battle against the Moors at, 127

ROON, COUNT VON. The statesman, 4

ROSE GARDEN, THE. A legend of Worms, 258–261

ROSEBACH. 1. A village in the valley of Hammerstein; a legend of, 141–144. 2. The castle of, 142, 143. 3. The Abbey of; story of the founding of, 144

ROTH, COUNT VON. Governor of Pfalzgrafenstein; in the legend of Pfalz, 185–188

RÜDESHEIM. The town; its many legendary associations, 212; favoured by Charlemagne, 213; famous for its wines, 213; the legend of Minna of, 213–215

RÜDIGER. Margrave of Bechlarn; in the legend of the Rose Garden of Worms, 260; in the *Nibelungenlied*, his embassy to the Burgundian court to seek the hand of Kriemhild for Etzel, 285; receives Gunther and Hagen on their journey to Etzel's court, and accompanies them, 290; and the conflict in Etzel's banqueting-hall, 293–294; slain by Gernot, 294; Dietrich's lament for, 295; in the *Klage*, 309, 310

RUDOLPH. A knight of Linz; in a legend of Okkenfels, 155–158

RUSSIA. Combats the monopoly of the Hanseatic League, 50

RUTHARD. A smith; in the legend of the Sword-slipper of Solingen, 101–102, 104

RYSWICK, TREATY OF. *See* Treaty

S

SÄCKINGEN. The town, 6; the legend of the Trumpeter of, 346–351

ST. CLEMENT. Church of; in a legend of Rheinstein, 198

ST. FRIDOLIN. The festival of, celebrated at Säckingen, 347

ST. GOAR. 1. The town; the haunt of the Lorelei near, 59; the habitation of the hermit St. Goar near, 174. 2. A hermit, 174–176; at the court of Sigebert, 174–175; the patron saint of hospitality, 175; Charlemagne at the shrine of, 176–177; Karloman and Pepin reconciled at the shrine of, 177–178. 3. The monastery of, 175

ST. GOTTHARD. Pass of, 5

ST. PETER. The Apostle, 227

ST. PETER'S. Cathedral at Rome; in the legend of the Trumpeter of Säckingen, 350

ST. URSULA. Probably the Teutonic goddess Ursa, or Hörsel, 77; the legend of, 75–77

SAND GEWIRR. A dangerous eddy in the Rhine, 174

SANTEN, or XANTEN. The town; in the *Nibelungenlied*, Siegfried and Kriemhild go to, after their marriage, 275

SARACENS. Mentioned, 213, 215, 216

SATAN. In Rhenish legend, 78; in the legend of the Architect of Cologne Cathedral, 106–108; in a legend explaining why Cologne Cathedral was never completed, 110–111; in the legend of the Fire-bell of Cologne, 113–114; as Master Urian, in the legend of the cathedral of Aix-la-Chapelle, 130–133; in a legend of Rheingrafenstein, 211–212; as the Yellow Dwarf, in a legend of Elfeld, 226–227; in a legend of Worms, 261–262; in the legend of the Klingelkapelle, 333

SAXONS, THE. In the Rhine-country, 24; a story of Charlemagne's wars with, 29–37; mentioned, 248; Siegfried helps the Burgundians against, 269

SAYN. A village; Kuno of; in a legend of Falkenstein Castle, 233–236

SCANDINAVIA. And the origin of the *Nibelungenlied*, 265, 298

SCHAFFHAUSEN. The town, 6

SCHAMS VALLEY. The Rhine flows through, 5

375

Glossary & Index

377

Glossary & Index

A CATALOG OF SELECTED
DOVER BOOKS
IN ALL FIELDS OF INTEREST

A CATALOG OF SELECTED DOVER
BOOKS IN ALL FIELDS OF INTEREST

CONCERNING THE SPIRITUAL IN ART, Wassily Kandinsky. Pioneering work by father of abstract art. Thoughts on color theory, nature of art. Analysis of earlier masters. 12 illustrations. 80pp. of text. 5⅜ × 8½.   23411-8 Pa. $3.95

ANIMALS: 1,419 Copyright-Free Illustrations of Mammals, Birds, Fish, Insects, etc., Jim Harter (ed.). Clear wood engravings present, in extremely lifelike poses, over 1,000 species of animals. One of the most extensive pictorial sourcebooks of its kind. Captions. Index. 284pp. 9 × 12.   23766-4 Pa. $11.95

CELTIC ART: The Methods of Construction, George Bain. Simple geometric techniques for making Celtic interlacements, spirals, Kells-type initials, animals, humans, etc. Over 500 illustrations. 160pp. 9 × 12. (USO)   22923-8 Pa. $9.95

AN ATLAS OF ANATOMY FOR ARTISTS, Fritz Schider. Most thorough reference work on art anatomy in the world. Hundreds of illustrations, including selections from works by Vesalius, Leonardo, Goya, Ingres, Michelangelo, others. 593 illustrations. 192pp. 7⅛ × 10¼.   20241-0 Pa. $8.95

CELTIC HAND STROKE-BY-STROKE (Irish Half-Uncial from "The Book of Kells"): An Arthur Baker Calligraphy Manual, Arthur Baker. Complete guide to creating each letter of the alphabet in distinctive Celtic manner. Covers hand position, strokes, pens, inks, paper, more. Illustrated. 48pp. 8¼ × 11.
24336-2 Pa. $3.95

EASY ORIGAMI, John Montroll. Charming collection of 32 projects (hat, cup, pelican, piano, swan, many more) specially designed for the novice origami hobbyist. Clearly illustrated easy-to-follow instructions insure that even beginning papercrafters will achieve successful results. 48pp. 8¼ × 11.   27298-2 Pa. $2.95

THE COMPLETE BOOK OF BIRDHOUSE CONSTRUCTION FOR WOOD-WORKERS, Scott D. Campbell. Detailed instructions, illustrations, tables. Also data on bird habitat and instinct patterns. Bibliography. 3 tables. 63 illustrations in 15 figures. 48pp. 5¼ × 8½.   24407-5 Pa. $1.95

BLOOMINGDALE'S ILLUSTRATED 1886 CATALOG: Fashions, Dry Goods and Housewares, Bloomingdale Brothers. Famed merchants' extremely rare catalog depicting about 1,700 products: clothing, housewares, firearms, dry goods, jewelry, more. Invaluable for dating, identifying vintage items. Also, copyright-free graphics for artists, designers. Co-published with Henry Ford Museum & Greenfield Village. 160pp. 8¼ × 11.   25780-0 Pa. $9.95

HISTORIC COSTUME IN PICTURES, Braun & Schneider. Over 1,450 costumed figures in clearly detailed engravings—from dawn of civilization to end of 19th century. Captions. Many folk costumes. 256pp. 8⅜ × 11¾.   23150-X Pa. $11.95

CATALOG OF DOVER BOOKS

STICKLEY CRAFTSMAN FURNITURE CATALOGS, Gustav Stickley and L. & J. G. Stickley. Beautiful, functional furniture in two authentic catalogs from 1910. 594 illustrations, including 277 photos, show settles, rockers, armchairs, reclining chairs, bookcases, desks, tables. 183pp. 6½ × 9¼. 23838-5 Pa. $8.95

AMERICAN LOCOMOTIVES IN HISTORIC PHOTOGRAPHS: 1858 to 1949, Ron Ziel (ed.). A rare collection of 126 meticulously detailed official photographs, called "builder portraits," of American locomotives that majestically chronicle the rise of steam locomotive power in America. Introduction. Detailed captions. xi + 129pp. 9 × 12. 27393-8 Pa. $12.95

AMERICA'S LIGHTHOUSES: An Illustrated History, Francis Ross Holland, Jr. Delightfully written, profusely illustrated fact-filled survey of over 200 American lighthouses since 1716. History, anecdotes, technological advances, more. 240pp. 8 × 10¾. 25576-X Pa. $11.95

TOWARDS A NEW ARCHITECTURE, Le Corbusier. Pioneering manifesto by founder of "International School." Technical and aesthetic theories, views of industry, economics, relation of form to function, "mass-production split" and much more. Profusely illustrated. 320pp. 6⅛ × 9¼. (USO) 25023-7 Pa. $8.95

HOW THE OTHER HALF LIVES, Jacob Riis. Famous journalistic record, exposing poverty and degradation of New York slums around 1900, by major social reformer. 100 striking and influential photographs. 233pp. 10 × 7⅞. 22012-5 Pa $10.95

FRUIT KEY AND TWIG KEY TO TREES AND SHRUBS, William M. Harlow. One of the handiest and most widely used identification aids. Fruit key covers 120 deciduous and evergreen species; twig key 160 deciduous species. Easily used. Over 300 photographs. 126pp. 5⅜ × 8½. 20511-8 Pa. $3.95

COMMON BIRD SONGS, Dr. Donald J. Borror. Songs of 60 most common U.S. birds: robins, sparrows, cardinals, bluejays, finches, more—arranged in order of increasing complexity. Up to 9 variations of songs of each species. Cassette and manual 99911-4 $8.95

ORCHIDS AS HOUSE PLANTS, Rebecca Tyson Northen. Grow cattleyas and many other kinds of orchids—in a window, in a case, or under artificial light. 63 illustrations. 148pp. 5⅜ × 8½. 23261-1 Pa. $3.95

MONSTER MAZES, Dave Phillips. Masterful mazes at four levels of difficulty. Avoid deadly perils and evil creatures to find magical treasures. Solutions for all 32 exciting illustrated puzzles. 48pp. 8¼ × 11. 26005-4 Pa. $2.95

MOZART'S DON GIOVANNI (DOVER OPERA LIBRETTO SERIES), Wolfgang Amadeus Mozart. Introduced and translated by Ellen H. Bleiler. Standard Italian libretto, with complete English translation. Convenient and thoroughly portable—an ideal companion for reading along with a recording or the performance itself. Introduction. List of characters. Plot summary. 121pp. 5¼ × 8½. 24944-1 Pa. $2.95

TECHNICAL MANUAL AND DICTIONARY OF CLASSICAL BALLET, Gail Grant. Defines, explains, comments on steps, movements, poses and concepts. 15-page pictorial section. Basic book for student, viewer. 127pp. 5⅜ × 8½. 21843-0 Pa. $3.95

BRASS INSTRUMENTS: Their History and Development, Anthony Baines. Authoritative, updated survey of the evolution of trumpets, trombones, bugles, cornets, French horns, tubas and other brass wind instruments. Over 140 illustrations and 48 music examples. Corrected and updated by author. New preface. Bibliography. 320pp. 5⅜ × 8½. 27574-4 Pa. $9.95

HOLLYWOOD GLAMOR PORTRAITS, John Kobal (ed.). 145 photos from 1926–49. Harlow, Gable, Bogart, Bacall; 94 stars in all. Full background on photographers, technical aspects. 160pp. 8⅜ × 11¼. 23352-9 Pa. $11.95

MAX AND MORITZ, Wilhelm Busch. Great humor classic in both German and English. Also 10 other works: "Cat and Mouse," "Plisch and Plumm," etc. 216pp. 5⅜ × 8½. 20181-3 Pa. $5.95

THE RAVEN AND OTHER FAVORITE POEMS, Edgar Allan Poe. Over 40 of the author's most memorable poems: "The Bells," "Ulalume," "Israfel," "To Helen," "The Conqueror Worm," "Eldorado," "Annabel Lee," many more. Alphabetic lists of titles and first lines. 64pp. 5³⁄₁₆ × 8¼. 26685-0 Pa. $1.00

SEVEN SCIENCE FICTION NOVELS, H. G. Wells. The standard collection of the great novels. Complete, unabridged. First Men in the Moon, Island of Dr. Moreau, War of the Worlds, Food of the Gods, Invisible Man, Time Machine, In the Days of the Comet. Total of 1,015pp. 5⅜ × 8½. (USO) 20264-X Clothbd. $29.95

AMULETS AND SUPERSTITIONS, E. A. Wallis Budge. Comprehensive discourse on origin, powers of amulets in many ancient cultures: Arab, Persian, Babylonian, Assyrian, Egyptian, Gnostic, Hebrew, Phoenician, Syriac, etc. Covers cross, swastika, crucifix, seals, rings, stones, etc. 584pp. 5⅜ × 8½. 23573-4 Pa. $12.95

RUSSIAN STORIES/PYCCKNE PACCKA3bI: A Dual-Language Book, edited by Gleb Struve. Twelve tales by such masters as Chekhov, Tolstoy, Dostoevsky, Pushkin, others. Excellent word-for-word English translations on facing pages, plus teaching and study aids, Russian/English vocabulary, biographical/critical introductions, more. 416pp. 5⅜ × 8½. 26244-8 Pa. $8.95

PHILADELPHIA THEN AND NOW: 60 Sites Photographed in the Past and Present, Kenneth Finkel and Susan Oyama. Rare photographs of City Hall, Logan Square, Independence Hall, Betsy Ross House, other landmarks juxtaposed with contemporary views. Captures changing face of historic city. Introduction. Captions. 128pp. 8¼ × 11. 25790-8 Pa. $9.95

AIA ARCHITECTURAL GUIDE TO NASSAU AND SUFFOLK COUNTIES, LONG ISLAND, The American Institute of Architects, Long Island Chapter, and the Society for the Preservation of Long Island Antiquities. Comprehensive, well-researched and generously illustrated volume brings to life over three centuries of Long Island's great architectural heritage. More than 240 photographs with authoritative, extensively detailed captions. 176pp. 8¼ × 11. 26946-9 Pa. $14.95

NORTH AMERICAN INDIAN LIFE: Customs and Traditions of 23 Tribes, Elsie Clews Parsons (ed.). 27 fictionalized essays by noted anthropologists examine religion, customs, government, additional facets of life among the Winnebago, Crow, Zuni, Eskimo, other tribes. 480pp. 6⅛ × 9¼. 27377-6 Pa. $10.95

FRANK LLOYD WRIGHT'S HOLLYHOCK HOUSE, Donald Hoffmann. Lavishly illustrated, carefully documented study of one of Wright's most controversial residential designs. Over 120 photographs, floor plans, elevations, etc. Detailed perceptive text by noted Wright scholar. Index. 128pp. 9¼ × 10¾.
27133-1 Pa. $11.95

THE MALE AND FEMALE FIGURE IN MOTION: 60 Classic Photographic Sequences, Eadweard Muybridge. 60 true-action photographs of men and women walking, running, climbing, bending, turning, etc., reproduced from rare 19th-century masterpiece. vi + 121pp. 9 × 12. 24745-7 Pa. $10.95

1001 QUESTIONS ANSWERED ABOUT THE SEASHORE, N. J. Berrill and Jacquelyn Berrill. Queries answered about dolphins, sea snails, sponges, starfish, fishes, shore birds, many others. Covers appearance, breeding, growth, feeding, much more. 305pp. 5¼ × 8¼. 23366-9 Pa. $7.95

GUIDE TO OWL WATCHING IN NORTH AMERICA, Donald S. Heintzelman. Superb guide offers complete data and descriptions of 19 species: barn owl, screech owl, snowy owl, many more. Expert coverage of owl-watching equipment, conservation, migrations and invasions, etc. Guide to observing sites. 84 illustrations. xiii + 193pp. 5⅜ × 8½. 27344-X Pa. $7.95

MEDICINAL AND OTHER USES OF NORTH AMERICAN PLANTS: A Historical Survey with Special Reference to the Eastern Indian Tribes, Charlotte Erichsen-Brown. Chronological historical citations document 500 years of usage of plants, trees, shrubs native to eastern Canada, northeastern U.S. Also complete identifying information. 343 illustrations. 544pp. 6½ × 9¼. 25951-X Pa. $12.95

STORYBOOK MAZES, Dave Phillips. 23 stories and mazes on two-page spreads: Wizard of Oz, Treasure Island, Robin Hood, etc. Solutions. 64pp. 8¼ × 11.
23628-5 Pa. $2.95

NEGRO FOLK MUSIC, U.S.A., Harold Courlander. Noted folklorist's scholarly yet readable analysis of rich and varied musical tradition. Includes authentic versions of over 40 folk songs. Valuable bibliography and discography. xi + 324pp. 5⅜ × 8½. 27350-4 Pa. $7.95

MOVIE-STAR PORTRAITS OF THE FORTIES, John Kobal (ed.). 163 glamor, studio photos of 106 stars of the 1940s: Rita Hayworth, Ava Gardner, Marlon Brando, Clark Gable, many more. 176pp. 8⅜ × 11¼. 23546-7 Pa. $10.95

BENCHLEY LOST AND FOUND, Robert Benchley. Finest humor from early 30s, about pet peeves, child psychologists, post office and others. Mostly unavailable elsewhere. 73 illustrations by Peter Arno and others. 183pp. 5⅜ × 8½.
22410-4 Pa. $5.95

YEKL and THE IMPORTED BRIDEGROOM AND OTHER STORIES OF YIDDISH NEW YORK, Abraham Cahan. Film Hester Street based on Yekl (1896). Novel, other stories among first about Jewish immigrants on N.Y.'s East Side. 240pp. 5⅜ × 8½. 22427-9 Pa. $6.95

SELECTED POEMS, Walt Whitman. Generous sampling from *Leaves of Grass*. Twenty-four poems include "I Hear America Singing," "Song of the Open Road," "I Sing the Body Electric," "When Lilacs Last in the Dooryard Bloom'd," "O Captain! My Captain!"—all reprinted from an authoritative edition. Lists of titles and first lines. 128pp. 5³⁄₁₆ × 8¼. 26878-0 Pa. $1.00

THE BEST TALES OF HOFFMANN, E. T. A. Hoffmann. 10 of Hoffmann's most important stories: "Nutcracker and the King of Mice," "The Golden Flowerpot," etc. 458pp. 5⅜ × 8½. 21793-0 Pa. $8.95

FROM FETISH TO GOD IN ANCIENT EGYPT, E. A. Wallis Budge. Rich detailed survey of Egyptian conception of "God" and gods, magic, cult of animals, Osiris, more. Also, superb English translations of hymns and legends. 240 illustrations. 545pp. 5⅜ × 8½. 25803-3 Pa. $11.95

FRENCH STORIES/CONTES FRANÇAIS: A Dual-Language Book, Wallace Fowlie. Ten stories by French masters, Voltaire to Camus: "Micromegas" by Voltaire; "The Atheist's Mass" by Balzac; "Minuet" by de Maupassant; "The Guest" by Camus, six more. Excellent English translations on facing pages. Also French-English vocabulary list, exercises, more. 352pp. 5⅜ × 8½. 26443-2 Pa. $8.95

CHICAGO AT THE TURN OF THE CENTURY IN PHOTOGRAPHS: 122 Historic Views from the Collections of the Chicago Historical Society, Larry A. Viskochil. Rare large-format prints offer detailed views of City Hall, State Street, the Loop, Hull House, Union Station, many other landmarks, circa 1904–1913. Introduction. Captions. Maps. 144pp. 9⅜ × 12¼. 24656-6 Pa. $12.95

OLD BROOKLYN IN EARLY PHOTOGRAPHS, 1865–1929, William Lee Younger. Luna Park, Gravesend race track, construction of Grand Army Plaza, moving of Hotel Brighton, etc. 157 previously unpublished photographs. 165pp. 8⅞ × 11¾. 23587-4 Pa. $13.95

THE MYTHS OF THE NORTH AMERICAN INDIANS, Lewis Spence. Rich anthology of the myths and legends of the Algonquins, Iroquois, Pawnees and Sioux, prefaced by an extensive historical and ethnological commentary. 36 illustrations. 480pp. 5⅜ × 8½. 25967-6 Pa. $8.95

AN ENCYCLOPEDIA OF BATTLES: Accounts of Over 1,560 Battles from 1479 B.C. to the Present, David Eggenberger. Essential details of every major battle in recorded history from the first battle of Megiddo in 1479 B.C. to Grenada in 1984. List of Battle Maps. New Appendix covering the years 1967–1984. Index. 99 illustrations. 544pp. 6½ × 9¼. 24913-1 Pa. $14.95

SAILING ALONE AROUND THE WORLD, Captain Joshua Slocum. First man to sail around the world, alone, in small boat. One of great feats of seamanship told in delightful manner. 67 illustrations. 294pp. 5⅜ × 8½. 20326-3 Pa. $5.95

ANARCHISM AND OTHER ESSAYS, Emma Goldman. Powerful, penetrating, prophetic essays on direct action, role of minorities, prison reform, puritan hypocrisy, violence, etc. 271pp. 5⅜ × 8½. 22484-8 Pa. $5.95

MYTHS OF THE HINDUS AND BUDDHISTS, Ananda K. Coomaraswamy and Sister Nivedita. Great stories of the epics; deeds of Krishna, Shiva, taken from puranas, Vedas, folk tales; etc. 32 illustrations. 400pp. 5⅜ × 8½. 21759-0 Pa. $9.95

BEYOND PSYCHOLOGY, Otto Rank. Fear of death, desire of immortality, nature of sexuality, social organization, creativity, according to Rankian system. 291pp. 5⅜ × 8½. 20485-5 Pa. $7.95

A THEOLOGICO-POLITICAL TREATISE, Benedict Spinoza. Also contains unfinished Political Treatise. Great classic on religious liberty, theory of government on common consent. R. Elwes translation. Total of 421pp. 5⅜ × 8½. 20249-6 Pa. $8.95

MY BONDAGE AND MY FREEDOM, Frederick Douglass. Born a slave, Douglass became outspoken force in antislavery movement. The best of Douglass' autobiographies. Graphic description of slave life. 464pp. 5⅜ × 8½.   22457-0 Pa. $8.95

FOLLOWING THE EQUATOR: A Journey Around the World, Mark Twain. Fascinating humorous account of 1897 voyage to Hawaii, Australia, India, New Zealand, etc. Ironic, bemused reports on peoples, customs, climate, flora and fauna, politics, much more. 197 illustrations. 720pp. 5⅜ × 8½.   26113-1 Pa. $15.95

THE PEOPLE CALLED SHAKERS, Edward D. Andrews. Definitive study of Shakers: origins, beliefs, practices, dances, social organization, furniture and crafts, etc. 33 illustrations. 351pp. 5⅜ × 8½.   21081-2 Pa. $8.95

THE MYTHS OF GREECE AND ROME, H. A. Guerber. A classic of mythology, generously illustrated, long prized for its simple, graphic, accurate retelling of the principal myths of Greece and Rome, and for its commentary on their origins and significance. With 64 illustrations by Michelangelo, Raphael, Titian, Rubens, Canova, Bernini and others. 480pp. 5⅜ × 8½.   27584-1 Pa. $9.95

PSYCHOLOGY OF MUSIC, Carl E. Seashore. Classic work discusses music as a medium from psychological viewpoint. Clear treatment of physical acoustics, auditory apparatus, sound perception, development of musical skills, nature of musical feeling, host of other topics. 88 figures. 408pp. 5⅜ × 8½. 21851-1 Pa. $9.95

THE PHILOSOPHY OF HISTORY, Georg W. Hegel. Great classic of Western thought develops concept that history is not chance but rational process, the evolution of freedom. 457pp. 5⅜ × 8½.   20112-0 Pa. $9.95

THE BOOK OF TEA, Kakuzo Okakura. Minor classic of the Orient: entertaining, charming explanation, interpretation of traditional Japanese culture in terms of tea ceremony. 94pp. 5⅜ × 8½.   20070-1 Pa. $2.95

LIFE IN ANCIENT EGYPT, Adolf Erman. Fullest, most thorough, detailed older account with much not in more recent books, domestic life, religion, magic, medicine, commerce, much more. Many illustrations reproduce tomb paintings, carvings, hieroglyphs, etc. 597pp. 5⅜ × 8½.   22632-8 Pa. $10.95

SUNDIALS, Their Theory and Construction, Albert Waugh. Far and away the best, most thorough coverage of ideas, mathematics concerned, types, construction, adjusting anywhere. Simple, nontechnical treatment allows even children to build several of these dials. Over 100 illustrations. 230pp. 5⅜ × 8½.   22947-5 Pa. $7.95

DYNAMICS OF FLUIDS IN POROUS MEDIA, Jacob Bear. For advanced students of ground water hydrology, soil mechanics and physics, drainage and irrigation engineering, and more. 335 illustrations. Exercises, with answers. 784pp. 6⅛ × 9¼.   65675-6 Pa. $19.95

SONGS OF EXPERIENCE: Facsimile Reproduction with 26 Plates in Full Color, William Blake. 26 full-color plates from a rare 1826 edition. Includes "The Tyger," "London," "Holy Thursday," and other poems. Printed text of poems. 48pp. 5¼ × 7.   24636-1 Pa. $4.95

OLD-TIME VIGNETTES IN FULL COLOR, Carol Belanger Grafton (ed.). Over 390 charming, often sentimental illustrations, selected from archives of Victorian graphics—pretty women posing, children playing, food, flowers, kittens and puppies, smiling cherubs, birds and butterflies, much more. All copyright-free. 48pp. 9¼ × 12¼.   27269-9 Pa. $5.95

PERSPECTIVE FOR ARTISTS, Rex Vicat Cole. Depth, perspective of sky and sea, shadows, much more, not usually covered. 391 diagrams, 81 reproductions of drawings and paintings. 279pp. 5⅜ × 8½. 22487-2 Pa. $6.95

DRAWING THE LIVING FIGURE, Joseph Sheppard. Innovative approach to artistic anatomy focuses on specifics of surface anatomy, rather than muscles and bones. Over 170 drawings of live models in front, back and side views, and in widely varying poses. Accompanying diagrams. 177 illustrations. Introduction. Index. 144pp. 8⅜ × 11¼. 26723-7 Pa. $7.95

GOTHIC AND OLD ENGLISH ALPHABETS: 100 Complete Fonts, Dan X. Solo. Add power, elegance to posters, signs, other graphics with 100 stunning copyright-free alphabets: Blackstone, Dolbey, Germania, 97 more—including many lower-case, numerals, punctuation marks. 104pp. 8⅛ × 11. 24695-7 Pa. $7.95

HOW TO DO BEADWORK, Mary White. Fundamental book on craft from simple projects to five-bead chains and woven works. 106 illustrations. 142pp. 5⅜ × 8. 20697-1 Pa. $4.95

THE BOOK OF WOOD CARVING, Charles Marshall Sayers. Finest book for beginners discusses fundamentals and offers 34 designs. "Absolutely first rate . . . well thought out and well executed."—E. J. Tangerman. 118pp. 7¾ × 10⅝. 23654-4 Pa. $5.95

ILLUSTRATED CATALOG OF CIVIL WAR MILITARY GOODS: Union Army Weapons, Insignia, Uniform Accessories, and Other Equipment, Schuyler, Hartley, and Graham. Rare, profusely illustrated 1846 catalog includes Union Army uniform and dress regulations, arms and ammunition, coats, insignia, flags, swords, rifles, etc. 226 illustrations. 160pp. 9 × 12. 24939-5 Pa. $10.95

WOMEN'S FASHIONS OF THE EARLY 1900s: An Unabridged Republication of "New York Fashions, 1909," National Cloak & Suit Co. Rare catalog of mail-order fashions documents women's and children's clothing styles shortly after the turn of the century. Captions offer full descriptions, prices. Invaluable resource for fashion, costume historians. Approximately 725 illustrations. 128pp. 8⅜ × 11¼. 27276-1 Pa. $11.95

THE 1912 AND 1915 GUSTAV STICKLEY FURNITURE CATALOGS, Gustav Stickley. With over 200 detailed illustrations and descriptions, these two catalogs are essential reading and reference materials and identification guides for Stickley furniture. Captions cite materials, dimensions and prices. 112pp. 6½ × 9¼. 26676-1 Pa. $9.95

EARLY AMERICAN LOCOMOTIVES, John H. White, Jr. Finest locomotive engravings from early 19th century: historical (1804–74), main-line (after 1870), special, foreign, etc. 147 plates. 142pp. 11⅜ × 8¼. 22772-3 Pa. $8.95

THE TALL SHIPS OF TODAY IN PHOTOGRAPHS, Frank O. Braynard. Lavishly illustrated tribute to nearly 100 majestic contemporary sailing vessels: Amerigo Vespucci, Clearwater, Constitution, Eagle, Mayflower, Sea Cloud, Victory, many more. Authoritative captions provide statistics, background on each ship. 190 black-and-white photographs and illustrations. Introduction. 128pp. 8⅞ × 11¾. 27163-3 Pa. $13.95

EARLY NINETEENTH-CENTURY CRAFTS AND TRADES, Peter Stockham (ed.). Extremely rare 1807 volume describes to youngsters the crafts and trades of the day: brickmaker, weaver, dressmaker, bookbinder, ropemaker, saddler, many more. Quaint prose, charming illustrations for each craft. 20 black-and-white line illustrations. 192pp. 4⅝ × 6. 27293-1 Pa. $4.95

VICTORIAN FASHIONS AND COSTUMES FROM HARPER'S BAZAR, 1867-1898, Stella Blum (ed.). Day costumes, evening wear, sports clothes, shoes, hats, other accessories in over 1,000 detailed engravings. 320pp. 9⅜ × 12¼. 22990-4 Pa. $13.95

GUSTAV STICKLEY, THE CRAFTSMAN, Mary Ann Smith. Superb study surveys broad scope of Stickley's achievement, especially in architecture. Design philosophy, rise and fall of the Craftsman empire, descriptions and floor plans for many Craftsman houses, more. 86 black-and-white halftones. 31 line illustrations. Introduction. 208pp. 6½ × 9¼. 27210-9 Pa. $9.95

THE LONG ISLAND RAIL ROAD IN EARLY PHOTOGRAPHS, Ron Ziel. Over 220 rare photos, informative text document origin (1844) and development of rail service on Long Island. Vintage views of early trains, locomotives, stations, passengers, crews, much more. Captions. 8⅞ × 11¾. 26301-0 Pa. $13.95

THE BOOK OF OLD SHIPS: From Egyptian Galleys to Clipper Ships, Henry B. Culver. Superb, authoritative history of sailing vessels, with 80 magnificent line illustrations. Galley, bark, caravel, longship, whaler, many more. Detailed, informative text on each vessel by noted naval historian. Introduction. 256pp. 5⅜ × 8½. 27332-6 Pa. $6.95

TEN BOOKS ON ARCHITECTURE, Vitruvius. The most important book ever written on architecture. Early Roman aesthetics, technology, classical orders, site selection, all other aspects. Morgan translation. 331pp. 5⅜ × 8½. 20645-9 Pa. $8.95

THE HUMAN FIGURE IN MOTION, Eadweard Muybridge. More than 4,500 stopped-action photos, in action series, showing undraped men, women, children jumping, lying down, throwing, sitting, wrestling, carrying, etc. 390pp. 7⅞ × 10⅝. 20204-6 Clothbd. $24.95

TREES OF THE EASTERN AND CENTRAL UNITED STATES AND CANADA, William M. Harlow. Best one-volume guide to 140 trees. Full descriptions, woodlore, range, etc. Over 600 illustrations. Handy size. 288pp. 4½ × 6⅜. 20395-6 Pa. $5.95

SONGS OF WESTERN BIRDS, Dr. Donald J. Borror. Complete song and call repertoire of 60 western species, including flycatchers, juncoes, cactus wrens, many more—includes fully illustrated booklet. Cassette and manual 99913-0 $8.95

GROWING AND USING HERBS AND SPICES, Milo Miloradovich. Versatile handbook provides all the information needed for cultivation and use of all the herbs and spices available in North America. 4 illustrations. Index. Glossary. 236pp. 5⅜ × 8½. 25058-X Pa. $5.95

BIG BOOK OF MAZES AND LABYRINTHS, Walter Shepherd. 50 mazes and labyrinths in all—classical, solid, ripple, and more—in one great volume. Perfect inexpensive puzzler for clever youngsters. Full solutions. 112pp. 8⅛ × 11. 22951-3 Pa. $3.95

PIANO TUNING, J. Cree Fischer. Clearest, best book for beginner, amateur. Simple repairs, raising dropped notes, tuning by easy method of flattened fifths. No previous skills needed. 4 illustrations. 201pp. 5⅜ × 8½. 23267-0 Pa. $5.95

A SOURCE BOOK IN THEATRICAL HISTORY, A. M. Nagler. Contemporary observers on acting, directing, make-up, costuming, stage props, machinery, scene design, from Ancient Greece to Chekhov. 611pp. 5⅜ × 8½. 20515-0 Pa. $11.95

THE COMPLETE NONSENSE OF EDWARD LEAR, Edward Lear. All nonsense limericks, zany alphabets, Owl and Pussycat, songs, nonsense botany, etc., illustrated by Lear. Total of 320pp. 5⅜ × 8½. (USO) 20167-8 Pa. $6.95

VICTORIAN PARLOUR POETRY: An Annotated Anthology, Michael R. Turner. 117 gems by Longfellow, Tennyson, Browning, many lesser-known poets. "The Village Blacksmith," "Curfew Must Not Ring Tonight," "Only a Baby Small," dozens more, often difficult to find elsewhere. Index of poets, titles, first lines. xxiii + 325pp. 5⅜ × 8¼. 27044-0 Pa. $8.95

DUBLINERS, James Joyce. Fifteen stories offer vivid, tightly focused observations of the lives of Dublin's poorer classes. At least one, "The Dead," is considered a masterpiece. Reprinted complete and unabridged from standard edition. 160pp. 5³⁄₁₆ × 8¼. 26870-5 Pa. $1.00

THE HAUNTED MONASTERY and THE CHINESE MAZE MURDERS, Robert van Gulik. Two full novels by van Gulik, set in 7th-century China, continue adventures of Judge Dee and his companions. An evil Taoist monastery, seemingly supernatural events; overgrown topiary maze hides strange crimes. 27 illustrations. 328pp. 5⅜ × 8½. 23502-5 Pa. $7.95

THE BOOK OF THE SACRED MAGIC OF ABRAMELIN THE MAGE, translated by S. MacGregor Mathers. Medieval manuscript of ceremonial magic. Basic document in Aleister Crowley, Golden Dawn groups. 268pp. 5⅜ × 8½. 23211-5 Pa. $8.95

NEW RUSSIAN-ENGLISH AND ENGLISH-RUSSIAN DICTIONARY, M. A. O'Brien. This is a remarkably handy Russian dictionary, containing a surprising amount of information, including over 70,000 entries. 366pp. 4½ × 6⅛. 20208-9 Pa. $9.95

HISTORIC HOMES OF THE AMERICAN PRESIDENTS, Second, Revised Edition, Irvin Haas. A traveler's guide to American Presidential homes, most open to the public, depicting and describing homes occupied by every American President from George Washington to George Bush. With visiting hours, admission charges, travel routes. 175 photographs. Index. 160pp. 8¼ × 11. 26751-2 Pa. $10.95

NEW YORK IN THE FORTIES, Andreas Feininger. 162 brilliant photographs by the well-known photographer, formerly with *Life* magazine. Commuters, shoppers, Times Square at night, much else from city at its peak. Captions by John von Hartz. 181pp. 9¼ × 10¾. 23585-8 Pa. $12.95

INDIAN SIGN LANGUAGE, William Tomkins. Over 525 signs developed by Sioux and other tribes. Written instructions and diagrams. Also 290 pictographs. 111pp. 6⅛ × 9¼. 22029-X Pa. $3.50

ANATOMY: A Complete Guide for Artists, Joseph Sheppard. A master of figure drawing shows artists how to render human anatomy convincingly. Over 460 illustrations. 224pp. 8⅜ × 11¼. 27279-6 Pa. $9.95

MEDIEVAL CALLIGRAPHY: Its History and Technique, Marc Drogin. Spirited history, comprehensive instruction manual covers 13 styles (ca. 4th century thru 15th). Excellent photographs; directions for duplicating medieval techniques with modern tools. 224pp. 8⅜ × 11¼. 26142-5 Pa. $11.95

DRIED FLOWERS: How to Prepare Them, Sarah Whitlock and Martha Rankin. Complete instructions on how to use silica gel, meal and borax, perlite aggregate, sand and borax, glycerine and water to create attractive permanent flower arrangements. 12 illustrations. 32pp. 5⅜ × 8½. 21802-3 Pa. $1.00

EASY-TO-MAKE BIRD FEEDERS FOR WOODWORKERS, Scott D. Campbell. Detailed, simple-to-use guide for designing, constructing, caring for and using feeders. Text, illustrations for 12 classic and contemporary designs. 96pp. 5⅜ × 8½. 25847-5 Pa. $2.95

OLD-TIME CRAFTS AND TRADES, Peter Stockham. An 1807 book created to teach children about crafts and trades open to them as future careers. It describes in detailed, nontechnical terms 24 different occupations, among them coachmaker, gardener, hairdresser, lacemaker, shoemaker, wheelwright, copper-plate printer, milliner, trunkmaker, merchant and brewer. Finely detailed engravings illustrate each occupation. 192pp. 4⅝ × 6. 27398-9 Pa. $4.95

THE HISTORY OF UNDERCLOTHES, C. Willett Cunnington and Phyllis Cunnington. Fascinating, well-documented survey covering six centuries of English undergarments, enhanced with over 100 illustrations: 12th-century laced-up bodice, footed long drawers (1795), 19th-century bustles, 19th-century corsets for men, Victorian "bust improvers," much more. 272pp. 5⅜ × 8¼. 27124-2 Pa. $9.95

ARTS AND CRAFTS FURNITURE: The Complete Brooks Catalog of 1912, Brooks Manufacturing Co. Photos and detailed descriptions of more than 150 now very collectible furniture designs from the Arts and Crafts movement depict davenports, settees, buffets, desks, tables, chairs, bedsteads, dressers and more, all built of solid, quarter-sawed oak. Invaluable for students and enthusiasts of antiques, Americana and the decorative arts. 80pp. 6½ × 9¼. 27471-3 Pa. $7.95

HOW WE INVENTED THE AIRPLANE: An Illustrated History, Orville Wright. Fascinating firsthand account covers early experiments, construction of planes and motors, first flights, much more. Introduction and commentary by Fred C. Kelly. 76 photographs. 96pp. 8¼ × 11. 25662-6 Pa. $8.95

THE ARTS OF THE SAILOR: Knotting, Splicing and Ropework, Hervey Garrett Smith. Indispensable shipboard reference covers tools, basic knots and useful hitches; handsewing and canvas work, more. Over 100 illustrations. Delightful reading for sea lovers. 256pp. 5⅜ × 8½. 26440-8 Pa. $7.95

FRANK LLOYD WRIGHT'S FALLINGWATER: The House and Its History, Second, Revised Edition, Donald Hoffmann. A total revision—both in text and illustrations—of the standard document on Fallingwater, the boldest, most personal architectural statement of Wright's mature years, updated with valuable new material from the recently opened Frank Lloyd Wright Archives. "Fascinating"—*The New York Times.* 116 illustrations. 128pp. 9¼ × 10¾. 27430-6 Pa. $10.95

CATALOG OF DOVER BOOKS

PHOTOGRAPHIC SKETCHBOOK OF THE CIVIL WAR, Alexander Gardner. 100 photos taken on field during the Civil War. Famous shots of Manassas, Harper's Ferry, Lincoln, Richmond, slave pens, etc. 244pp. 10⅝ × 8¼.
22731-6 Pa. $9.95

FIVE ACRES AND INDEPENDENCE, Maurice G. Kains. Great back-to-the-land classic explains basics of self-sufficient farming. The one book to get. 95 illustrations. 397pp. 5⅜ × 8½. 20974-1 Pa. $7.95

SONGS OF EASTERN BIRDS, Dr. Donald J. Borror. Songs and calls of 60 species most common to eastern U.S.: warblers, woodpeckers, flycatchers, thrushes, larks, many more in high-quality recording. Cassette and manual 99912-2 $8.95

A MODERN HERBAL, Margaret Grieve. Much the fullest, most exact, most useful compilation of herbal material. Gigantic alphabetical encyclopedia, from aconite to zedoary, gives botanical information, medical properties, folklore, economic uses, much else. Indispensable to serious reader. 161 illustrations. 888pp. 6½ × 9¼. 2-vol. set. (USO) Vol. I: 22798-7 Pa. $9.95
Vol. II: 22799-5 Pa. $9.95

HIDDEN TREASURE MAZE BOOK, Dave Phillips. Solve 34 challenging mazes accompanied by heroic tales of adventure. Evil dragons, people-eating plants, bloodthirsty giants, many more dangerous adversaries lurk at every twist and turn. 34 mazes, stories, solutions. 48pp. 8¼ × 11. 24566-7 Pa. $2.95

LETTERS OF W. A. MOZART, Wolfgang A. Mozart. Remarkable letters show bawdy wit, humor, imagination, musical insights, contemporary musical world; includes some letters from Leopold Mozart. 276pp. 5⅜ × 8½. 22859-2 Pa. $6.95

BASIC PRINCIPLES OF CLASSICAL BALLET, Agrippina Vaganova. Great Russian theoretician, teacher explains methods for teaching classical ballet. 118 illustrations. 175pp. 5⅜ × 8½. 22036-2 Pa. $4.95

THE JUMPING FROG, Mark Twain. Revenge edition. The original story of The Celebrated Jumping Frog of Calaveras County, a hapless French translation, and Twain's hilarious "retranslation" from the French. 12 illustrations. 66pp. 5⅜ × 8½.
22686-7 Pa. $3.95

BEST REMEMBERED POEMS, Martin Gardner (ed.). The 126 poems in this superb collection of 19th- and 20th-century British and American verse range from Shelley's "To a Skylark" to the impassioned "Renascence" of Edna St. Vincent Millay and to Edward Lear's whimsical "The Owl and the Pussycat." 224pp. 5⅜ × 8½.
27165-X Pa. $4.95

COMPLETE SONNETS, William Shakespeare. Over 150 exquisite poems deal with love, friendship, the tyranny of time, beauty's evanescence, death and other themes in language of remarkable power, precision and beauty. Glossary of archaic terms. 80pp. 5 3/16 × 8¼. 26686-9 Pa. $1.00

BODIES IN A BOOKSHOP, R. T. Campbell. Challenging mystery of blackmail and murder with ingenious plot and superbly drawn characters. In the best tradition of British suspense fiction. 192pp. 5⅜ × 8½. 24720-1 Pa. $5.95

THE WIT AND HUMOR OF OSCAR WILDE, Alvin Redman (ed.). More than 1,000 ripostes, paradoxes, wisecracks: Work is the curse of the drinking classes; I can resist everything except temptation; etc. 258pp. 5⅜ × 8½. 20602-5 Pa. $5.95

SHAKESPEARE LEXICON AND QUOTATION DICTIONARY, Alexander Schmidt. Full definitions, locations, shades of meaning in every word in plays and poems. More than 50,000 exact quotations. 1,485pp. 6½ × 9¼. 2-vol. set.
Vol. 1: 22726-X Pa. $15.95
Vol. 2: 22727-8 Pa. $15.95

SELECTED POEMS, Emily Dickinson. Over 100 best-known, best-loved poems by one of America's foremost poets, reprinted from authoritative early editions. No comparable edition at this price. Index of first lines. 64pp. 5³⁄₁₆ × 8¼. 26466-1 Pa. $1.00

CELEBRATED CASES OF JUDGE DEE (DEE GOONG AN), translated by Robert van Gulik. Authentic 18th-century Chinese detective novel; Dee and associates solve three interlocked cases. Led to van Gulik's own stories with same characters. Extensive introduction. 9 illustrations. 237pp. 5⅜ × 8½. 23337-5 Pa. $6.95

THE MALLEUS MALEFICARUM OF KRAMER AND SPRENGER, translated by Montague Summers. Full text of most important witchhunter's "bible," used by both Catholics and Protestants. 278pp. 6⅝ × 10. 22802-9 Pa. $10.95

SPANISH STORIES/CUENTOS ESPAÑOLES: A Dual-Language Book, Angel Flores (ed.). Unique format offers 13 great stories in Spanish by Cervantes, Borges, others. Faithful English translations on facing pages. 352pp. 5⅜ × 8½. 25399-6 Pa. $8.95

THE CHICAGO WORLD'S FAIR OF 1893: A Photographic Record, Stanley Appelbaum (ed.). 128 rare photos show 200 buildings, Beaux-Arts architecture, Midway, original Ferris Wheel, Edison's kinetoscope, more. Architectural emphasis; full text. 116pp. 8¼ × 11. 23990-X Pa. $9.95

OLD QUEENS, N.Y., IN EARLY PHOTOGRAPHS, Vincent F. Seyfried and William Asadorian. Over 160 rare photographs of Maspeth, Jamaica, Jackson Heights, and other areas. Vintage views of DeWitt Clinton mansion, 1939 World's Fair and more. Captions. 192pp. 8⅞ × 11. 26358-4 Pa. $12.95

CAPTURED BY THE INDIANS: 15 Firsthand Accounts, 1750–1870, Frederick Drimmer. Astounding true historical accounts of grisly torture, bloody conflicts, relentless pursuits, miraculous escapes and more, by people who lived to tell the tale. 384pp. 5⅜ × 8½. 24901-8 Pa. $8.95

THE WORLD'S GREAT SPEECHES, Lewis Copeland and Lawrence W. Lamm (eds.). Vast collection of 278 speeches of Greeks to 1970. Powerful and effective models; unique look at history. 842pp. 5⅜ × 8½. 20468-5 Pa. $13.95

THE BOOK OF THE SWORD, Sir Richard F. Burton. Great Victorian scholar/adventurer's eloquent, erudite history of the "queen of weapons"—from prehistory to early Roman Empire. Evolution and development of early swords, variations (sabre, broadsword, cutlass, scimitar, etc.), much more. 336pp. 6⅛ × 9¼. 25434-8 Pa. $8.95

AUTOBIOGRAPHY: The Story of My Experiments with Truth, Mohandas K. Gandhi. Boyhood, legal studies, purification, the growth of the Satyagraha (nonviolent protest) movement. Critical, inspiring work of the man responsible for the freedom of India. 480pp. 5⅜ × 8½. (USO)　　　　24593-4 Pa. $7.95

CELTIC MYTHS AND LEGENDS, T. W. Rolleston. Masterful retelling of Irish and Welsh stories and tales. Cuchulain, King Arthur, Deirdre, the Grail, many more. First paperback edition. 58 full-page illustrations. 512pp. 5⅜ × 8½.
26507-2 Pa. $9.95

THE PRINCIPLES OF PSYCHOLOGY, William James. Famous long course complete, unabridged. Stream of thought, time perception, memory, experimental methods; great work decades ahead of its time. 94 figures. 1,391pp. 5⅜ × 8½. 2-vol. set.
Vol. I: 20381-6 Pa. $12.95
Vol. II: 20382-4 Pa. $12.95

THE WORLD AS WILL AND REPRESENTATION, Arthur Schopenhauer. Definitive English translation of Schopenhauer's life work, correcting more than 1,000 errors, omissions in earlier translations. Translated by E. F. J. Payne. Total of 1,269pp. 5⅜ × 8½. 2-vol. set.　　　　Vol. 1: 21761-2 Pa. $11.95
Vol. 2: 21762-0 Pa. $11.95

MAGIC AND MYSTERY IN TIBET, Madame Alexandra David-Neel. Experiences among lamas, magicians, sages, sorcerers, Bonpa wizards. A true psychic discovery. 32 illustrations. 321pp. 5⅜ × 8½. (USO)　　　　22682-4 Pa. $8.95

THE EGYPTIAN BOOK OF THE DEAD, E. A. Wallis Budge. Complete reproduction of Ani's papyrus, finest ever found. Full hieroglyphic text, interlinear transliteration, word-for-word translation, smooth translation. 533pp. 6½ × 9¼.
21866-X Pa. $9.95

MATHEMATICS FOR THE NONMATHEMATICIAN, Morris Kline. Detailed, college-level treatment of mathematics in cultural and historical context, with numerous exercises. Recommended Reading Lists. Tables. Numerous figures. 641pp. 5⅜ × 8½.　　　　24823-2 Pa. $11.95

THEORY OF WING SECTIONS: Including a Summary of Airfoil Data, Ira H. Abbott and A. E. von Doenhoff. Concise compilation of subsonic aerodynamic characteristics of NACA wing sections, plus description of theory. 350pp. of tables. 693pp. 5⅜ × 8½.　　　　60586-8 Pa. $13.95

THE RIME OF THE ANCIENT MARINER, Gustave Doré, S. T. Coleridge. Doré's finest work; 34 plates capture moods, subtleties of poem. Flawless full-size reproductions printed on facing pages with authoritative text of poem. "Beautiful. Simply beautiful."—*Publisher's Weekly*. 77pp. 9¼ × 12.　　　　22305-1 Pa. $5.95

NORTH AMERICAN INDIAN DESIGNS FOR ARTISTS AND CRAFTS-PEOPLE, Eva Wilson. Over 360 authentic copyright-free designs adapted from Navajo blankets, Hopi pottery, Sioux buffalo hides, more. Geometrics, symbolic figures, plant and animal motifs, etc. 128pp. 8⅜ × 11. (EUK)　　　　25341-4 Pa. $7.95

SCULPTURE: Principles and Practice, Louis Slobodkin. Step-by-step approach to clay, plaster, metals, stone; classical and modern. 253 drawings, photos. 255pp. 8⅛ × 11.　　　　22960-2 Pa. $10.95

THE INFLUENCE OF SEA POWER UPON HISTORY, 1660–1783, A. T. Mahan. Influential classic of naval history and tactics still used as text in war colleges. First paperback edition. 4 maps. 24 battle plans. 640pp. 5⅜ × 8½.
25509-3 Pa. $12.95

THE STORY OF THE TITANIC AS TOLD BY ITS SURVIVORS, Jack Winocour (ed.). What it was really like. Panic, despair, shocking inefficiency, and a little heroism. More thrilling than any fictional account. 26 illustrations. 320pp. 5⅜ × 8½.
20610-6 Pa. $7.95

FAIRY AND FOLK TALES OF THE IRISH PEASANTRY, William Butler Yeats (ed.). Treasury of 64 tales from the twilight world of Celtic myth and legend: "The Soul Cages," "The Kildare Pooka," "King O'Toole and his Goose," many more. Introduction and Notes by W. B. Yeats. 352pp. 5⅜ × 8½. 26941-8 Pa. $8.95

BUDDHIST MAHAYANA TEXTS, E. B. Cowell and Others (eds.). Superb, accurate translations of basic documents in Mahayana Buddhism, highly important in history of religions. The Buddha-karita of Asvaghosha, Larger Sukhavativyuha, more. 448pp. 5⅜ × 8½. 25552-2 Pa. $9.95

ONE TWO THREE . . . INFINITY: Facts and Speculations of Science, George Gamow. Great physicist's fascinating, readable overview of contemporary science: number theory, relativity, fourth dimension, entropy, genes, atomic structure, much more. 128 illustrations. Index. 352pp. 5⅜ × 8½. 25664-2 Pa. $8.95

ENGINEERING IN HISTORY, Richard Shelton Kirby, et al. Broad, nontechnical survey of history's major technological advances: birth of Greek science, industrial revolution, electricity and applied science, 20th-century automation, much more. 181 illustrations. ". . . excellent . . ."—Isis. Bibliography. vii + 530pp. 5⅜ × 8¼.
26412-2 Pa. $14.95

Prices subject to change without notice.

Available at your book dealer or write for free catalog to Dept. GI, Dover Publications, Inc., 31 East 2nd St., Mineola, N.Y. 11501. Dover publishes more than 500 books each year on science, elementary and advanced mathematics, biology, music, art, literary history, social sciences and other areas.